BAGS TO RICHES

Pg. 53 -- Do my Research = what are other ads doing?

Pg 73 - Log - Business Plan

Start Out W/ An End In Mind

What IS your End?

Pg. 76 - Income Statement

Pg 85 - Patents

Corporate Partnerships

Amy,

Bags to Riches

7 Success Secrets for Women in Business

Linda Hollander,
the Wealthy Bag Lady

Bag Your Dreams!

CELESTIAL ARTS
BERKELEY — TORONTO

Celestial Arts
an imprint of Ten Speed Press
P.O. Box 7123
Berkeley, California 94707
www.tenspeed.com

Distributed in Australia by Simon and Schuster Australia, in Canada by Ten Speed Press Canada, in New Zealand by Southern Publishers Group, in South Africa by Real Books, and in the United Kingdom and Europe by Publishers Group UK.

Cover design by Chloe Nelson and Larissa Pickens
Text design by Lynn Bell, Monroe Street Studios
Wealthy Bag Lady illustration by Jon Demos

Library of Congress Cataloging-in-Publication Data
Hollander, Linda.
   Bags to riches : 7 success secrets for women in business / Linda Hollander.
      p. cm.
   ISBN-13: 978-1-58761-148-3 / ISBN-10: 1-58761-148-1
   1. Businesswomen—Life skills guides. 2. Women executives—Life skills guides. 3. Success in business—Handbooks, manuals, etc. 4. Women-owned business enterprises—Management—Handbooks, manuals, etc. 5. New business enterprises—Management—Handbooks, manuals, etc. I. Title.

   HD6053.H63 2002
   658.1'1'082—dc21   2002156178

Reprint 2008
Printed in Canada

2 3 4 5 6 7 8 9 10 — 12 11 10 09 08

DEDICATION

I am truly surrounded by love.

This book is dedicated to Leslie Greenfield, my loving husband, for sharing my vision and to Sheryl Felice, my best friend and business partner, for believing in the dream.

myvalleytrust.com

Acknowledgments

I don't know how it happened, but incredible people have helped me grow this book from a fleeting fantasy into a reality. This book was truly a "success team" effort. I feel like I'm in Hollywood, accepting the Academy Award and desperately hoping I won't forget to mention any of the visionaries who made this book possible.

I wish to thank my husband, Leslie Greenfield, for putting up with my craziness, for seeing me at my worst and still loving me. I always wanted a great love in my life. Now I have one.

"Thank you" doesn't seem like enough for my best friend and business partner, Sheryl Felice. Your sacrifice and loyalty made it all possible. You held my vision in light. We are truly friends for life, and I cherish our friendship every day.

I would like to thank my parents, Robert and Blossom Hollander, for their love and support. You've instilled wonderful values in me that have guided my life's choices. I couldn't ask for better role models in my "other parents," Howard and Rhoda Goldie. My beautiful and talented sister, Patty Hollin, has always encouraged me to be strong and go for my dreams. Everyday I hope to make you all proud of me.

I have the deepest admiration and gratitude for the members of my "You-Can-Do-It" team: Maria Carter, who has the most beautiful heart; Jared Silver, one of the most talented and giving people I know; Patricia Pastor, who taught me to be brave; Pamela Exum, my constant cheerleader; and Denise Michaels, a fountain of wisdom and a great coach. My Internet marketing buddies—Joel Christopher, Cordell Vail, Hagen Hartung, and Bret Essing—have endowed me with brilliant brainstorming.

Kay Briski is smart, loyal, and a good friend. Eddy Rivera's talents are remarkable. They both meet challenges with style and grace.

The other members of my family success team have always supported me and shared their love: Steve and Monica Huss, Barbara Hartmann, James Hartmann, Charlene Endes, Arlene Gibberman, Pam and Jay Gibberman, the Rodsteins, as well as Curtis, Georgina, Matthew, and Emily Shapiro. You are some of the most loving and courageous people I know.

I have little furry writing companions, my beautiful cats, the dynamic mother and daughter duo, Carmella and Sneakers.

Sharing laughs and delicious Italian food with my girlfriends has kept me sane throughout the crazy writing process. I would like to extend a heartfelt thanks to my friends Diane Schoessow, Janet Goldman, and Rhonda Heldman Raider.

I've been blessed with many wonderful mentors. Robert Allen ignited the spark that led to the creation of this book. Mark Victor Hansen taught me to dream big and to break down the stumbling blocks in my path. Ken Kerr taught me how to think more creatively. Claude Diamond was only a phone call away when I needed help desperately. Al Lapin Jr. is a business maverick and a source of unwavering support and motivation.

Wendy Keller is the most incredible literary consultant and agent. She is one of the only people who talks faster than I do and always astonishes me with the store-house of knowledge in her mind. Her advice was nothing short of amazing.

Lydia Bird, my wonderful manuscript consultant, is a delight. She is kind and talented, with the patience of a saint. Our brainstorming sessions were phenome-nal, and we made a great success team. She is a true entrepreneurial empress.

I had many publishing mentors at Ten Speed Press. Jo Ann Deck and Philip Wood took on this project, believed in me, provided support, and shared good food and laughter with me. You both are an author's dream and I was truly lucky to find you. Gonzalo Ferreyra, Mark Anderson, and Kara Van de Water were dedi-cated collaborators. Meghan Keeffe, my amazing editor, had incredible patience and wisdom. Meghan was a great sounding board, confidant, and trusted adviser.

All of the wonderful small business owners who shared their stories with me have inspired every page of this book. The Millionaire Mentors who shared their secrets have a true desire to empower others and make the world a better place. My clients and students have trusted me and let me into their lives. I learned so much from their experiences. Thank you all for your generosity and graciousness.

Finally, I would like to thank you, the reader, for believing that entrepreneurship can transform your life. If you would like to share your stories and comments, write me at P.O. Box 83639, Los Angeles, CA 90083; phone 888-286-0602; or visit my website, www.WealthyBagLady.com. Best of luck on your incredible journey!

Contents

INTRODUCTION 1

PART I BAG OF DREAMS: SETTING THE STAGE 8

Success Secret #1 *You've Already Got What It Takes* 9

Chapter 1 GO FOR IT! 10
Are You a Natural Entrepreneur? 10
Benefits of Being Your Own Boss 12
Wealth Is Not Just Nice—It's Necessary 15
Bust through the Roadblocks 18

Chapter 2 ATTITUDE IS (ALMOST) EVERYTHING 23
Determination 23
The Awesome Power of the Subconscious 24
Dream Big Dreams 27
Sensory Anchoring 31
Breakthroughs 33

Chapter 3 YOUR SUPPORTING CAST 34
Your "You-Can-Do-It" Team 34
Success Teams 35
Mentors 39
Your Circle of Influence 40
Professionals 42
Organizations 42

PART II BREAK OUT OF THE BAG: GETTING UP AND RUNNING 46

Success Secret #2 *Your Business Is a Lifetime Self-Improvement Course* 47

Chapter 4 FINDING YOUR PERFECT BUSINESS 48
A Wealth of Possibilities 49
Location, Location, Location 54
Alone or in Partnership? 56
Who Else Is Concerned? 61

Chapter 5   STARTING OFF RIGHT   63
   Make It Real   63
   Choose a Great Name   65
   Decide on a Legal Structure   68
   Find the Right Bank   70
   Write a Knockout Business Plan   72
   A Few Additional Hoops   76

Chapter 6   OPERATING SMOOTHLY   77
   Systems and Equipment   77
   Time Management   80
   Take Risks, Stay Protected   81
   Protect Your Ideas   85

Chapter 7   PACKAGING YOUR IMAGE   87
   Your Personal Brand   87
   Brand Your Place of Business   88
   Look Good in Print   91
   Look Bigger Than You Are   94
   Gifts and Promotional Items   95

Chapter 8   BRINGING IN EMPLOYEES   97
   Assess Your Needs and Resources   97
   Create a Positive Work Environment   100
   Know When to Let Go   105

Success Secret #3   *A Woman's Yardstick Is Different Than a Man's*   107

PART III   BROWN BAGS TO MONEY BAGS: CONTROLLING YOUR FINANCES   108

Success Secret #4   *Wealth Only Corrupts the Corruptible*   109

Chapter 9   THE MONEY'S IN YOUR HANDS   110
   Sound Accounting   111
   Taming the Tax Beast   112
   Running Lean and Mean   113
   Turbulent Economic Times   117

Chapter 10   GETTING THE FINANCING YOU NEED   120
              What Lenders and Investors Want to See   122
              Bootstrapping   122
              Equity Financing   126
              Debt Financing   128
              Government Loans   131
              Other Financing Options   132

Chapter 11   MULTIPLE STREAMS OF INCOME   134
              Internal Profit Centers   134
              Licensing and Royalties   135
              Coaching   137
              Investments   138

PART IV BAG OF TRICKS: ATTRACTING YOUR IDEAL CUSTOMERS   142
Success Secret #5   *Selling Is Nurturing*   143

Chapter 12   COMMUNICATING YOUR PASSION   144
              Conquering Shyness   144
              Communicating Face to Face   145
              Communicating on the Phone   146
              Public Speaking—Oh No!   149
              Networking Power   153

Chapter 13   PRICING FOR PROFIT   157
              Know Your Costs   157
              Acknowledge Your Worth   158
              The Perils of Pricing Too Low   159
              Pricing Strategies   161
              When It's Time to Raise the Bar   164

Chapter 14   THE LURE OF MARKETING   166
              Target Your Market   167
              Word of Mouth   168
              Free Publicity   170
              Advertising   173
              Direct Mail   176
              Internet Marketing   180
              Trade Shows   185
              Measure Your Results   187

Chapter 15   THE HOOK OF SALES   189
Set the Stage   190
Present with Confidence   193
Perfect Your Follow-Up   196
Close with Aplomb   198
Land the Trophy Client   201

Chapter 16   CREATING LIFETIME CUSTOMERS   203
Five-Star Customer Service   204
Your Fortune Is in Your Follow-Up   205
Court the Dissatisfied Customer   207
Loyalty and Referral Programs   209

Success Secret #6   *The Octopus Is Mightier than the Elephant*   211

PART V   BAG OF LOVE: CREATING YOUR LEGACY   212

Success Secret #7   *The Heart Weighs More than the Wallet*   213

Chapter 17   BALANCE YOUR MIND, BODY, AND SPIRIT   214
The Importance of Relationships   214
An Active Mind   219
A Healthy Body   220
An Open Spirit   222

Chapter 18   BE THE HERO OF YOUR OWN LIFE   226
Your Hero's Journey   227
Give Back to Others   228
Give Wings to Your Dreams   230

AUTHOR'S NOTE   231
REFERENCES   232
RESOURCES   236
INDEX   238

Success Secrets These secrets speak directly to the hearts and goals of women. They encourage you to break free of conventional thinking, capitalize on your feminine strengths, crank up your business, and grow.

Learn from the Stars These are motivational stories about famous men and women who overcame obstacles and discovered their greatness through business ownership. These legends of entrepreneurship will elevate and inspire you.

Winning Women These are stories of everyday women just like you who pushed through their fears and summoned up the courage to move ahead with their dreams. If they can do it, so can you.

Hazardous to Your Wealth These are warnings about very costly problems to avoid. It's your chance to learn from trial and error of the business mavericks.

Introduction

I'm known as the "Wealthy Bag Lady." I own a thriving business in partnership with my best friend. I work as a small business consultant, speak internationally to groups on business success, and am the founder of Women's Small Business Month and the Women's Small Business Expo, which are massive empowerment events for female entrepreneurs.

If you think I'm a natural businesswoman, think again! Before I started my own business, I was so deeply in debt I didn't know which end was up. For most of my life I thought business was intimidating, not to mention boring. It was something for men, not for me. I never took one business class in college—all of my college studies were in art. But I've achieved an exciting, successful life through business, and I'm here to help you do the same.

THE ARTIST'S PATH

As a child I loved to draw and paint. This passion and talent continued well into my teenage years, and my mother encouraged me to study art in college. Of course, she also thought the answer to my financial future was to find a good husband. My father was more practical, reminding me that being an artist would probably relegate me to a meager existence.

I listened to my mother, not my father. Art was the perfect career choice for me. I was painfully shy, and it let me hide from the world. In school, I was the kid in the back of the classroom who was constantly hiding and in fear of raising her hand. Parties, job interviews, even getting my hair done were stressful events because of my shyness. I didn't even start dating until I was in my twenties. Being left alone all day to work on my collages and paint my large canvases suited me just fine.

After graduating from college, I actually sold some of my artwork but only earned enough money to go to the grocery store . . . one time. I wanted to do some strange things, like eat, buy clothing, pay rent, and breathe. Fewer than 5 percent of artists make their living from their art, and I was not one of this 5 percent.

I took a sales position at a gallery to support my "habit." My first sale was the ultimate high. I realized that I had talents other than art. I could actually develop rapport with people and convince them to buy something. I learned the techniques of prospecting, building relationships, and closing. One day, the manager, Mike, said to me, "Kiddo, I like the way you handle your customers. Even if an art piece is $25,000, you say, 'It's only $25,000.' It actually turns the conversation away from price and onto the benefits."

Unfortunately, at that point I didn't recognize and make use of my talents. Burdened with low self-esteem and lacking the guts to create my own success plan and start my business, I bounced from job to job. I took the easy way out, following other people's directions and living from paycheck to paycheck. I sold housewares, furniture, and advertising. I desperately tried to measure up to my boss's standard of performance, but I was constantly frustrated. I would come up with ideas of how to improve each company I worked for, but I could not implement them. I saw many capable people passed up for promotions and many less deserving people move up the corporate ladder because they mastered the art of office politics.

THE ABYSS

The lowest point of my life was in 1988. I was worse than broke. I was buried in major debt, afraid to go to my mailbox because of the bills I couldn't afford to pay. Credit card companies and their lovely debt collectors were constantly harassing me on the phone. I was working like a dog in a dead-end job as a giftware sales representative, battling the horrendous Los Angeles traffic to get to the office. My bosses were obnoxious, overbearing, alpha males from another culture, almost another planet.

I was living in a low-rent apartment, concealing the whereabouts of my "family"—my beautiful cat Tuffy—from my landlord, constantly worried about being discovered. I couldn't afford to live anywhere else. I couldn't even imagine buying a house of my own.

On the highway of men, I was constantly getting off on the "Jerk Exit," and during that period I was dating a temperamental and abusive man. He never abused me physically, but he certainly did emotionally. He was prone to tremendous mood swings. He was jealous of the time I spent with my girlfriends. Unfortunately, my self-confidence at the time was so low that I thought this relationship was better than no relationship at all.

One day, my boss announced that he was moving into my office and checking all my work. That was the last straw. I knew that I couldn't take this kind of violation of my personal space and privacy eight hours a day. I wanted more. I didn't believe we were put on this earth to work our fingers to the bone—and never see the light at the end of the tunnel.

I went home, assessed my core values while Tuffy purred on my lap, and made some critical life decisions. I decided that it was absolutely essential to my mental well-being to be surrounded by supportive people. I vowed that if I ever had employees, I would respect them as people with feelings, emotions, sensitivity, intelligence, and a life outside the company. I decided to fire my idiot boss and dump my jerky boyfriend. The next thing I did was to pick up the phone and call my best friend, Sheryl Felice.

THE BAG LADIES ARE BORN

In some ways, the story of my life began at age thirteen, on the playground at recess, when a classmate named Sheryl asked me to have lunch with her. We didn't know it at the time, but the unstoppable girl power that has guided our lives had been officially put into motion.

It's hard to believe that the little geeky kid in the school cafeteria has grown into the beautiful woman who is my business partner today. Sheryl and I have gone through incredible life experiences together. Whenever a boyfriend dumped me or a boss treated me badly, Sheryl was a comforting shoulder to cry on. Whenever something momentous happened in my life, she was there to share in the excitement.

Sheryl and I quickly became closer than sisters, and her mother, whom I adored, was very different from my own. I loved my mother more than anything and she was truly amazing. She was nurturing, sensitive, romantic, and creative, but she mostly cared about making a beautiful home. My "other mother," Rhoda, cared about her career. She was fiercely loyal to her family and friends, but she needed the stimulation of working outside the home.

In the seventies, when the first wave of feminism was making a controversial impact on America, it was Sheryl who told me, excitedly, that we could do and be anything we desired. We needed to acknowledge our worth as women. Our identity was no longer based on being someone's wife, mother, or daughter. We could go after success in our own right and claim our part of the American dream.

Her message was echoing in my mind that night, in 1988, when I called her, told her the woes and discoveries of my day, and begged her to quit her job so we could go into business together.

She was game.

We didn't know where to start. We thought about opening a restaurant, but neither of us could cook. We thought about opening a retail store, but it didn't inspire us. Then one day I opened a closet and my collection of shopping bags with beautiful graphics cascaded out and almost buried me. It was a breakthrough moment. I thought, "Wait a minute. Sheryl and I have been collecting great shopping bags for years. Here's something we know *and* love." We had chosen our business.

Next came an exciting period of researching precisely what it meant to produce promotional bags. Where would we get the bags? Who would print the graphics? How would we let prospective clients know about our business? At least we had a wonderful business name: The Bag Ladies.

Our first client came entirely by chance. I had been referred to a woman who might know where I could buy sturdy rope to use as the handles for bags. It turned out she knew nothing about rope, but she asked about my business. Swallowing my trepidation, I announced that my partner and I produced promotional bags—even though we'd never produced a bag in our lives. It turned out this woman was looking for a company to create promotional bags for the City of San Antonio, Texas.

After I hung up the phone, Sheryl and I looked at each other and burst out laughing. We had an order, but now—oh no!—we had to figure out how to do it.

We figured it out, and kept doing so. We learned to promote our business through direct mail and other marketing strategies, creating our first handwritten mailing lists by poring through business journals. We underpriced some jobs and had to eat our costs. Even my passion for art came into play—my life came full circle when my art training allowed me to run the graphics department of our company.

We identified a need, among small companies, of short print runs of bags and developed a way to fill it while our competitors required a minimum run of five thousand bags. We'd found a niche. Before long we were doing short runs for big names. Movie studios needed a small number of bags for one-night events such as parties and openings. The Bag Ladies became purveyors to the stars, and we haven't stopped since. Our client list has grown to include names such as Ocean Spray, Infiniti, Revlon, Yamaha, Sanyo Fisher, Sears, and Nissan.

FROM ONE BUSINESS SPRINGS ANOTHER

Because we were one of the only women-owned promotional-bag firms in the country, women entrepreneurs were attracted to our business. I got to know these fabulous females intimately. They confided to me their hopes, dreams, challenges, concerns, and motivations. I knew what made these women get out of bed in the morning, and what really rocked their world.

I saw certain women entrepreneurs setting the world on fire. Their businesses started small, and their growth was fast and furious. Other women's businesses seemed doomed to failure, or in a continual struggle to stay afloat.

I wanted to know why some businesses thrived and others failed. My thirst for knowledge had begun. I was insatiable. My library of business and investing books grew. If there was a seminar on how to close more sales, I was there. If a real estate guru wanted to tell people how to buy income properties creatively with no money down, count me in. If there was a class on how to start your own business, I was one of the first to enroll. What I never found was a seminar for women that addressed their special challenges and issues about business.

As I exchanged ideas with the women who did business with The Bag Ladies, I frequently found myself in the role of offering advice. I'd learned so much in my own company—and through all those seminars and books—and it was wonderful to share this knowledge. I really enjoyed looking at other businesswomen's problems and arriving at solutions.

Finally I recognized that what I was doing had value, and people might even be willing to pay me for it. The shy girl who used to be afraid to raise her hand in class started a consulting business. One day, one of my clients said to me, "You're not just a bag lady, you're a Wealthy Bag Lady." I'd found the name for my new business.

The next step on my entrepreneurial path was teaching seminars. I could hardly believe that I was getting up in front of crowds of strangers, but I had so much to share. And much to my amazement, I discovered that public speaking was stimulating, rewarding, and fun.

Radio interviews were harder, because I couldn't see who I was talking to. On my first radio interview, I was so nervous I wore a hole in the carpet from pacing. But I was on a roll. I wanted to do more. I wanted to affect women's lives on a wider scale. The next step was to create Women's Small Business Month and the Women's Small Business Expo, events and celebrations where women could learn success skills and acknowledge the accomplishments of the remarkable women business owners who preceded them. From one step to the next to the next—what an exhilarating ride!

And, by the way, I met the man of my dreams at one of those real estate seminars. We are now happily married and Leslie is the best man I've ever known.

Bags to Riches

As I've already confessed, I'm a book and seminar junkie. I've read tons of business books, but as a woman, many of these didn't speak to me. Swimming with the sharks, guerrilla business tactics, ripping the heads off the competition—these are not comfortable concepts for women. Winning women are more comfortable with collaboration than competition.

When I discovered I couldn't find a book that fully spoke to my needs, I decided it was time to write one. Through my business I had talked to thousands of women. I had come to know their challenges, motivations, and dreams. To add to this knowledge, I interviewed multimillionaires, CEOs, celebrities, authors, psychologists, international speakers, and leading authorities on finance and business. Their marvelous advice and wisdom forms the backbone of this book.

Bags to Riches is for women just starting out in business as well as for those who are already traveling the entrepreneurial road but need a little help around the curves. In this book you will learn how to choose a business that's right for you, get through the hoops of making it legal, find financing, hire employees, and create lifetime customers. You will also learn how to break through the roadblocks to your dreams—even (especially!) if they are inside your head. In the midst of all this information and advice are seven secrets of success that speak specifically to the dreams and hearts of women.

Most business book authors put themselves on a pedestal and try to tell you how great they are. I've knocked the pedestal down and thrown it out the window.

I've revealed the many mistakes I've made in business, and I'll tell you how to avoid those pitfalls. Trial and error is great, but it's very expensive. If I can take away some of the hard knocks of business for you, my mission is accomplished.

I have peppered these pages with real-life success stories of people just like you who were inspired to knock down their obstacles, start successful businesses, and move ahead with their dreams. I wrote this book to empower women, but I did not interview women exclusively. As a woman, you don't want to be discriminated against because of an accident of your gender. Men have learned incredible business lessons from women ever since feminism brought fearless females into the workplace. Empowered women can also learn wonderful things from men.

The success concepts in *Bags to Riches* are explained in plain English. My mission is to help you live well and discover your greatness, not to impress you with fancy schmancy terms.

I also want you to have fun while you read. What a concept for a business book! Well, I'm here to tell you that business can be stimulating, creative, challenging, rewarding, and yes—*fun!* When I give seminars, I throw a girl's party. We play music, solve puzzles, dance, do makeovers, and give away prizes. I've even thought of asking my students to show up in their nightgowns so that we can have a good old-fashioned pajama party. People take life and business much too seriously. The only way to keep your sanity is to be able to laugh at life and yourself.

Reading this book is a giant step toward starting your business and claiming your power. But you are going to have to take an active role in your success and wealth-building. You can't just sit back in your comfy armchair and expect your Fairy Godmother to wave her magic wand of success. The more you put into anything, the more you'll get out of it.

Fear is the biggest hurdle you need to overcome. You need to believe deep down in your soul that you can do it. You need to discover and celebrate your greatness, so that you can share it with the world.

Let's get started!

PART I

BAG OF DREAMS

Setting the Stage

You've Already Got What It Takes

It's true: You've got what it takes to succeed as an entrepreneur. Many women simply don't believe this. They don't believe they can compete with men. But the fact is, you were born with the ability to make your dreams into reality.

Being a woman is your base of power, not your weakness. Women entrepreneurs are the fastest growing segment of the economy. We are starting businesses at twice the rate of men and claiming our true economic power. We are a force to be reckoned with. This isn't just because we've been held back so long—it's because we're good at it.

Capitalize on your feminine strengths. Some of the most talented businesspeople can read profit and loss statements, but they neglect to pay attention to their intuition. Use that famous female sixth sense. If you get a bad feeling about the character of a prospective customer or business associate, heed your body's warning instead of ignoring it. Your first impression is usually right. Listen to your inner voice.

Winning women are more likely than men to admit when they don't know something and ask for help. Being natural networkers, they seek out mentors and develop a great supporting cast. Within their companies, employee-management relationships form into supportive teams, rather than hierarchical structures.

From birth, women are relationship-oriented. They create powerful bonds and connections. In business, this translates to nurturing clients and providing great customer service. In sales, women are able to focus on helping others rather than pushing products. They ask poignant questions, learn their customer's needs, and offer extraordinary solutions. To skyrocket your business, cash in on the feminine.

CHAPTER 1

Go for It!

My life changed when I went into business for myself. I became fulfilled creatively, financially, and emotionally. Instead of dreading my dead-end job, I flew out of bed in the morning with a kazillion new ideas for my business. Rather than just earning a living, I became the architect of my own life.

Some women certainly achieve success and do good work without starting their own businesses. Professionals such as doctors and judges work well within established hospitals and courts. Teachers and professors contribute tremendously in their communities and gain benefits and tenure in the bargain. An accomplished chef may be more suited to running just the back kitchen rather than the entire restaurant.

Still, you're reading this book because somewhere in your heart you want to strike out on your own. You may be worrying that you aren't a natural entrepreneur. Some people are certainly more suited to starting their own businesses than others, but in my work with women entrepreneurs, I've come to recognize that we're all a lot more suited than we might at first believe.

You'll face challenges, but you can overcome them. You'll run into roadblocks, but you can bust through them. The rewards are enormous. Go for it!

ARE YOU A NATURAL ENTREPRENEUR?

To see if you have the right stuff to fly solo in your own business, take this short quiz. Answer each question honestly with a number between 1 and 5.

1 = NEVER   2 = RARELY   3 = SOMETIMES   4 = USUALLY   5 = ALWAYS

1. I'm a self-starter.

2. I'm organized.

3. I'm creative.

4. I'm competitive.

5. I have adequate resources.

6. I finish the projects I start.

7. I'm excited about meeting new challenges.

8. My spouse, friends, and family are supportive.

9. I'm willing to make short-term sacrifices for long-term rewards.

10. I create rapport with people.

11. I'm comfortable with selling myself.

12. I'm comfortable asking for help.

13. I'm able to take rejection.

14. I'm able to learn from my mistakes.

15. I listen to my intuition.

Now add up your points and determine your entrepreneurial profile:

- **Less than 35: Lady-in-Waiting.** Fear may be holding you back from starting a business or taking your business to the next level. You need to stop thinking small and expand your horizons. You may have negative people in your life who have chipped away at your self-worth. The good news is that with the right information, a great supporting cast, and a shot of self-confidence, you will take the entrepreneurial leap and succeed!

- **35 to 50: Daring Dame.** You have wonderful ideas, energy, and motivation. You have received shining praise from others. You have a natural rapport with people and a sincere desire to help others. Success is yours if you are aware of distractions on your journey toward your goals and dreams. Feel the fear and do it anyway!

- **More than 50: Entrepreneurial Empress.** You are a freedom fighter with amazing leadership skills. You may not be the one who was voted "Most Likely to Succeed," but your inner strength and resiliency will surprise everyone—even you. A maverick like you breaks down the roadblocks in your way and leaves the losers in the dust. You dream big and your world has no boundaries. Taking risks and meeting challenges are like adrenaline to you. You go, girl!

BENEFITS OF BEING YOUR OWN BOSS

Let me tell you a secret: If I had taken that entrepreneurial test before I started my business, I only would have scored as a Lady-in-Waiting. Sure, it helps to have the deck stacked in your favor, but you don't have to be a natural entrepreneur to be a successful one.

I believe every woman should start her own business, even if it's only part-time, even if it's just to get a taste of it. Here are a few of the reasons.

Freedom and Independence

Liberty is so precious to Americans that it's written on every one of our coins. Claim your power. You want it. Go ahead and get it! Freedom and independence are the number-one reasons why women start businesses.

The true measure of success is being able to live on your own terms. Only then are you able to live your passionate life and do it bravely. When I was an employee, my boss decided on my hours, my salary, and my vacation days. He even had control over my weekends and free time. By going to work for myself, I claimed my freedom and determined my true worth.

The burning desire for freedom may also foretell your accelerated growth. The National Foundation for Women Business Owners and Fleet Boston Financial wanted to know more about the differences between fast-growth women-owned firms and the laggards. They found that 46 percent of the "gazelles"—women owners of fast-growth firms—cited "wanting to be independent" as their prime motivator in starting their businesses.

Entrepreneurship allows you to do the work you want, with the people you want. When you work for someone else, you may need to deal not only with Bozo the Boss but also with Toxic Tina the employee, whose negative attitude affects others and destroys their motivation. But what can you do? Since you don't own the company, you can't fire her. You would like her to do the same disappearing act your last boyfriend did, but you're forced to deal with her.

Flexibility

Has your son or daughter been rehearsing for weeks for the school play and wants you desperately to be there? Does the performance take place during business hours? With your own business, you can rearrange client meetings and work obligations so that you can see your child portray a stop sign in the school play.

For example, Jan Brogniez and Stacey Hall of Perfect Customers Unlimited decided that they only wanted to work Monday through Thursday. They felt that they would not serve their customers well if they were burned out and exhausted. Fridays would be their day to recharge and plan for the upcoming week. By starting their own firm, they could arrange their work hours around their unique styles and values.

As the visionary of your company, you can create a family-friendly environment. Your pets can be your furry little office companions. You can take vacations whenever you want—why confine yourself to the traditional two weeks a year? Even if your business demands long hours when you first get it started, you can choose what hours you work, and keep the rest of your life in perspective.

> *I snapped out of my commuter daydream only to discover that I had been dreaming I had pneumonia, was in the hospital, and had a big smile on my face because I was resting peacefully and didn't have to go to work.*
> —Beth Sirull, coauthor, *Creating Your Life Collage*

Financial Potential

Business ownership is the fast track to wealth. It always has been and always will be. In the book *The Millionaire Next Door,* 99 percent of the millionaires interviewed by authors Thomas J. Stanley and William D. Danko owned their own businesses. Most of the wealthiest people in the world are entrepreneurs. Oprah Winfrey is a great talk show host, but she is also the CEO of her own company, Harpo Productions. Bill Gates of Microsoft, Ruth Handler of Mattel, and Michael Dell of Dell Computer all rose to mega-wealth through entrepreneurship.

This is not to say that all small businesses succeed. Many don't, and many take years and years to become profitable. But the fact remains that when you work for someone else, the amount you earn is dictated by your employer. Despite the challenges, the potential for financial gain is far greater when you work for yourself.

Empowerment

Women are all about connections and relationships. We need approval. A caustic relationship with a boss or a superior affects our entire psyche. I once heard a radio show moderated by a husband-and-wife team of radio psychologists. A caller named Mona said she was thinking of leaving her job, because of the abrasive relationship she was having with her boss. The husband psychologist told Mona not to look for emotional satisfaction and personal growth from her job. "Your job is the place you go to advance your career and pay the bills. Got it?" The wife understood that experiencing this kind of stress for forty hours a week would lower Mona's self-esteem and affect her other relationships. Her advice to Mona was that she should start a business of her own where she could feel good about herself.

I still miss my ex, but my aim is improving.
—bumper sticker

Starting your own business is a passport to self-esteem and empowerment. It is a rite of passage into a kind of adulthood that has nothing to do with age. In many ways, a superior-subordinate relationship with a boss is similar to a parent-child relationship. In a disagreement, you can argue your point, but you have to defer to the authority figure. Just as rebellion is part of growing up, you may feel the need as an adult for what psychologists call "creative rebellion." When you start your own business, you grow into a second adulthood by deciding on the direction of your own life.

Becoming a business owner gets you into an exclusive club. It's a gutsy move and your reward is to associate with other mavericks who will share their business strategies with you. You will meet them through your business and at industry meetings, conventions, associations, chambers of commerce, and networking functions. Associating with these visionaries is truly empowering.

And let's not forget the revenge factor. Hey, don't knock it. We've all had the "I'll show them" fantasy. We walk into our high school reunion and the music and dancing stops like in *West Side Story*. All eyes are on us. We are a perfect size 6 and the other women, who have developed thunder thighs and are starting to sag everywhere, look at us and our gorgeous hunk-of-the-month, regretting all the cruel things they did and said to us. The ex-boyfriend who cheated on us, treated us bad, and chose someone else suddenly sees the error of his ways. Best of all, we have a successful business and have gone further in life than any of these losers ever dreamed of. Ha!

WEALTH IS NOT JUST NICE— IT'S NECESSARY

Women are making huge strides toward financial equality with men. But face it: the glass ceiling still exists. Many women continue to earn less than they're worth, and less than their male counterparts. This is particularly aggravating since women frequently need more money than men. Sound ridiculous? Think about it . . .

Girl Stuff

Remember the scene in the movie *Tootsie,* where Dustin Hoffman goes to the department store and buys all the "girl stuff" so he can dress like his soap-opera character Dorothy? In his vain attempt to measure up to the television standard of beauty, he buys dresses, panty hose, scarves, cosmetics, depilatories, hand bags, hair products, jewelry, perfume, and control-top underwear. He tells his friend, "I don't know how a woman can be attractive without spending a fortune."

Just the "girl stuff" adds up to thousands of dollars a year. A shoe sale turns meek and mild women into Darwinian predators. A feeding frenzy ensues where only the strongest survive and walk away victorious with the spoils of war.

MADISON AVENUE MANIPULATION

We're told that our skin isn't soft enough. Our teeth aren't white enough. Our hair is the wrong color. Our breasts are too flat, but our stomachs need to be flatter. We're told we need to slim down our thighs but fatten up our eyelashes. There's even a 2000 Calorie Mascara. Give me a break!

Don't make the Feminine Mistake. Spend enough on girl stuff to feel good about yourself, but don't be manipulated by Madison Avenue into spending more money than you can afford.

Some of the costs of being female are frivolous—and should be resisted—but others aren't. A friend of mine who lives in New York spends a small fortune every month to ride in taxicabs rather than on the subway because she feels safer that way. Women spend more for dry cleaning and hairstyling. Studies by online car marketplace autobytel.com even report that women pay more than men for the same car.

Divorce

One of the most devastating experiences for women is divorce. Some women never recover financially and emotionally from this trauma. I applaud all the women who want to be full-time moms to their children. It is the hardest job you will ever do,

THE DETERMINATION TO THRIVE

Terri Murphy is an entrepreneur and expert on real estate and technology. She is a regular guest commentator on ABC, NBC, and CNN. This beautiful bombshell also has a truly magnificent home. But it wasn't always that way.

Terri is the first to admit she made poor choices in men. Her husband was abusive and deceitful. One day, he did the unthinkable. Terri came home to find herself locked out of her own home.

For the next three years, she lived out of her car. Ironically, during the time she was homeless, she was still working in real estate, selling opulent million-dollar properties. She didn't admit to any of her coworkers that she didn't have a roof over her own head. She showered at her gym. She became a professional speaker, partly so she could spend a night in a hotel when her clients flew her to out-of-town engagements.

Terri could have drifted into a deep depression and let the anger over her divorce eat her alive. Instead, she used her intense determination to survive and thrive. She now has a wonderful man in her life. She has the gorgeous home of her dreams, but she lets people know that even accomplished women can become homeless. Her mission is to tell women how to protect themselves so that they will never become victims.

but please don't paint yourself into a corner by relying solely on your husband's income. Even if you're currently happily married, the hard statistics make a strong case for learning about business and laying the groundwork for taking care of yourself. You can start with such simple steps as helping your husband handle family finances and establishing credit in your own name.

Half of all women married in the past twenty years will eventually divorce. According to *Divorce Magazine,* 45 percent of divorced women experience a drop in their income from when they were married. The average woman's standard of living drops dramatically in the first year after a divorce, but the average man's standard of living rises after a marital split. Of the women who go through a divorce, only 23 percent will be granted an award of ongoing financial support from their ex-husbands. As if that isn't bad enough, more than a third of the women who are entitled to alimony or child support will never see a penny of the money that's due them.

Childcare and Eldercare

After a divorce, the woman usually takes care of the children's financial needs, a substantial burden since single mothers often earn less than their married counterparts. In addition, as marvelous as motherhood is, it frequently means that women take time off from working and don't pay into the Social Security system. At retirement, this gives them less money to live on every single month.

Women are also more likely than men to care for an aging parent, which often includes financial support. According to a recent study, as many as two-thirds of working people who try to help their aging parents feel they have lost out on promotions and pay raises because they can't give a full commitment to their jobs. It's been called the "glass ceiling of caregivers," and it's likely to become more widespread as thousands more families face the experience of helping their aging parents maintain a satisfactory quality of life.

Longevity

The most compelling reason that women need more money than men is that, on average, women outlive men by seven years. If a woman needs $30,000 a year to live, that's an extra $210,000 over her lifetime.

The average age at which a woman becomes a widow is only fifty-six. Almost four times as many widows live in poverty as wives of the same age. Of those widows who are now living in poverty, some 80 percent hadn't been poor while their husbands were still alive. It wasn't supposed to be that way. In their golden years, women thought they would be traveling with their husbands, doing the things they couldn't do when they were working and raising the kids. Instead, they find themselves living on a shoestring so that they don't outlive their money.

Clearly, starting your own business isn't a one-step solution to these challenges, but it's certainly a good place to start.

Bust through the Roadblocks

I absolutely believe that women can be hugely effective and find tremendous satisfaction through business. I also acknowledge that we face more roadblocks to our success than men. Recognizing these roadblocks is the first step to breaking through them. Here are some of the most common roadblocks for women:

Fear

In our early childhood, we have no fear of failure or fear of rejection. We want to start walking, so we take a couple of clumsy steps, only to fall flat on our face. But do we quit? No. We just get up again and take some more steps with no thoughts of failure, embarrassment, or looking foolish. We don't worry about people not loving us because we failed. Failure is part of learning and growing as a person. There are no points for playing it safe.

Fear wears many different masks: procrastination, perfectionism, and even arrogance. It is the most expensive habit you will ever have. If you think you can't do something, you'll always be right. If you think you *can* do it, you'll also always be right.

Fear of the unknown is universal. Human beings are creatures of habit and, by nature, afraid of change. Starting your business is a huge change. I've talked with many women over the years, and I know there's a lot of fear out there—fear of success as well as fear of failure. I often ask women to write down their fears about success. One woman thought that if she were successful, her friends would become resentful and she would be alone. It would be like sixth grade all over again.

Another woman feared that her alcoholic brother would always be on her doorstep asking for money.

Breaking past the roadblock of fear is about breaking out of your comfort zone. When I first started my business, I had to go out and make sales presentations. It was definitely out of my comfort zone. Sometimes I had to do what's affectionately known as a "dog and pony show," presenting to many people at one time around a conference table. These people would ask many tough questions and put me on the spot. Oh no! What if I start stuttering? What if I don't make the sale? What if I have a gross pimple on my nose that day? And the scariest thought of all . . . What if I get rejected?

> *Once I decide to do something, I can't have people telling me I can't. If there's a roadblock, you jump over it, walk around it, or crawl under it.*
> —Kitty Kelley,
> celebrity biographer

Talking to multimillionaires, celebrities, business leaders, and experts on success was very scary for me. I was in awe of many of the people I interviewed. They were my heroes. I had witnessed their brilliance when they inspired large crowds. I had read their books. I studied them for years. What if they didn't like me? What if they thought I was a bad interviewer? What if I came off as stupid?

We may not be happy putting out maximum effort for minimum pay, but it sure is familiar. The fear of the unknown is so powerful that most people never get out of their comfort zones. Think about it. The thermostat in your home is based on the concept of a comfort zone. When it is too cold, the heat is activated. When it is too hot, the air-conditioning comes on. When the thermostat is in its comfort zone, nothing happens.

A technique of Robert G. Allen, author of *Nothing Down and Multiple Streams of Income,* in his Master System is to do your "feared thing first." We all know about procrastination. We open the refrigerator door again and again, hoping the cheesecake we want will magically appear. We feel an urgent need to clean out the sock drawer. When you procrastinate, a lot of psychological baggage gets attached to the scary task you're avoiding. After doing the feared task, you realize it wasn't as difficult or as scary as you thought it would be. You become filled with a sense of accomplishment. You give yourself permission to succeed.

Naysayers

When you announce your intentions to start your own business, your family and friends may not always respond with enthusiasm. You might be greeted with something like, "Don't you know that practically all small businesses fail?" "Don't you know that it's not the right time to start a business?" "Don't you remember what happened to Aunt Sally?"

Going in a new direction requires courage. You must protect your fragile dreams in their early stages. The media gives us the impression that our dreams are thwarted by gigantic forces outside ourselves, like the state of the economy. In reality, the danger lies much closer at hand. Instead of being your allies, your friends and family may be critical of your entrepreneurial dreams. They aren't trying to throw a wet blanket on your fire because they're cruel. They care about you and they don't want to see you fail or get hurt.

For me, the naysayer was my father. When I started The Bag Ladies, I had a terrible fight with him. My father is five feet six inches tall, but to me he was always larger than life. I love my father dearly and I needed his approval more than anything in the world. I didn't get it.

When I started my business, my father told me that I was "living in a fantasy world." Who was I to think that I could run a business, when the only training I had in college was art classes? To add insult to injury, he yelled, "You're not qualified to do anything!"

His words were like daggers to me, but I made a decision. I could believe him, take his words to heart, or I could show him that he was wrong about me. I knew that it was my time to strike out on my own. I built my business and traveled the world.

> *If the idea of making a living without a job doesn't make you feel a bit fearful, check your pulse.*
>
> —Barbara J. Winter, entrepreneur and author, *Making a Living without a Job*

The rift with my father lasted for years and left a tremendous hole in my heart. My life was great, but I was missing one thing: my father's approval. When I started teaching small business success seminars to women, I sent him an audio tape of one of my classes. Then one day I answered the phone to a gruff, familiar voice. My father made a special call to tell me he was proud of me, and he apologized for all the hurtful things he said in the past. I was filled with so much love that I thought my heart would burst. Now my father and I have a great relationship. He is my biggest fan, and he and I have been close ever since.

Lack of Knowledge

Lack of knowledge is an enormous roadblock to success for women entrepreneurs. There's so much we don't know and think we can't learn. You may feel you don't know enough about business in general, or your field in particular. You may feel you don't know enough about the world of finance.

It's really not the lack of money that keeps women's businesses from flourishing, but the lack of capital-raising skills and knowledge. Unless the Financing Fairy Godmother graces them with unlimited funds, most women lack the necessary information about how to put together business plans, how to do projections, and who to approach as possible financing sources.

Lack of knowledge about technology is another big one for women. The rules are changing constantly. New technology makes the old stuff marginal. Worse yet, every new technology has a learning curve. By the time you learn that blasted new computer program, it seems that something better always comes along to replace it.

Don't be discouraged by lack of knowledge. Just get out there and learn. Go to seminars. Take evening classes. Hire coaches. Read books. You're reading a book right now—you can do it!

Personality Traps

In my success coaching, I talk to many women who are just too sensitive about business. Every rejection becomes a devastating blow. It takes them days to pick themselves up and start over again. The likes of a potential buyer who wouldn't even call them back can crush and distract them for days.

I'm a victim of this oversensitivity as well. I get insulted if someone doesn't want to be on my email newsletter anymore. How dare they? Don't they know what they're missing?

The truth is these people who reject us are really doing us a favor. They are not our ideal customers. They are freeing us. We will not waste our time on them, but concentrate on our top-priority customers. Remember the guy you had a crush on in school who didn't return your feelings? At the time it was the ultimate horrible rejection, but he was really doing you a gigantic favor by not leading you on so you could focus your romantic energy on a truly willing participant.

> *The difference between a winner and a loser is that the winner has failed more.*
> —Claude Diamond, author, The Mentor: A Story of Success

Another personality trap is perfectionism. I fell into it for years. Needing to have everything perfect is just another way to put off the things you are afraid of. Ramon Williamson, business coach and author of *Live Your Best Life* says, "Strive for completion, not perfection."

Do you think other people really notice if everything's perfect? Probably not; they're too busy thinking about themselves. Have you ever met a perfect person? Did you like that person? Enough said.

CHAPTER 2

Attitude Is (Almost) Everything

*E*very woman who reads this book comes to the table with vastly different backgrounds, limitations, talents, circumstances, perceptions, thoughts, and belief systems. And each of you has the capacity to succeed, not because of the facts you'll learn in these pages, but because you have it inside you. Success is 80 percent attitude and only 20 percent strategy.

DETERMINATION

What makes a successful woman entrepreneur? Is it talent? Is it intelligence? What is the mystical ingredient?

It's determination. It's that certain little spirit that compels you to stick it out just when you're at your most tired. It's that quality that forces you to persevere, find the route around the stone wall. It's the immovable stubbornness that will not allow you to cave in when everyone says give up.

In Chérie Carter-Scott's book, *If Life Is a Game, These Are the Rules,* one of the rules of being human is that there are no mistakes, only lessons. When disappointments occur, you are immediately faced with a choice. You have one of two options. You can fall down, weighted by self-recrimination and an attitude of defeat. Or you can process the disappointment, persevere, and eventually learn and grow from what happened. In other words, you can either give up or move forward.

Most people feel great disappointment and anger when the plans in which they've invested a great deal of energy, time, and money fall through. The first reaction for most of us is to feel that we've failed. The failed experiments, however, are no less valuable than the experiments that ultimately prove successful; in fact, you usually learn more from your failures than you do from your successes.

THE AWESOME POWER OF THE SUBCONSCIOUS

Your body will produce what your mind believes. Within your subconscious depths lie infinite wisdom, infinite power, an infinite supply of everything you need. It's waiting there for you to give it development and expression. Once you learn to contact and release the hidden power of your subconscious mind, you can bring into life more wealth, more health, more happiness, and more joy than you ever thought possible.

TRIUMPH OF THE HUMAN SPIRIT

Jackie Nink Pflug has lived through horrors that most of us cannot imagine. In 1985, she was a young newlywed and a special education teacher in Cairo, Egypt. She and her husband had spent Thanksgiving weekend in Greece, and she was to fly back to Cairo ahead of him. Ten minutes after her flight left Athens, however, the plane was hijacked by three brutal terrorists.

Like four hostages before her, Jackie was shot in the head at point-blank range, execution style, thrown from the plane onto the tarmac in Malta, and left for dead. The hijacking of EgyptAir flight 648 turned into one of history's deadliest airline attacks. Fifty-nine passengers died during the ordeal. Miraculously, Jackie lived.

Jackie went through years of physical and emotional healing. Her marriage ended in divorce. She went into debt to write her book, *Miles to Go before I Sleep,* which propelled her into her current role as an inspirational speaker and entrepreneur.

During her recovery, the doctors told Jackie that she would never be able to teach again, drive a car, or have a baby. She proved them wrong and did all three. Now she is remarried with a beautiful son. When people hear her speak, they witness firsthand the triumph of the human spirit.

You do not need to acquire this power. You already possess it. But you will have to learn how to use it. You must understand it so you can apply it in all areas of your life. Unlike the conscious mind, the deeper subconscious is noncritical and nonjudgmental. If you feed it a constant diet of positive self-talk, it will respond with positive actions.

Positive Self-Talk

Nothing will stop you from achieving your dreams more quickly than negative self-talk. The inner beast inside your head says, "I'm going to fail. Everyone will think I'm a loser. I'm not ready. I'm not good enough."

Women tend to pay more attention to this inner beast than men do. Our challenge is to maintain our sensitivity and empathy, while learning not to take everything so personally. We need to develop a thicker skin for business.

Here is some negative self-talk your inner beast may be whispering in your ear:

- I can't do it.
- I'm too young.
- I'm too old.
- Everyone else is better than me.
- I'm not smart enough.
- Nobody cares.
- I'll get rejected.
- I don't know what to do.
- I don't have enough money.
- I'll fail.
- I'll be sorry.
- I just can't win.

Does any of this sound familiar? If so, it's time to banish your inner beast and start listening to the positive self-talk of your inner hero.

- I can do it.
- This is precisely the right time in my life to do it.
- I'm going to do it better than anyone else.
- I'm smart enough.
- I'm loved for who I am.

- If people reject me, that's their loss.
- If I don't have the answers, someone else will.
- If I don't have the money, someone else will.
- If I fail, I'll analyze what I did wrong and learn for the future.
- If I go for my dreams, I'll have nothing to regret.
- If it is to be, it's up to me.

The Mental Bank

Here's a tremendous tool I learned from Danielle Durant in her seminar "Success is Not an Accident." As a means of building self-esteem, honoring your worth, and training your subconscious, pay yourself in a "mental bank." The bank isn't a real bank and the money isn't real money, but the profits are immeasurable.

You will pay yourself in your mental bank by the event, the hour, or a combination of the two. Let's say you're just beginning to explore the possibility of starting your own business. You could pay yourself $1,000 for attending a seminar on small business ownership, or $300 for buying a new book about business, then an hourly rate for reading it. You can decide on your rate, but I suggest you pay yourself at least $500 an hour.

At the end of the day, add up the money you earned in your mental bank. Write down the total in the same place every day. At the end of the week, add up the mental bank money. Paying yourself well in your mental bank gets your brain into the habit of receiving abundance and not apologizing for it. You will upgrade your sense of self worth so fast your head will spin.

Your subconscious does not know the difference between a real payday and a make-believe one. Did you get that? To your subconscious you are already rich, making thousands of dollars a day. And if you really want to whip yourself into shape and maximize your time, you can deduct money from your mental bank account for time zappers such as disorganization, gossip, sleeping late, and perfectionism.

I absolutely swear by paying myself in my mental bank and keep track of my mental bank earnings in a special spiral-bound book called the "Success Planner." If my ultimate goal is to make a sale to a customer, I might pay myself $1,000 for making the initial contact, $2,000 for giving a presentation, $500 for writing up the purchase order, another $500 for getting the purchase order signed by the customer, and $1,000 for receiving payment, for a grand total (All Right!) of $5,000. In the real world, I only get paid for making the sale, the final step, but in my mental bank I get paid every step of the way.

Not only has my confidence grown with my mental bank account, but adding up all those numbers has really improved my math skills!

DREAM BIG DREAMS

Just as most women want to fit into a dress size that's too small, they also put themselves in a bag that's too small and never achieve their dreams. Breaking out of the bag means having the courage to deal with your fears. Successful people have big dreams. Break through all of the false limitations you've placed on yourself and create your vivid vision.

Mission Statement

Most successful corporations have their mission statements emblazoned on their annual reports. Some have them hanging on the wall. It is their company philosophy that guides all their important decisions and keeps them on track for achieving their goals.

Even if you haven't yet started your business, you can create a mission statement. It can be a few sentences or a few pages. Look at it every day. Live it. Breathe it. Change it as you change.

My mission statement was once a page long. I've shortened it to one sentence: "I want to live well, have fun, and help others achieve their greatness." It can be that simple.

Be sure your goals are aligned with your mission statement. I've turned down some lucrative business opportunities because I didn't want to deal with offensive people. The opportunity was not aligned with my mission statement. Working with difficult clients who make my life and my staff miserable would have violated my mission statement about having fun. After I turned down these projects, the coast was clear for better and more profitable projects to come my way. The mission statement gives your life clarity and purpose.

Affirmations

Many women have heard about the power of affirmations. They say to themselves, "I am beautiful," "I am smart," "I am wealthy." The reason these affirmations don't always work is that the conscious mind takes over and believes that you are lying to yourself, creating mental conflict.

> *The future belongs to those who believe in the beauty of their dreams.*
> —Eleanor Roosevelt, American First Lady

Your affirmation succeeds best when it is specific and when it does not produce a mental conflict or argument. Your subconscious accepts what you really feel to be true, not just idle words or statements. The dominant idea or belief is always accepted by the subconscious mind.

Instead of "I am prosperous," you can try, "Every day I am becoming more and more prosperous." Instead of chanting, "My sales are phenomenal," you can try, "My sales are improving every day." Instead of declaring, "I am wealthy," say, "I am advancing, progressing, and getting wealthier every day."

Goals and Visions

According to Maria Nemeth in her inspired work *The Energy of Money*, everyone has at least ten or twenty life's intentions locked inside their hearts. Here are some examples:

- To be a better mate.
- To be healthy.
- To be happy.
- To be wealthy.
- To be an adventurer.
- To be compassionate.

What are your life intentions? Feel free to dream and fantasize about your future. Think of where you want your business to be in three years. How do the employees greet you? What is the feeling when you see the sign, open the door to something you've created? How do your customers respond to you? What car are you driving? Where are you living? Involve all your senses in your visioning. Think about the sights, smells, sounds, even the feel of your plush office chair.

Your business is the fulcrum that lets you make a huge impact on society. How do you want to make a difference? Ending world hunger? Eradicating illiteracy? Stamping out domestic violence? Cleaning up the environment? Making child abuse a thing of the past? Ending animal cruelty? Improving the condition of women in third-world countries?

These seem like grandiose fantasies, don't they? Thomas Edison wanted to bring light to the world. Crazy, huh? What do outrageous goals have to do with building your business? When you align yourself to a higher purpose, you are guided by your life's mission. Your mission is the beacon of safety in the cold harbor at night. Your mission is the key to getting through the maze of life. Your mission keeps you on track and on purpose.

Are you an adventurer? One of the reasons I got into business was for the travel. I love to explore new places. Your business gives you the passport to fulfill your adventurous spirit. Imagine all the places you will travel to in the next three years. Who will you travel with? What will you explore there?

Do you want to make the lives of the people you love better? Think about how you can provide a better life for your children because of your business. Fantasize about how you can arrange your schedule to spend time with them during weekdays. You can send them to the best schools and plan for their futures. Maybe you want to help out your parents, friends, other family members. Envision how you will help and impact their lives.

Goals are meaningless without purpose. Oprah Winfrey's mission was not to become one of the richest women in America. It was to inspire and motivate others. She has done that through her show, her movies, her charitable donations, and her business. In fact, one of the common traits of successful people is that they have found something they love to do and figured out how to get paid for it. The millionaire mentors I've talked to say things like, "I can't believe I get paid for this," "I wake up excited every morning about what I do," "I can't wait to start working." Goals/ Visions

Goals are measurable. They have a beginning, middle, and end. Visions are your dreams. Perhaps your vision is to be wealthy so that you can have financial freedom and be able to give freely to those you love. Your wealth goal may be to have a net worth of a million dollars and to be earning $100,000 annually in the next three years. Your fitness vision may be to get in better shape. Perhaps your fitness goal is to lose fifteen pounds in the next three months and work out four times a week.

A CEO of one of the most successful computer companies has his job title as "Visionary" on his business card. To reach your goal, you must first visualize it. When you acquire the wealth and success you deserve, it is already familiar, not scary. Your goals and visions will evolve as your life evolves. I've gone from just wanting a business so I could pay my bills to wanting to empower the lives of women entrepreneurs so that they can achieve their greatness and the success they deserve.

PERSEVERING TO GREATNESS

Mary Cassatt wanted to be a painter from the time she was a young girl in Pennsylvania, but she encountered great opposition. In the mid 1800s, women of her wealthy social background were not encouraged to be anything but wives and mothers.

Even when the young Mary traveled to the more "enlightened" Paris and began realizing her vision, she still had to overcome strong prejudice and bias. Edgar Degas, one of her strongest supporters, once said, "I am not yet ready to accept that a woman can paint this well."

Mary persevered, developing a unique blend of American and European influences. Through both her stubbornness and her competence, she became one of the best and most successful Impressionist painters and was considered the greatest female American artist of her time.

Mary's strong belief in the family is reflected in her brilliant paintings. The themes of her art are woman-centered. She is best known for her sensitive documentation of the bond between a mother and her child.

Exhibitions of Mary Cassatt continue to draw thousands of viewers all over the world. Her admirers come to see her immense talent and to marvel at her courage for defying the enormous ignorance and prejudice against women in her generation.

SENSORY ANCHORING

Sensory anchoring means imprinting feelings of self-confidence onto your subconscious through your senses. In replaces stress and fear with power and self-worth. Sensory anchoring turns music, scents, clothing, physical gestures, and colors into powerful emotional triggers. It's a marvelous tool for empowerment.

Theme Songs

Music soothes your inner beast and affects your subconscious in mysterious ways. It elevates your mood, changes your outlook, affects your heart rate, and can even change your cell structure.

I love the great girl-power songs like "Respect" by Aretha Franklin and "I Will Survive" by Gloria Gaynor. A recent survey of the top dance songs by cable music station VH1 placed "I Will Survive" in the number-one position. When I play these songs in my seminars, the whole class gets up, dances, and has a good ol' time. The seminar is transformed into a Girl Power Party. The Disco Divas are great for motivation. When people are in my car, it's like the Twilight Zone. My passengers think they're in the 1960s and 1970s.

I'm a big advocate of personal theme songs. Choose a song that energizes you. It could be a song from your youth that gives you a nostalgic feeling of power and confidence. Maybe a beautiful song from your wedding has a special significance to you. Countless songwriters and poets have written songs with the name Sarah in the title. If you're lucky enough to have a name that has inspired musicians, you might use one of those tunes as your theme song.

Music changes the body's physiology from stress and fear to creativity and inspiration. It creates hope and positivity. When you're doing something scary or uncomfortable, play your theme song. While driving to a sales appointment, blast your song to give you energy and motivation.

Peak Experiences

For unshakable self-confidence and power, think back to a peak experience in your past. It could be a time when you conquered a fear and were really on top of your game, or a time when you made other people extremely proud of you. You realized all your hard work had paid off. You not only rose to the occasion, but you nailed it. You felt the ultimate confidence and euphoria. Peak experiences such as these are imprinted in your subconscious. Through sensory anchoring, you can call them up at will. You can summon your confidence and courage to the fore as easily as you can retrieve a file from your computer.

Once when I was on television and nailed the interview, I had a powerful peak experience. An overwhelming feeling of confidence came over me, so I anchored the experience. I was wearing a royal blue dress, so blue became my power color. I reinforced the feeling of confidence by forming my arms into the shape of a "V" above my head, doing a victory dance, literally reaching for the stars and signaling

BREAKTHROUGH AT KRISPY KREME

On a hot July day in 1937, Vernon Rudolph and two of his friends came to Winston-Salem, North Carolina, with $25 and a handwritten recipe scribbled on a piece of paper. They rented the front of a store and talked the grocer into loaning them the ingredients to make their first doughnuts.

For years Krispy Kreme was a high-volume, low-margin business that whole-saled doughnuts by the boxload to local supermarkets. Most of the profit came from selling the dough mix, not the doughnuts. Even after the company opened retail outlets, sales remained sleepy.

Then came the breakthrough. An outlet in Chattanooga, Tennessee, began putting out a sign reading HOT DOUGHNUTS NOW when a new batch of dough-nuts was ready, and sales went through the roof. Customers loved the idea of knowing when the doughnuts were cooking and buying them while they were hot. Company headquarters took the idea and ran with it. HOT DOUGHNUTS NOW became the focus of the Krispy Kreme experience. In time, doughnut-making machines were moved right into the middle of the stores.

Now Krispy Kreme has a cultlike following, and the company is worth over $2 billion. People camp out overnight to await a new store opening. Can you believe all the hoopla for a doughnut shop?

victory, and shouting out loud the word "Yes!" In the years since that peak experience, my physical-sensory anchor has empowered me numerous times.

Close your eyes and remember in detail your peak confidence experience. Think about the sights, the feel of the room or setting, the people around you. Attach a power color to that event. Play your theme song as an auditory anchor and use a body movement to create a physical anchor.

The next time you feel scared or anxious, think of your power color, play your theme song, and repeat your physical anchor. You'll be amazed by the results.

BREAKTHROUGHS

On your journey to success you will discover many things along the way. Your mind will become an open fertile ground for new discoveries and revelations. Someone once asked Warren Buffet, a great American investor and entrepreneur, what kind of computer he used. He answered, "The most powerful computer is the one that sits on top of my shoulders."

Once you fire up that amazing computer between your ears, you will collect many new thoughts and observations. Carry a tape recorder, a personal digital assistant such as a Palm Pilot, or a note pad with you at all times. Any one of these lightning-bolt thoughts can be your next million-dollar idea. When you see information-packed articles and motivational quotes, cut them out and save them.

A mistake that many business owners make is tunnel vision, not looking beyond their limited scope of the everyday to see miraculous opportunities. Many successful people are not on their original path. The course they embarked on years ago was merely a way of leading them to their destiny.

Throughout your hero's journey to success you will be presented with opportunities. These life-changing discoveries are not always clearly defined, but be ready to recognize and act on them.

CHAPTER 3

Your Supporting Cast

Women thrive on connections and relationships. According to the book *Brain Sex,* by Anne Moir and David Jessel, the differences between the male and the female brains "are apparent in the very first hours after birth. It has been shown that girl babies are much more interested than boys in people and faces; the boys seem just as happy with an object dangled in front of them."

If you capitalize on this inborn talent and need for relationships, becoming an entrepreneur won't be a one-woman show. An entire cast is waiting to support you as you make your decision to go for it and then move through the adventure of your business life.

YOUR "YOU-CAN-DO-IT" TEAM

Before you even start your business, you probably have a wonderful network of family, friends, and colleagues who believe in you and will push you to achieve excellence. The husband or parents who love and respect you, the girlfriend you meet for margaritas and guacamole, these are your Rocks of Gibraltar, your touchstones in life, your source of grounding and energy. They will hold your dreams in the light. When you want to quit, they will tell you to raise the bar and not settle for the ordinary.

> *The most important single ingredient in the formula of success is knowing how to get along with people.*
> —Theodore Roosevelt, twenty-sixth president of the United States

Sometimes they know you even better than you know yourself.

One of my clients, a fashion designer named Susan, told me that her younger sister, the same little girl who ripped the heads of her dolls when they were kids, was her best ally in business. As adults, the two sisters were confidants, cheerleaders, and trusted advisers. Susan's sister pushed her to start her business, explore her talents, and push on when the going got tough.

SUCCESS TEAMS

A more formal team of cheerleaders I call a "success team," a group of people who gather at regular intervals to help each other achieve their goals. The group intelligence activates imagination and creative energy. Being with successful people who have confidence in you and who are actively working on behalf of your success instills tremendous confidence and initiative. The members of your success team balance out your strengths, weaknesses, experience, and expertise, and widen your horizons.

You can have anything in the world you want if you'll just help enough other people get what they want.

—Zig Ziglar, sales trainer, author, and motivational speaker

When I first came up with the idea for the Women's Small Business Expo, the first people I ran it past were the members of my success team. They were encouraging, straightforward, and wonderful. They told me about the holes in my idea and asked me some really important questions that I hadn't even thought about. Effective success team members are straight shooters.

THE CLOSENESS OF COUSINS

Iris Rainer Dart would call her cousin Sandy when anything important happened in her life: a new job, her boyfriend proposing, the birth of her son. Iris and Sandy went through school, boyfriends, jobs, parenting, and life together. All their triumphs and tribulations were shared. If you hurt one woman, the other would come to her defense. Inspired by her closeness with her cousin Sandy, Iris wrote a great book about two women who became lifelong friends. She created the memorable characters C. C. Bloom and Hillary Whitney in her poignant novel *Beaches*. Her success became all the sweeter when *Beaches* was made into a major motion picture starring Bette Midler and Barbara Hershey.

Everyone respects the other person's ideas, but they don't give rubber-stamp approval to everything that's presented. They challenge you and inspire you, as you do them.

Success Team Benefits

The benefits of success teams are myriad. You will tap into the resources, skills, and knowledge of the other members. The group intelligence of your team will help you accelerate your goal attainment, giving you a fresh perspective on projects that you are extremely close to. Synergy is created when the whole is greater than the sum of its parts. You'll be amazed by the degree to which a success team works on a synergy level to inspire breakthroughs.

Here are some other benefits of success teams:

- **Problem solving.** Success teams will help you find solutions to your challenges. According to Albert Einstein, "Problems cannot be solved at the same level of consciousness that created them." With the group intelligence you can tap into resources, develop ideas, gain feedback, and bring forward your brilliance.

- **Confidentiality.** The success team gives you a safe forum to share your dreams, goals, and desires. To keep the members protected, confidentiality must be respected. What is said in the group stays there.

- **Banishment of entrepreneurial isolation.** At times business owners operate in a vacuum. This is especially true if you are running a home-based business. Success teams offer a marvelous opportunity to meet with other individuals of like mind.

- **Dynamic brainstorming sessions.** There's no better place to brainstorm than with your success team. Marvelous ideas and solutions emerge from these brainstorming sessions.

- **Accountability to yourself and others.** Women, perhaps more than men, tend to let down themselves before they would let down their esteemed colleagues. The accountability factor is a tremendous force in moving members of the success team along their path toward their goals.

- **Strong relationships.** Even if the success team starts out with the goal of fast-tracking business accomplishments, you will become friends with your group members. An incredible bond is created when harmony of purpose exists.

Forming Dynamic Success Teams

You may want to form more than one success team, for achieving a variety of goals. One team might help you with financial issues, another with creative issues. I've been on success teams with people I've never met in person. We just talk on the phone at regular intervals. Many people prefer to meet with their success team partners in person. It helps strengthen the bond and the achievements.

During meetings, success team members share their accomplishments on their goals from the last meeting, state their new goals, and say with what they need help and support from the group. If you have a project such as a business plan or marketing piece that needs time for review, send it to the group members in advance of the meeting. The quality of the input tends to be higher when people have time to evaluate your project and write down their suggestions in advance.

Here are some additional tips for creating success teams that live up to their full potential:

- **Name your success team.** The name should reflect the common interests, goals, or values of the group, such as the Magnificent Mentors or Future Millionaires.

- **Create a purpose statement.** One of the best ways to run a success team is to develop a group purpose statement that is read at the beginning of each meeting. The purpose statement will be constantly growing and evolving according to the visions of the group members. Here is an example: "To help each member get more focus in less time, more growth with less effort, and more profits with less stress. By elevating and stimulating the minds of each member, we will all live well, have fun, and help each other achieve personal success by transforming other people's lives. The team members will give first, then receive. Each success team partner understands that the power of the group is greater than the sum of its parts. All members of the success team will be encouraged to be their highest and best selves."

- **Limit the number of members.** Four to six people is a good number for a success team. If your group has dramatic results, word will spread and others will want to join, but it's best to keep the group small so that everyone gets a fair share of personal attention and brainstorming.

- **Qualify your members.** New success team members could be nominated by someone in the group, then voted on by the other members. Or you could ask prospective members to write their individual mission statements and tell what they will bring to the group. People have a greater respect for groups if they have to do some work to join them.
- **Meet regularly.** Whether you meet weekly, biweekly, or monthly, regular meeting dates will give the group a sense of structure. One to two hours is a good length for success team meetings. (Conference lines are great for phone meetings.) Be respectful of time differences if you meet by phone from opposite sides of the country.

PROSPERITY CIRCLES

Paige Grant of www.wealthywomen.com did not have parents who taught her about money, so she "married well." Unfortunately, her fairy-tale marriage crumbled and ended up in divorce. Paige vowed to take back her power and get smart about money. To help other women live financially free, she created a brilliant concept called "prosperity circles." A prosperity circle is a group of like-minded women who are committed to achieving financial independence by supporting each other. The prosperity circle members meet regularly and are accountable to themselves and each other.

Women will do more for others than they will for themselves. In the prosperity circle, you are assigned a partner whom you will speak to each week to see if she needs any support in accomplishing her goals, and she will help you with yours. Your partner will hold you accountable when the circumstances of your life seem to be conspiring against you. This revolutionary approach is helping women all over the world achieve their financial and personal goals.

- **Assign a team leader.** Meetings run more smoothly when someone moderates. The leader reads the purpose statement, monitors each person's contributions so that nobody monopolizes, assigns action items for the next meeting, and wraps up the session with a conclusion. To create a sense of fairness, rotate the role of team leader, either every meeting or every few meetings.

- **Make use of a hot seat.** One of the great benefits of a success team is assistance on specific projects. The person who gets her project reviewed is in the hot seat. To be fair to the other members of the group, rotate the hot seat so that everyone gets the advantage of the group dynamic.

MENTORS

Finding a mentor is the fast track to success. It allows you to tap into the skills and knowledge of visionaries at a higher level, in positions you aspire to attain. Many successful businesspeople have had mentors who believed in them and pushed them to excel. Without their mentors, they believe they'd be flipping burgers in a fast-food joint. Mentors come in many forms. A concerned teacher can change the course of a young person's life. A supportive boss can give an employee a whole new take on the world of work.

Some women are lucky enough to find mentors within their own families. My parents have been amazing mentors for me, and my partner, Sheryl Felice, has an incredible mom with a keen business sense. Over the years, she has offered Sheryl great advice, inspiration, insight, and breakthroughs. For Patti Regan of the Regan Group, a full-service marketing firm, it was her father who told her she could do anything and helped her build her business by strategizing on how she could get clients.

Many successful entrepreneurs have found their mentors high in the echelons of business. Doug Mellinger, CEO of PRT Group, a global software engineering services company headquartered in New York, didn't start out with a board of advisers, because "I didn't know what a board of advisers was. I needed mentors."

He called the "number-one guy at Merrill Lynch" and kept calling for months until he got an appointment. When the meeting finally took place, Doug simply asked the man at Merrill Lynch to be his mentor, requesting that they meet every six to eight weeks so that he could ask for advice and get feedback. The man was flattered by the request and impressed by Doug's persistence. He said "Sure!" Today, PRT has approximately nine hundred employees and eleven locations worldwide.

Pegine Echevarria, who holds a master's degree in social work, is a speaker and author on motivation, leadership, sales, and customer service. She gives this advice on how to find a mentor:

- Define what you need help with.
- Join professional associations and networking groups to meet and identify potential mentors.
- Get involved. Talk to a variety of people.
- Identify who has what you want or need.
- Offer to help them with a project (volunteer for them).
- Ask for help.
- Then listen, use, or discard the advice.
- Share about your decisions and outcomes. (There is nothing more frustrating for mentors than not knowing what you did and if you are successful after they helped you.)

> *Connecting with a mentor is like connecting to a higher power than yourself.*
> —Robin Fisher Roffer,
> author, *Make a Name for Yourself*

Although the classic mentor relationship is personal and ongoing, any time you seek out guidance and advice from people you respect you are gaining from a mentoring experience. I've talked to multimillionaires, business experts, celebrities, psychologists, international speakers, and authors—many of whom have overcome tremendous adversity in their lives—and put these incredible discussions on tape. I call this extraordinary group the Millionaire Mentors and I apply the wisdom I've gained from them on a daily basis.

YOUR CIRCLE OF INFLUENCE

Your circle of influence includes your friends, family, acquaintances, customers, prospects, mentors, success team, business associates, and company cheerleaders.

Studies have found that most people have 250 people in their circle of influence, which happens to be the average number of invitations to a wedding.

See if you can double your circle of influence from 250 to 500. This gives you twice the power base and connections to grow in your business and your life.

Key Influencers

The wider your circle of influence, the more likely it is to include key influencers. These people have power and clout. They can make purchasing decisions, refer you to major players, and make quality introductions. Try to expand your circle of influence to reach more key influencers. Attend networking meetings, teach seminars, write books and special reports, join associations for the industry you want to penetrate. By joining groups where the power brokers hang out, you can gain entry into their circles.

Quality Introductions

A wonderful service any person in your circle of influence can provide is a quality introduction. A quality introduction not only opens doors, it breaks down barriers. The introducer could be a personal friend, relative, adviser, colleague, vendor, or banker of the person you're trying to contact, or a respected person in the industry and the community. He or she will act as your intermediary by calling your prospect or writing a letter or email and giving you a glowing recommendation. You can even offer to write the letter yourself, so all your influencer needs to do is sign it. (This is also a great way to get past the mental block of self-promotion!) Your liaison could also provide a simple Post-it note to stick on a letter you've written to your prospect. The note might say, "I thought you'd be interested in this," or even better, "I know these people and can recommend them highly."

A quality introduction could be as simple as giving you the name of someone you want to reach. You can then say, "Mary Jones suggested I call you" when you make contact. And if you're lucky, you might get a number not otherwise attainable. High-ranking executives often have a private number they give only to family, friends, and members of their inner circle.

Remember, everyone has his or her own circle of influence, and your radar for people who can give you quality introductions needs to be laser sharp. You will come across excellent intermediaries in the course of doing business. Always ask, "Do you know anyone else who can use my products and services?" The answers will surprise you. You may find out that your client Sue plays tennis with one of the top executives for the Mega Great Corporation. The power networking techniques described later in chapter 12, "Communicating Your Passion," will help you meet more quality liaisons.

PROFESSIONALS

To benefit from the wisdom of certain members of your supporting cast, you'll need to take out your wallet and invest in your success. Professional advisers don't cost you money, they save you money. An insurance agent who truly understands the needs of small businesses can help you create a fortress around your company. The advice of a trusted attorney will at times be absolutely indispensable. Knowing how to tame the tax beast is essential for survival in the business world, and a great accountant will show you how to minimize your taxes, which will more than justify the fee. He or she can also help you set up your books, manage your money, and make decisions about important issues such as incorporation or buying versus leasing your business space.

> *Get a coach! You can't run the race, wave the flags, take photos, run the stop watch, and win by yourself. A coach can be your greatest asset (besides your hairdresser).*
>
> —Terri Murphy, author, columnist, and television producer

You may also want to pay for the services of coaches and consultants to help you close the gaps in your knowledge and achieve your goals. Whatever professionals you work with, choose them carefully. Listen to your instincts. Get recommendations from people you trust. Interview several candidates before you make your final decision. Hire professionals you admire and with whom you have a strong rapport.

ORGANIZATIONS

The great thing about organizations is that most of them are populated by marvelous people, many of whom will become members of your supporting cast.

You'll find many organizations to help you along your entrepreneurial path. Here are just a few:

- **National Association of Women Business Owners (NAWBO).** This wonderful association has local chapters, so you can find one wherever you live. NAWBO has regular meetings, luncheons, awards ceremonies, and conventions. It provides support and resources to help you grow your business and enrich your life. Membership in NAWBO also provides you with listings of other women-owned businesses in your area and lets you post your business in its directory so that people can find you. NAWBO is dedicated to accelerated learning, networking, and empowering women. It has tremendous political clout and access to the media. For more information, go to www.nawbo.org.

- **National Association for Female Executives (NAFE).** The membership of this vast organization includes women business owners as well as high-powered executive women in corporations. NAFE provides education, public advocacy, resources, and networking to empower its members to achieve career success and financial security. For more information, go to www.nafe.com.

- **eWomenNetwork.** This organization was founded by a powerful husband and wife success team, Kym and Sandra Yancey. Their slogan is, "It takes teamwork to make the dream work," and their network is the embodiment of this credo. This organization has international members who meet for regular telephone conference calls. You can also look up other women-owned businesses and post your profile on the site, so that people can find you. The organization also holds live events in cities as well as an annual conference. For more information, go to www.eWomenNetwork.com.

- **American Woman's Economic Development Corporation (AWED).** This organization offers small business courses, one-on-one coaching, and group support to women business owners of all socioeconomic levels, ages, and backgrounds. Their talented and approachable staff members are active executives and entrepreneurs, not just business theorists. The AWED alumnae are extremely bonded to their mentors and welcoming to newcomers. I like this organization because they have "brown bag lunches," informal and informative ways to get valuable business information, to engage in enlightening discussions, and to enjoy an opportunity to meet with peers, make new friends, and benefit from the experiences of expert presenters. Their website is www.awed.org.

- **Springboard Enterprises.** The primary function of Springboard is helping women business owners claim their power by giving them access to capital. Springboard offers Venture Capital Forums, Boot Camps, VC Tune-Ups, and Online Learning Centers that give women both the skills and the confidence to present their high-growth businesses to venture capital groups. Springboard has an active community of venture partners, investors, vendors, and mentors with high octane business connections. Springboard conferences include great speakers, accelerated learning, and power networking. For more information, go to www.springboardenterprises.org.

- **Small Business Administration (SBA).** The SBA is Uncle Sam's way of helping you with your business. I'll tell you all about SBA loans in chapter 10, "Getting the Financing You Need." In the meantime, their business centers are a marvelous resource.

    In partnership with local colleges and universities, the SBA has set up Small Business Development Centers (SBDCs) to provide free management and educational help to current and prospective small business owners. These centers are very women-friendly and offer one-stop assistance. Your local SBDC can help you apply for a loan, write a business plan, do your income statements and balance sheets, price your products and services, develop your sales skills, and market your business. The list is endless. In addition to classes, you can make appointments with the wonderful SBDC counselors. These advisers are top-notch business pros and I highly recommend them.

    The SBA also offers business training and technical assistance specifically for women at Women's Business Centers (WBCs). These centers provide assistance and training in areas such as finance, management, marketing, and e-commerce. They also address the issues and challenges specific to women and offer specialized topics such as home-based businesses and business plan training. All provide individual business counseling and access to the SBA's programs and services; a number of the WBCs are also intermediaries for the SBA's microloan and loan prequalification programs. Diversity is addressed at the WBC, and some centers even offer programs in different languages. For more information, go to www.onlinewbc.gov.

The SBA has offices located throughout the country. For the one nearest you, consult the telephone directory under "U.S. Government," call the Small Business Answer Desk at 1-800-8-ASK-SBA, or go to www.sba.gov.

PART II

BREAK OUT OF THE BAG

Getting Up and Running

Your Business Is a Lifetime Self-Improvement Course

Let's say you sign up for a seminar entitled "Bring Abundance into Your Life." You arrive at the given time, find a seat in the room, and take a look around. Are most of the other members of the audience women? Probably so.

There's a reason that women are more likely to ask for directions than men. We're willing to learn. We're also willing to change. We seek out ways to better our lives and the lives of the people we care about. Sometimes change can be frightening, but if you're looking for a sure route to personal growth, the best kick-butt self-improvement course you can ever sign up for is your own business.

Becoming an entrepreneur will take you into worlds you never imagined inhabiting. You will make decisions about everything from your phone system to the branded image of your company. You will deal with high-level professionals to move your business forward. By meeting challenges and taking risks, you will grow every day and feel truly alive.

Practice lifetime learning. Don't ever become complacent and think that you know it all. Part of your self-improvement course involves investing time and money in yourself without guilt or apology. Finding mentors, attending seminars, reading books, and forming success teams are all a part of the curriculum. Develop the mind-set of a wide-eyed child always eager to learn new things. Each day brings you new problems to solve, new challenges, new things to learn.

The first step of your journey is always the hardest. Don't worry about making mistakes. Experience really is the best teacher. Once you sign up for the seminar of entrepreneurship, it will continue to enrich your life for decades to come.

CHAPTER 4

Finding Your Perfect Business

It started with an idea you couldn't get out of your head. You tried to push it down, but it wouldn't let go of your gut. You woke up and went to sleep thinking about your vivid vision. You're ready to get started, impatient for success. You know exactly what kind of business you want to own.

Or maybe you're working at a steady job. You've been a good employee, but you're tired of putting out maximum effort for minimum pay. You're thinking, "If this dufus I'm working for can do it, then I can do it better."

Or you may have been downsized or laid off. At first you were terrified, but then for the first time in your adult life, you found yourself in charge of your own schedule—and you loved it. You've recognized the entrepreneurial dream buried deep within your soul. If you hadn't lost your job, you might not be exploring this wonderful opportunity of working for yourself.

Finding your ideal business is very personal and life-changing. Many women ask me to tell them about the new, hot business opportunities for emerging entrepreneurs. Just as I wouldn't hand-pick a husband for you, I can't prescribe a business for your future. But here are some questions you can ask yourself to kick-start the wonderful process of discovery:

- What has my life been the laboratory for?
- What do I love to do? What do I love to talk about?
- What am I passionate about, committed to, proud of?
- What is important to me? Independence? Money? Doing what I love?

- Do I need to be around people? Am I happier alone?
- What is the problem that I am the answer to? Who has this problem?
- What is the cost of not using my solutions?
- How can I provide a better solution than anyone else?

These questions become the keys to discovering your true business calling.

A WEALTH OF POSSIBILITIES

There are so many wonderful business ideas out there waiting for you to explore them. As you move about your life, keep your heart and mind open to possibilities. How do you feel when you walk into a retail store? Do you wish it were you behind the cash register? When you walk into a restaurant, do you imagine yourself designing the menus and mingling with customers? Flip through the yellow pages or a business directory; is anything calling out your name?

A RECIPE FOR SUCCESS

A good friend of mine is Wally "Famous" Amos. Wally was born into a poor family back in the 1930s. For most of his young life, he couldn't even read or write. When he was twelve years old, his parents divorced and Wally was sent to live with his Aunt Della. He and Aunt Della would bake chocolate chip cookies together in her Manhattan apartment, which eased the tragedy and hurt of his parents' divorce.

Wally earned his general school equivalency diploma in the Air Force and went on to work in show business—first as a theatrical agent, then as an actor. But what really catapulted him to fame was when he took his aunt's recipe and opened his first Cookie Shack on Sunset Boulevard and Formosa Avenue in Hollywood in 1975. Wally's friends in entertainment helped him out with seed money. He couldn't afford advertising, so these staunch supporters hand-delivered invitations for his grand opening and alerted the media. Before long, Wally had reinvented himself as "Famous Amos," an entrepreneur, master promoter, and inspirational leader.

This wonderful man is always optimistic, wears a giant grin, and has a truly magnetic personality. He never let the obstacles in his life hold him back.

Great wealth is possible with your own business. You shouldn't be afraid of getting rich, as some women are, but you also shouldn't go into business just for the money. Choose a business that will allow you to live your passion and your purpose. Many successful people say that they found what they love to do and then found someone to pay them for doing it.

Hobby? Lifestyle? Growth?

According to Brian Hill and Dee Power, authors of *Attracting Capital from Angels*, businesses fall into three broad categories of hobby, lifestyle, and growth:

- **The hobby business.** This is a part-time or full-time endeavor that never replaces the owner's full-time income. For the hobbyist, creative and emotional fulfillment are prime motivators.
- **The lifestyle business.** This business creates a constant cash flow and supports the lifestyle of one or two people. It may turn a profit or just break even.
- **The growth business.** This is what many people dream of. The growth business takes off quickly and may change its entire industry. It grows rapidly in sales every year, creates jobs, uses technology, and has rapid access to capital.

It may be that you truly want to make jewelry, and sell it a few times a year at craft shows to bring in some extra cash and express your creativity. That's great. It's also great if you adore weddings and are pretty sure you can support yourself as a wedding planner. And if you've spent years developing a breakthrough technology and are ready to see it shoot to the stars, what a tremendous opportunity. The main thing is to look at your needs and desires and get under way to realize your dreams. Who knows, that hobby or lifestyle business of yours may grow, and the next thing you know, you're selling your jewelry or planning weddings all over the world.

Service? Retail? Wholesale? Manufacturing?

Another way to look at business is by the type of product or service you sell. This breaks down into four broad categories, with a certain degree of overlap. For example, if you knit handmade sweaters and sell them over the Internet, you're both a manufacturer and a retailer.

- **The service business.** Service businesses are favorites of entrepreneurial women. They're easy to start, require minimal seed capital, and make use of your skills and talents. If you're doing public relations work for a large company, you can hang out a shingle and start your own firm. If you're an experienced stylist, you can open your own hair and makeup salon. A drawback of the service business is that it's sometimes harder to sell a service than a product, but as you forge relationships with your clients and word of mouth spreads, your business will grow.

- **The retail business.** Retail businesses sell products to the general consumer. They usually have a storefront location or an Internet site. Bricks-and-mortar businesses require more start-up capital than service businesses, but don't require extensive training or advanced skills. Retail businesses may also require working on weekends. People skills and the ability to build rapport is a must for the bricks-and-mortar retail queen, although if you like to travel and visit clients personally you may feel tied down. Product display, atmosphere, visual branding, and a helpful staff will keep the cash register ringing. Smart buying and pricing are vital to your success.

- **The wholesale business.** Wholesaling entails selling products to a retailer or a business that marks up the price and sells to the end-user. Wholesale products are usually sold in bulk, and businesses must qualify to purchase from a wholesaler or distributor. Wholesaling is great because it builds relationships and repeat sales, and your schedule is more flexible than with retailing. You may find yourself making presentations to potential clients or traveling to important meetings and conventions.

- **The manufacturing business.** This could be as simple as making pottery and selling it on Saturdays in your frontyard, or as complicated as producing fine-tolerance computer parts in a giant factory. Manufacturing companies can be expensive to start and complicated to run. You're often a wholesaler as well as a manufacturer, and you'll probably need a substantial workforce. The upside, if you're not doing the production with your own two hands, is that once up and running, the company can yield big profits without you, the owner, always needing to be on the job.

Consider the Tried and True

Your business doesn't have to be revolutionary. People will always need their dogs groomed or their taxes done; if you're a dog lover or a CPA, you may need to look no further. It's easier to follow an established business model than to reinvent the wheel. Many of the most successful businesses today took tried-and-true concepts and added their own unique twist to them. Think about Amazon.com or Kinko's.

> *Whenever I have to choose between two evils, I always like to try the one I haven't tried before.*
> —Mae West,
> entertainer and
> humorist

You might also consider buying a franchise or an existing business. These businesses have a good chance of success because the infrastructure is already in place. The owners have spent lots of time and money testing their business model to see if it works. An existing business has customers, support staff, name recognition, and systems in place. You can start turning a profit immediately.

When buying a business or franchise, consider a venture that is at least five years old. Tour the facility and have your accountant look over the financials with a fine-tooth comb. Find out why the owner is selling so that you don't buy someone else's problem. Your ideal business is a strong financial concern that is being sold to solve a people problem. The owner may want to retire or there may be personality problems among the partners.

Many businesses will consider taking a down payment and regular payments until the purchase price is reached. You may also want the current owner to stay on as a consultant for a specified amount of time until you've learned the business.

Think toward the Future

When Anita Roddick first started The Body Shop she only had one store, and she was in sales, shipping, marketing, and packaging. She put the labels on the containers and even swept up the floor at the end of the day. Then she moved from being a drone—working *in* her business rather than *on* her business—to being the Queen Bee. Eventually, she developed a system that could be replicated so that she could franchise her business and replicate her vision.

A coaching client of mine named Marcella told me she wanted to open a day spa. "Only one?" I asked. She stared at me incredulously. I told her that one spa was only the beginning for her. Marcella was hanging on my every word. I told her that she could set up her first spa, then expand to the next one, and then another one. After a while she could own a worldwide franchise.

When you start your business, think about setting up systems so that you can eventually sell it to someone else. The reason people eagerly pay millions of dollars for a McDonald's franchise is because the system is so brilliant that even with high turnover and a young labor force, the business survives and grows every year. Wouldn't it be nice to be sipping tropical drinks on the beach on the French Riviera while your business runs itself and sends you streams of cash?

> *What I wanted to be when I grew up was—in charge.*
> —Wilma Vaught,
> Brigadier General of
> the U.S. Air Force

Some businesses simply aren't suited to this kind of future expansion, but there's no reason not to think big. Give some thought to what kind of systems and infrastructure would allow your business to operate without your presence. Who knows, you may be starting the next Starbucks or Supercuts!

Do Your Research

Once you're pretty sure what kind of business you want to start, but before you actually leap into the fray, you'll want to learn as much as you can about your new endeavor. Don't, however, get caught in the "paralysis of overanalysis." Some business gurus say that you should do one year of research before you start your business. Unfortunately, society, trends, and technology move so fast that by the time you've researched the business so thoroughly for one whole year, everything might have changed, or somebody else might have taken your idea and run with it.

Here are some ways to research your prospective business:

- Search the Internet for articles.
- Interview industry professionals.
- Subscribe to trade magazines.
- Go to the library.
- Study annual reports from competitors.

- Visit your potential competition.
- Attend trade shows.
- Order start-up guides from *Entrepreneur* and *Inc.* magazines.

LOCATION, LOCATION, LOCATION

Do you want to work at home? Have you always dreamed of owning a shop on a busy walking street, where lots of relaxed customers drop in to check out the wares? Before you make a final decision on your business, give some thought to the environment you'll work in most productively.

The Home Office

Women have changed the workforce forever. The old patriarchal male model separated work and home. Women came along and forcefully changed all that. They said, "Hey, guys. You're really missing something by not seeing your children grow up."

At one time there was a stigma about working from home, but today the phrase "home office" has been coined into the popular lexicon. Now it seems everyone has a home office. Real estate sales are reflecting that couples and families want an extra room for telecommuting. Even large companies are offering telecommuting options to their prospective employees to stay competitive in today's marketplace.

Women entrepreneurs are particularly suited to working at home. A home-based business is the perfect vehicle for combining work and family. The twenty-second commute is an amazing time-saver, not to mention what you save on the cost of a lease. Your overhead is low and you can design your own work environment. You can plan your day around client meetings, taking the kids to their after-school activities and running errands.

Even if you work primarily at home, you might consider having a satellite office for client meetings. Some professional women with home offices meet once a week for brainstorming sessions and accelerated success. Networking meetings, webcasts, and teleconferencing with other entrepreneurs are also great.

People who run successful home-based businesses need to be self-starters and have excellent time-management skills. Otherwise, it's tempting to slack off and relax on the chaise lounge in the backyard. Don't look at the *TV Guide* and then decide if you want to work. It sounds laughable, but I used to do this. Okay, I still do, but I record the programs I want to watch and reward myself by watching them later.

Out in the World

Not everyone—or every business—is suited for a home-based office. Rieva Lesonsky, senior vice president and editorial director of *Entrepreneur* magazine, has also authored many books. She was working at home on her book writing, but found it oppressive. As a social being, she needed the stimulation of coworkers whom she could bounce ideas off. She missed brainstorming sessions, dressing up, and going out to lunch with the office gang. Some people need other people like oxygen. They have to be surrounded by other people for their mental well-being. If they are deprived of other adults all day, they go crazy.

If a home-based business isn't the best choice for either your personality or your particular business, you'll need to buy or lease space. For a bricks-and-mortar business, the location is paramount. You'll want to research it thoroughly before you decide on your location.

Most businesses begin by leasing. In the testing phase of your business, you can even sublease space from an established tenant, allowing you to try out a location to see if it works for your business. Remember that when you first lease your space, the empty building, store, or office looks huge, but once you fill it with desks, office equipment, and inventory, you may quickly outgrow your space.

If you can afford it, owning your building is great because you're building equity as you occupy the space. I'll discuss this option in more detail in the "Investments" section of chapter 11.

Executive Suites

Another great option is the executive suite, a shared-services concept for emerging entrepreneurs. An executive suite or business center has a private office for you with a shared receptionist, utilities, janitorial service, and conference rooms on-site. Many centers also offer shipping services, photocopy and fax equipment, high-speed Internet connections, and food service.

An executive suite is both productive and cost effective for the up-and-coming entrepreneur. In an executive suite office, your efforts are dedicated entirely to your business, while the suite owner is responsible for typical office management. It gives your company an extra added professionalism and presents a great image to clients.

ALONE OR IN PARTNERSHIP?

In the next chapter, "Starting Off Right," I'll cover the legal entity called a partnership. What I want to discuss here is the challenging, rewarding endeavor of running a business with another human being.

There are lots of good reasons to form a partnership. As the saying goes, two heads are better than one—and it takes a lot of brainpower to get a business up and running. Once you're established, your partner can keep things going when you're on vacation or out of town on business, or cover for you when you unexpectedly have to run to school to pick up your sick child. It's a great feeling to know someone's there through the good times and the bad times, in sickness and in health, for richer and for poorer (interesting how they sneak that one into the marriage vows). You may even spend more time with your business partner in the early years of the business than you do with your husband and family.

If you want ultimate control and need everything done your way, don't consider a partnership. It's all about compromise. And you absolutely must choose your partner wisely. The saying about marriages also applies to partnerships: "Marry in haste. Repent at your leisure." Many people are so anxious to start their businesses that they enter into partnerships hastily without thinking about compatibility issues. As with any intimate relationship, staying on course with a business partner requires patience, sacrifice, compromise, and a bit of good luck. Working in partnership requires different strengths, skills, and training than being successfully employed by a corporation or prosperously self-employed as a sole proprietor.

Qualities of a Great Partnership

I have the greatest business partnership ever, with a wonderful woman who's been my best friend since we were schoolgirls. We are alike yet different. Sheryl is strong in ways I'm weak, and I fill in her gaps. We really enjoy being together and have a unique kind of synergy. Often, words are not even necessary. I can look across the room at her in a meeting and know exactly what she's thinking. We finish each other's sentences. We like being together but respect each other's space.

I'm often asked if the "opposites attract" theory is good for business partners. The answer is yes and no. If you prefer to work behind the scenes and your partner is an aggressive sales and marketing person, that's a great match. Your personality traits can be opposite, but your core values have to be the same.

Think of the qualities you want in a partner: Someone who is respectful, kind, compassionate, honest (does this sound like a list of the qualities you would want in your perfect mate?), and above all trustworthy. You must trust in each other's ability, knowledge, and desire to succeed. Partners must have the same personal and business values. Goals for growing the business must be similar, integrity and

INCOMPATIBLE PARTNERSHIPS

Jan and Tina were business partners. They were both great entrepreneurs and had complementary skills, but they had very different core values about the clients for their marketing firm.

Jan believed in relationships. She felt the best way to expand the business was by obtaining a broad base of satisfied clients who would spread the word about their firm, even if it meant taking on certain projects at a discount. Tina had more of a checkbook mentality. She wanted to make a certain profit on every sale.

When Sheila, their top client, referred a friend named Sandy, it started a volcanic reaction within Jan and Tina's firm. Sandy could only afford the firm's services if they gave her a discount. Jan had encouraged Sheila to refer business whenever she could, but Tina insisted on turning Sandy down as a client. Sheila did not like the way her friend was treated and moved her account to another firm. This crippled Jan and Tina's growing business and caused a rift between them. Eventually, they dissolved their partnership.

Neither Jan nor Tina's approach was necessarily wrong, but their company was unable to thrive without compatibility of values.

professionalism must be high, communication must be clear and frequent, and adherence to deadlines is a must.

For Kathy Garland and Maxine Guli—partners of G II Design Group, a Glencoe, Illinois, interior design firm—another aspect of an in-sync partnership is similar priorities. Garland has two children; Guli has five. With all that responsibility, each has agreed that family comes first. "That's not to say we don't work hard," Garland says. "We do. But when something comes up in our families that requires our presence, it's important that we feel free to go."

For Better or for Worse

One of the most common partnerships in small business is between people who are already partners in marriage. This can be a wonderful arrangement, but it has unique challenges. Azriela Jaffe—author of *Honey, I Want to Start my Own Business: A Planning Guide for Couples* and *Let's Go Into Business Together: Eight Secrets to Successful Business Partnering*—discusses the danger of couples in business putting all their eggs in one basket and examines how sharing power, making joint decisions, and coping with different working styles can influence, both positively and negatively, interactions outside the office.

A good barometer of whether you would be compatible work partners with your husband is to think of the last time you did a household project together. If you planted a garden or painted the bathroom together, what was the experience like? Did you enjoy creating something together, or did you want to pull your hair out by the time the project was finished?

Are you starting off with a rewarding, enjoyable marriage and good communication skills? Do you have the same vision for your business and your relationship? Talk a lot with each other about your concerns and fears—before you start working together. No concern is too small or too petty. Take it slow and accept that there will be a learning curve in the process of forming a business/marriage partnership.

Diverse Partnerships

The visage of the American business partnership has undergone a radical change in a very short period of time. It ain't your father's partnership anymore. A typical partnership is no longer two middle-aged men of the same religion, race, socioeco-nomic level, and background. Now business partners can come from very different backgrounds and have vastly diverse life experiences. I've consulted businesses where the partners looked like the cast of Disneyland's "It's a Small World" (with-out the annoying music).

Partners might meet in high school or college, deciding to start businesses together while they're still in school or right after graduation. At the other end of the age spectrum, seniors are more active than ever and starting businesses even in their retirement years. As far as the distribution of equity, partnerships can be the traditional fifty-fifty split or a customized arrangement such as seventy-thirty. A partnership may be two people working together or many collaborators. The part-ners can work in the same office, out of their homes, or across the country—even across an ocean. Most important for women, we can now partner and travel with a man who is not our husband or significant other without stigma or apology.

The traditional model of partnership changed radically as technology spawned virtual partnerships we wouldn't have imagined ten years ago. In some cases, part-ners connected on the Internet and have never even met in person. They rely entirely on modern technology to connect them toward achieving their business goals and visions. The key to the success of a virtual partnership is excellent com-munication. For smooth day-to-day operations, virtual partners use every available technology to stay connected—fax machines, cell phones, voice mail, and of course email. Email is especially important for Tracy Mathieu, a virtual partner of WowGlobal, a Washington, D.C., digital Internet TV business that markets and sells products and services worldwide. "It's a kind of Baywatch meets Harrods," she says. Tracy's partners are two brothers, one in England and one in Spain. Email works especially well for them. "I'm a late-night person," Mathieu says. "So I can be out at a meeting during the day, and if there's an email from one of my partners that requires a response, I can work on it in the evening. By the time he gets to his computer in the morning, my email reply is waiting for him."

Similarly, Shelly Gore and Christina Gage, cofounders of the website MillionaireWomen.com, live on opposite ends of the country—Connecticut and California. Good communication is vital to the success of their partnership. Most virtual partners, even those in cities thousands of miles apart, agree that occasional personal contact is a necessary overlay to ongoing email and phone conversations. Technology is great, but there's nothing like meeting face to face.

Protecting Yourself and Your Partner

Even if you have a great relationship with your business partner, it's a good idea to draw up a partnership agreement. Sometimes the goals and desires of each partner are in perfect alignment when the business is created, but after a few years life gets in the way and one partner wants to grow the business faster, leave the business to concentrate on her family, or start another business of her own. The partners may disagree about which direction the business should take.

The time to draw up a partnership agreement is when you first start the business together. You are both idealistic and hopeful. Most important, you still like each other. When constructing a partnership agreement, experts say, nothing, nothing, nothing is more important (or more frequently overlooked) than a mechanism for ending the partnership—a way to extricate your partner, or yourself, from your company at a fair price. "It's kind of like your roll bar," explains Fort Worth management consultant Sam Lane. "You hope you never have to use it, but you want it in there." Think about possible scenarios and decide who will stay, who will go, and how much money will change hands if you and your partner decide to go your separate ways.

As difficult as it is to contemplate, the agreement should provide for continuing the business if one of the partners should die. It may also include everything from stock ownership and confidentiality/noncompete clauses to compensation and how phone bills are handled.

Here are some other suggestions for guarding your interests in a partnership:

- **Communication is key.** Have regular meetings with your partner. Discuss plans, issues, and concerns on a regular basis. Little concerns have a way of festering and growing into big resentments if they aren't dealt with by open communication.
- **Be clear about percentage ownership of the company.** Nowadays it's not always fifty-fifty. Your partnership may be sixty-forty ownership, or you may have other silent partners who are not active in the daily operations of the business.

- **Provide for life insurance and disability policies on all key partners.**
- **Keep an eye on your checkbook.** Write in an agreement for the bank that you need two signatures to withdraw more than $5,000.

WHO ELSE IS CONCERNED?

When you live with people who are important to you, remember that business decisions are not entirely yours to make. What you do for a living, and how you shape your workday, affects all who live with you, or rely on you, every day. Thoroughly discussing your business dreams and planning with your family will help you choose the entrepreneurial path with the most potential for satisfying your long-term individual, couple, and family goals.

WORKING TOGETHER FOR MATERIAL SUCCESS

More than thirty years ago, a young housewife in London invested $20 and started her own business from her kitchen table. She was fascinated by old-fashioned textile designs and wanted to duplicate them. At first she did all the silk-screening herself, using antiquated tools.

Her husband was enormously supportive. They relocated with their four children to a rural area, but just as the business was gathering steam, a nearby river overflowed its banks, destroying the barn they'd converted to a factory, along with all the inventory. The next move was to the woman's native country, Wales. Lacking the money to purchase both a house and a factory, they opted for the building to shelter their fledgling business and set up their family residence in a tent.

Soon they were able to open their own retail shop and be the exclusive purveyors of their signature textile line. The product line expanded to clothing, household accessories, and wallpaper. Their trademark style had enormous nostalgia appeal and, in time, attracted millions of devoted customers.

Today Laura Ashley, Ltd. has more than two hundred shops internationally, with annual sales of over $250 million. The London housewife who began with a $20 investment is now known throughout the world.

The most common mistake a married entrepreneur can make to endanger her relationship is either not involving her husband enough, or counting on him too much to be a sounding board and crisis manager. Other stumbling blocks include not planning for the possibility that your business might fail, or letting the business take over your life.

If you're married, find out ahead of time what your husband's bottom line is—the line you should not cross if you want to keep him sane and supportive, such as losing the house or prioritizing your business over the needs of your children. Promise not to cross that line no matter what.

The key—whether your "family" is a husband and children, a domestic partner, or a faithful dog or cat—is to keep your loved ones' needs in mind and the lines of communication open.

CHAPTER 5

Starting Off Right

You've decided on your business, and now it's time to roll up your sleeves and get to work. Starting a business can be totally overwhelming. Because the endeavor seems so big, and so much needs to get off the ground at one time, it's easy to procrastinate and put things off. Don't do it! Sure, the process is scary, but it's also exciting, and if you take things one step at a time you'll be fine.

MAKE IT REAL

Most women think about the business they want to start for years, allowing the thoughts to germinate and grow in their heads. Sometimes they finally take the necessary steps to move forward. Other times, the challenge seems too great and the idea simply melts away.

The sooner you make your business a legal and separate entity, the more likely you are to move forward with your dreams. The minute you think of your business, make it real by taking a few simple steps to set your future in motion.

> *Courage is the first of the human qualities because it is the quality that guarantees all the others.*
> —Sir Winston Churchill, British prime minister

Open Your Business Account

Open a business bank account as soon as possible. The longer you've been in business, the more stable you are to customers and lenders. It's better to say, "I've been in business for three years" than "I've been in business for three months." Don't even worry about the business name. You can always change that. The most important thing is to open a bank account, even if you only put in $100 or whatever the minimum amount is. For now, simply go to the bank where you already have a personal bank account. Later on in this chapter, we'll discuss choosing a bank that's truly right for your business needs.

Register Your Website

If your business is currently only a dream, a website probably seems like a virtual pipe dream. Still, as soon as you decide on your business name (or even if you're thinking of several possibilities), register the name of your future website before anyone else can steal it. Good website names are going quickly. With domains, if you snooze, you lose. There are companies who buy up blocks of good website names that are short and catchy and sell them later, for a lot of money. Recording your domain immediately will ensure that you don't pay thousands of dollars to get that perfect name.

The .com and .net names are the most desirable. If you have a website named www.MyCompany.ws (.ws stands for website), most people will not remember this domain name. When they get back to their home or office, they'll log on to www.MyCompany.com or www.MyCompany.net, which is probably the website of your competition. If you really want to brand your business name, register it as both a .com and a .net.

To register your name, just log on to any site that offers website registration. My favorite is Internexions.com. You can search online within seconds to see if your website name is available. If it is, just pay a low fee and register the name. That's it! You can register the name for one year or a few years. Most Internet experts recommend one year at a time, so that you can try out names at minimal cost. You'll be sent automatic emails when it is time to renew your website name.

DBA, EIN, and Other Initial Hoops

If the business name is different from your own name, you need to register and publish a fictitious business name or "DBA," which stands for "doing business as." For instance, a flower shop would be "Mary Jones DBA Castle Florist." The DBA is registered with your county and published in a newspaper to make it public record.

Most banks require a federal Employer Identification Number (EIN). To obtain this, simply call the IRS office in your state. In many cases, you can apply for the EIN over the phone. If they need to know why you want the EIN right away, just tell them you need it to open a bank account. That will usually do the trick.

After you open your bank account and publish your DBA, and the information becomes public record, a flood of solicitations will ensue. Your mailbox will be packed with offers for everything from legal and financial services to magazine subscriptions to credit cards. Keep all these solicitations in a file; they may come in handy!

CHOOSE A GREAT NAME

It all starts with a great name. My partner Sheryl's father, Howard, is quite a character. He has a wonderful sense of humor and he thought of the name The Bag Ladies for our custom bag company. We make bags and we're ladies, right? Initially I didn't like it. I wanted to be taken seriously and have a name like Sherlyn Enterprises. Big mistake! The name Bag Ladies has done more for our business than the most expensive advertising agency ever could have. The name is memorable, cute, controversial, and shows people that we don't take ourselves too seriously. There's enough seriousness in the world.

With a great name like The Bag Ladies, we established immediate rapport with our customers. I can't tell you the number of times I've answered the phone only to hear someone laughing on the other end of the line. "You really call yourselves 'Bag Ladies'?" I love it. Women say, "They call me 'the bag lady' too because I order bags for my company." Voilà! Instant rapport through humor, and rapport equals money.

Most business books tell you not to choose a name that's too cute. I disagree with this popularly held opinion. Two of the major search engines on the Internet are Yahoo! and Google, both cute and memorable names. Apple computer made technology friendly and fun. The name Apple also paved their way into the educational market—you give an apple to the teacher, right? For years, Apple was the major supplier of computers to schools.

I went to a party at a friend's house and the host said, "She's a Wealthy Bag Lady." Everyone wanted to know what the name meant, so I went right into my little speech about teaching women to start and succeed in their businesses so that the only bag ladies they will ever become are Wealthy Bag Ladies. It broke the ice and helped me establish rapport with a delightful young lady that led to a consulting project. Depending on your type of business, why not be cute and funny? If you're running a financial services company, you don't want a name like "Clowning Around," but it's great for a children's store.

Brainstorm the Possibilities

To simplify the process of creating a name for your new venture, begin with a brainstorming session, asking yourself the following questions.

- Who exactly are my target customers?
- What problems do I help solve for them?
- What words or phrases appeal to them?
- What are the three to five most attractive benefits my business brings to customers?
- Are there word pictures or metaphors that communicate what I do and that would be relevant to my customers?
- What names do my competitors go by? What kind of name would differentiate me from the crowd?

Pick the Finalists

Spend a few days jotting down possible business names. When you have your top contenders, test them on friends, family, and potential customers. Pick a name that's memorable and stands for quality, value, and continuity.

Ask yourself these questions:

- **Does the name appeal to my target customers?** Get feedback from customers or potential customers. What names appeal to them the most?
- **Does the name give me room to expand, or is it limiting?** The name Forever Flowers is great for a florist, but what if you decide to expand to chocolates and gifts?
- **Does the name distinguish me in the marketplace?** Most attorney firms are named according to their partners' last names, such as "Brock & Clay." But when Evelyn Ashley launched her high-tech law firm in Atlanta, she came up with something very different: "The Red Hot Law Group of

Ashley." This name has become a highly recognizable brand throughout the Southeast and has helped generate dozens of PR opportunities.

- **Does the name inspire trust?** If your name is Sarah Jane Roberts, don't name your company SJR Enterprises. It screams that you are a one person operation, and you always want to appear bigger than you are. Remember that you have a delicate trust relationship with your clients. They are trusting you with their hard-earned money and banking on the fact that you will deliver quality and value.

- **Is the name simple to spell?** If it's not, people will be much less inclined to send you referrals or log on to your website. Make things as easy as possible for your customers, prospects, and referral sources.

TRADEMARK INFRINGEMENT

In 1968, before expensive skin care salons came to America, Estée Lauder's son Leonard and his wife Evelyn took a trip to Paris. They kept noticing signs that said CLINIQUE AESTHETIQUE. These exclusive salons were devoted solely to skin care.

This was at the time when Estée was developing her first hypoallergenic cosmetics, but she didn't yet have a name for the new line. When Leonard and Evelyn told her about the French salons, Estée fell in love with the word *clinique*. It had a clean sound, made a great motif, and the French spelling gave it panache.

Estée Lauder spent an enormous amount of money secretly developing the Clinique line of cosmetics. She tested and finally decided on the perfect packaging, and produced thousands of Clinique jars and boxes for her revolutionary new product.

Just when she was ready to debut Clinique, a bombshell hit. Another company had a brand of skin care products called Astringent Clinique. Estée's new line was a definite trademark violation. She offered the owner of the Clinique name what seemed an enormous sum of money—$5,000—to own the name. He politely said no. They finally settled on the price of $100,000.

The moral? Do your search before you decide on your name.

- **Does the name elicit pride and enthusiasm within me?** Choose a name that makes you beam with excitement when you talk about your business. Prospects will notice your enthusiasm and want to do business with you.

Confirm Availability

After you've shortened your list of winning names, you need to check on name availability. This is particularly important if your business is likely to grow; your name can't be the same as—or often even similar to—the name of any other company operating in any state where you plan to do business.

A good first step is to type in the name on the Internet's major search engines of the Internet and see what comes up. You can then try phone books, business directories, and the U.S. Patent and Trademark Office (www.uspto.gov). To be absolutely certain the name isn't already taken, consider asking your attorney, accountant, or a private search company to help you verify name availability.

DECIDE ON A LEGAL STRUCTURE

Once your business has become reality, you'll need to decide what legal form best suits your needs. I'm frequently asked for advice on this subject; unfortunately, there's no one-size-fits-all answer. Your decision about a legal structure will depend on what kind of business you're starting. The various options all have their pros and cons, with issues of taxation, liability, and red tape coming into play. This is a subject you'll absolutely want to discuss with both your attorney and your accountant. Here, in the meantime, is a brief overview of the various legal entities.

Sole Proprietorship

This is the most common form of business organization. It's easy to form, requires very little paperwork—you don't even need to file a separate income tax return for your business—and offers you complete managerial control. The business is basically an extension of yourself.

The main problem with a sole proprietorship is the financial risk. Because you and the business are essentially one and the same, you're personally liable for all the debts of your company. Also, because a sole proprietorship does not survive the owner, it's difficult for your heirs to sell your business. If you're running a small home-based business, however, with virtually no risk of debts or lawsuits, a sole proprietorship may be the right choice.

Partnership

A partnership involves two or more people who agree to share in the profits or the losses of a business. A primary advantage is that the partnership does not bear the tax burden of profits or the benefit of losses—profits or losses are "passed through" to partners to report on their individual income tax returns. A huge disadvantage is liability. Each partner is personally liable for the financial obligations of the business, which means you could end up responsible not only for your own business mistakes, but for your partner's as well.

A limited liability partnership provides risk protection for some of the partners but requires at least one general partner to remain liable for the debts of the business. You should definitely get legal advice before forming a partnership; it's a complicated business! Like the sole proprietorship, the partnership does not survive its founders.

Corporation

Unlike sole proprietorships and partnerships, the corporation is a legal entity, separate from those who founded it. Like a person, the corporation can be taxed. More important, it can be held legally liable for its actions, thus protecting the assets of the owners.

The avoidance of personal liability is the key benefit of corporate status. Carol Baker, the owner of The Company Corporation—a firm based in Wilmington, Delaware, that offers incorporation services—points to the protection of personal assets as "the number-one reason our clients incorporate. In case of a lawsuit or judgment against your business, no one can seize your house or your car. It's the only rock-solid protection for personal assets that you can get in business." As additional benefits, more tax options are available to corporations than to sole proprietorships or partnerships, and a corporation can be easily sold.

The primary disadvantages of incorporation are the substantial costs involved, the record-keeping that is required, and the fact that corporations are subject to double taxation—the corporation pays taxes on its profits, and if you receive some of those profits as dividends, you'll be taxed, too.

Double taxation can be avoided by forming an S-corporation, rather than the "regular" C-corporation. The S-corporation allows income or loss to be passed through on individual tax returns, similar to a partnership. The S-corporation offers a number of advantages to small businesses. The paperwork is simpler than for a C-corporation, and you still avoid personal liability.

Corporations are not just for the big boys. You even can be a one-person corporation. However, if you plan to seek funding from venture capitalists, be aware that they prefer C-corporations to S-corporations. Be sure to talk to your accountant or attorney before you make a decision about incorporation, and plan to hire a professional to help you through the process.

> *Keep away from people who try to belittle your ambitions. Small people always do that. But the really great make you feel that you too can become great.*
>
> —Mark Twain,
> American writer

Limited Liability Company

The limited liability company, or LLC, is gaining in popularity because it allows owners to take advantage of the benefits of both the corporation and partnership forms of business. The paperwork isn't too daunting, and the owners are still shielded from personal liability. As with a partnership, profits and losses can be passed through to owners without taxation of the business itself. An LLC can have an unlimited number of members (owners). And while an S-corporation can't have non–U.S. citizens as shareholders, an LLC can. As with the sole proprietorship or the partnership option, the LLC does not survive its members, and selling the business is more difficult than with a corporation.

FIND THE RIGHT BANK

Not all banks make it a point to reach out to small businesses, or particularly to small businesses run by women. So where do you look, and what do you look for?

Call or visit different banks in your area. Get a feel for the bank's personality. Are they into relationship banking? Are they bogged down by bureaucracy? Do they decide everything by committee? Do they participate in community programs? Do they offer seminars and workshops for entrepreneurs? Are the employees friendly? Is the bank line longer than a line for a ride at Disneyland?

Banks are often divided into two sectors: commercial banking and retail banking. Retail banking usually focuses on personal accounts. Commercial banking is often segmented into three parts: small business (less than $3 million in sales), mid-market ($3 million to $20 million in sales), and large business (more than $20 million in sales). When you're just starting out, you'll probably want the bank that specializes in "relationship banking" for small businesses. Introduce yourself to all the bank personnel, the tellers, new accounts, and especially the loan officers.

Is the Bank Women-Friendly?

Many seasoned women CEOs have told me horror stories about how, many years ago, banks turned them down because of their gender. The only way they could secure financing was to have an established man with a strong financial statement cosign on the loan. Now banks are aggressively trying to reach the strong market of women entrepreneurs. Many banks have special departments that deal just with women. They realize that women-owned businesses are not just a niche but the fastest growing segment of the economy. As a woman entrepreneur, you will be courted by various financial institutions. Go to women's events and you'll probably see banks there handing out their information and beckoning you to open an account. It's actually kind of fun. Make the competitiveness between the banks work for you. Compare the various programs. If you like Bank X but they have more monthly garbage fees than Bank Y, bring Bank Y's information to Bank X and ask if they can waive some fees for you. If they can be flexible enough to handle your special requests, they may be a keeper.

Does the Bank Understand Your Industry?

Tell the bank about your type of business and inquire if they handle other businesses similar to yours. Every industry has certain characteristics not commonly understood. In the future, you may be asking the bank for a loan. When bankers don't understand how an industry operates, they don't understand how they'll be repaid on a loan. And when they don't understand how they'll be repaid, they may decline loan requests.

Is It Small Enough to Help?

A business consulting client of mine, Wendy, had a problem with check fraud. Someone got access to blank checks from her business and tried to cash them with phony-baloney signatures. Her small regional bank was vigilant and noticed that the signatures were amiss. They called her to come down and look at the checks before they would cash them. This wonderful watchdog bank saved her a lot of money and anguish, and she refers many of her friends there to open accounts.

With a small bank, it's more likely that loan requests for your business will be underwritten locally. In these days of mergers, acquisitions, and hostile takeovers, bank loans from larger banks are often decided by committees in other locations, even across the country. The staff of a small bank will take the time to spell out the requirements of their programs, and if your loan is turned down, they'll be there to help you understand why.

WRITE A KNOCKOUT BUSINESS PLAN

There is a twofold reason for writing a business plan. It will help you get financing and outside investors, and it will also serve as the internal roadmap and owner's manual for your business. The business plan is not a fancy schmancy cold document. It is a life force for your company, an extension of your goals and visions. As the old adage goes, "If you fail to plan, you plan to fail."

You can hire a capable person to write your business plan—and you'll probably want outside help for the trickier sections like financials—but the process of drafting the plan is at least as important as the final product. It forces you to delve deep into the heart of your proposed venture and think through the numerous questions that will arise when developing your business ideas into tangible components. It will actually help you fill in holes that you wouldn't normally realize were there.

Your plan can be a creative force to be reckoned with. You're not like anybody else, so don't do an ordinary business plan. Let your passion for your business jump out of the page. Is there a law that says business plans have to be dry and dull? Use humor and make it fun to read. Give it color. Put in photographs of the key management team. Write fictitious articles about what your business will look like in three years. Add anecdotes, news clippings, and relevant stories. The final result is a living, breathing document. Don't just place it in a file and forget about it. Take it out and review it every quarter, especially if you feel you're getting off course.

A great business plan starts with a picture of a well-defined future and then comes back to the present with the intention of changing it to match the vision.

The components of a knockout business plan include:

- Executive summary.
- Company description.
- Products and services.
- Operations.
- Target market and competition.
- Management and advisers.
- Financials.
- Attachments.

STARTING OUT WITH THE END IN MIND

IBM achieved its greatness by creating a template for the future. The founders envisioned what the business would look like in ten years, and worked backward from there. The vivid vision of their company as the country's technological leader was the fuel that drove them in the early years of the business.

Tom Watson, the principal founder of IBM, asked himself how a company that looked like his template would act, and he recognized that if the company didn't act that way from the very beginning, his vision would never be fulfilled. "In other words," Tom has said, "I realized that for IBM to become a great company it would have to act like a great company long before it ever became one."

Every day, the founders attempted to model the company after the template. If there was a disparity between the vision and the reality, they set out the following day to make up for the difference.

"We didn't do business at IBM," says Tom, "we built one."

Executive Summary

This must be scintillating and passionate. If you're seeking investors or bank financing, the executive summary has to hook readers and make them want more. A good executive summary touches on all the major issues that are explored in depth in your plan. Remember to be concise. Highlight the critical information that will make up the meat of your plan to best tell the story of your business and what you're trying to accomplish.

Company Description

The story of your company should begin with a short-and-sweet explanation of your business concept. After someone reads this, they should be able to easily tell someone else what your company is all about.

Products and Services

What is your widget? What services are you offering that your customers won't be able to live without? In this section, you want to give a very clear description of what your products and/or services are and how you plan to make money from them. Try to include actual photos or mock-up sketches of your product whenever possible. A great way to do this is to imagine you are creating a short TV infomercial.

Operations

This is the technical stuff. Describe your production process, quality control systems, location, and any proprietary technology.

Target Market and Competition

Illustrate your target demographic; explain who could realistically become your customers and who they are buying from right now.

Many women tell me that their new business will be so unique that they'll have no competition. Get real! There is *always* competition. Research your competition so that you're knowledgeable about the market conditions. You may also want to include some clear points of differentiation between you and your competitors, showing the unique attributes of what you will offer that will put you ahead of the curve. Charts, graphs, and photographs work great in this section.

Never put your competitors down. Give them honest credit for the job they've done. When you trash other people, you trash yourself.

Marketing and Promotions

In this section, your unique qualities and creativity can really shine. The most important question to answer here is how you are going to successfully make your potential customers aware of—and hungry for—your products and services.

The four P's of marketing are product, price, promotion, and placement. Let your imagination run wild and list a sampling of whatever clever marketing and promotional programs you can come up with. You may have some more traditional plans, like putting on a local fundraiser or offering discounts through print publications, or you may be more ambitious and send out teams of local athletes to pass out samples during busy city events.

> *You miss 100 percent of the shots you never take.*
> —Wayne Gretsky,
> hockey all-star

Management and Advisers

There is an old adage in business that says, "I'd take an 'A' team with a 'B' idea over a 'B' team with an 'A' idea any day!"

In the world of business this is absolutely true. Running a successful business is almost all about employing great people. Having a great idea is very important, but having great people to execute your plan is of paramount importance! In many cases, entrepreneurs don't start out with enough money or connections to pull together a stellar team. If that's the case for you, start with contractors, part-timers, interns, and your success team.

This section of your business plan should cover the relevant biographies of everyone who will come together to make this business a success. Remember that biographies are different from resumes. You should present not only the applicable background information and experience of each team member, but also the roles they each will play in your company. This helps investors justify the money you spend on staff and other related expenses. Include descriptions of your board of advisers with their biographies and relevant expertise.

Financials

As a rule of thumb, there are four key financial documents that convey the most critical financial information:

- Projected income statements.
- Balance sheet.
- Break-even analysis.
- Cash-flow analysis.

Be sure to also include notes and assumptions to your financial documents so that the sources of your information and data are clear. So much of the information in financials is already speculative that it's always better to give some reasonable explanations for your numbers. Lastly, detailed projections should be created for six months, one year, two years, and three years. List all the multiple streams of income and profit centers for the business.

Attachments

This is where you can put any additional information that doesn't quite fit into the body of your plan. For example, you might want to include press clippings, advertisements, your catalog or additional product sketches—anything that adds to your plan and strengthens your case for why your business is a good investment.

For more information on writing a business plan, go to www.sba.gov or www.capital-connection.com.

A Few Additional Hoops

Your final hoops will depend on the nature of your business. First, you'll probably need a local business license. Check with your state and local agencies for information on how to obtain this. If you're reselling goods, you'll also need to obtain a seller's permit with a resale number from the State Board of Equalization. With the resale number, you don't pay sales tax when you buy products, but you need to collect sales tax from your customers.

Certain businesses, such as restaurants, need to check health and fire department requirements. For some businesses, you may also need to check the zoning and permit requirements for your particular area and industry.

Voilà! Now you're in business.

CHAPTER 6

Operating Smoothly

The next step on your entrepreneurial path is to be sure your business runs efficiently. You need to equip it with the necessary tools so that you can do your work and your customers can find you when they need you. You also need to protect your investment and your ideas so that your business continues to run smoothly for years to come.

SYSTEMS AND EQUIPMENT

Clearly, the equipment, supplies, and services required to run your business will depend on your business. If you're a potter, you'll need a potter's wheel, kiln, clay, and glazes—hardly must-have items for a personal trainer! No matter what your business, you'll need some basics to operate efficiently in today's business climate.

Phone and Fax

Be sure to set up an efficient phone system. If you have more than one person in the office, you should have a rotating multiline phone. If you're a solo operator, get voice mail that picks up if you're talking to a client—call-waiting clicks are annoying and unprofessional. Also consider call forwarding—it's truly liberating: You can forward calls to your office, home, cell phone, or any location. If you're operating your business from home, install a separate phone line for your business. Always answer the phone with your business name. Never merely say "hello."

No matter where you operate your business, install a separate fax line. When I see a phone/fax number on a business card, I want to scream. Combined phone/fax machines are notoriously unreliable. Here's a typical scenario: A customer tries to fax a document to your shared phone/fax line. It doesn't go through. The customer calls back. You tell her to wait a few minutes so that you can run over to turn the fax machine on. Most people are too busy for this. When they send a fax, they expect it to go through the first time. Get a dedicated line to decrease frustration and increase credibility.

Finally, if you don't already have one, consider investing in a cell phone. When you're traveling on business, it is invaluable. For women, a big advantage of cell phones is security. No longer do you have to worry about being helplessly stuck in the middle of nowhere or getting lost. Help is a wireless call away. The cell phone is also a great time management tool. Instead of wasting valuable time waiting at your doctor's office, you can call business associates.

When choosing your cell phone, it's probably best to start with the phone that feels good in your hand and fits well in your purse or briefcase. Make sure the phone comes with the functions that you need, such as long battery life and phone number memory. If you travel, make sure to get a plan with roaming included. Typically these plans are more expensive, but they may include free nationwide long distance. If you don't travel much, look into a local wireless plan.

Whether you put your cell phone number on your business card is a personal choice. Instead of listing my mobile phone on my business card, I forward calls from my office to my cell phone.

Mail System

I'm always surprised at how many women put their home addresses on their business cards. To promote your home-based business, you want to give your business card out to as many people as possible, and you don't want to worry about whether it will land in the wrong hands.

A post office box is not the best solution, since you need a physical address to receive shipments by UPS and Federal Express, with someone there to sign for the packages. Mail box rental businesses are great. They provide a physical address for your business and they can accept and sign for all shipments. If your box number is 123, you can even use "Suite 123" rather than "Box 123" in your address so your business sounds bigger than it is. If you rent a post office box from the local post office, find out the address and use that on your correspondence.

When you are registering your website domain, never give your home address on the online application. Here it is okay to use a post office box or any location other than your home address. If you register your website with your home address, any World Wide Web weirdo with a computer and an Internet connection can find out where you live.

Computer System

Many women today are as comfortable at a computer keyboard as they are on a telephone. If you're not that comfortable yet, it's time to break through the roadblock of computer resistance and invest in this indispensable tool.

The best way to choose a computer system is to first write down what you'll be using it for. If you are only doing word processing, accounting, Internet activity, and email, you don't need an expensive system. However, if you want to use music, graphics, and web design programs, you will need to spend more.

Start with a computer system that will grow with your business. If you work with partners and employees, you may want a networked system where everyone has their own workstation. Keep an eagle eye on your checkbook. Many women let smart high-tech advisers talk them into spending more money than they need to.

CYBER DIVA

When Aliza Sherman was held up and kidnapped at gunpoint in Manhattan in 1994, the brush with death changed her life. Realizing her job would never give her satisfaction, she decided never to work for anyone else again. In 1995, before most people even knew the Internet existed, she took a $10 HTML class and started a successful Internet company, Cybergrrl Inc.

Aliza paved the way for the women's websites iVillage.com and Oxygen.com. Named by *Newsweek* as one of the "Top 50 People Who Matter Most on the Internet," she is a cyber celebrity, online marketing expert, published author, and international speaker. Aliza Sherman has played a major role in helping women become more cyber savvy.

Shop around for deals. Simply buying "the best" or most expensive choice is not a guarantee of success. You may be paying a lot of money for features you don't need and may never use. You will need to upgrade your system periodically and today's state-of-the-art system may be tomorrow's fossil.

One of the most important features of the computer system is support. A bargain-basement computer without support is a worthless paperweight. Make sure that a technician is available for questions and problems that arise. Nothing can put a crimp in your workday and profitability faster than when your computers are down.

TIME MANAGEMENT

Each day we are given a gift of 86,400 seconds. Time is the great equalizer for all of us. As a business owner, time is your inventory. You always want to be conscious of the highest and best use of your time. Oprah Winfrey has the same twenty-four hours in the day as you and I.

Slaying the dragon of delay is no sport for the short-winded.
—Sandra Day O'Connor, first woman appointed to the U.S. Supreme Court

Time management is really life management. According to Connie Brown Glaser, coauthor of *Swim with the Dolphins,* "Time is the currency of the new millennium." But once time is squandered, it cannot be reclaimed. Here are some strategies for managing your time.

Get Organized

An organized simpleton beats a disorganized genius every time. Searching for papers and files is a huge time waster. Decide on your filing method and make sure everyone in the business follows the same system.

Keep only one pad of paper by the phone for taking notes. Instead of little slips of paper, write all notes on the designated pad. If necessary, put clients on hold while you locate your central notepad. Transfer all important information to the computer immediately.

Another good way to stay organized is to buy a timer and set it up next to your workstation. Set it for the amount of time you think the task should take. You'll work more efficiently when you see the seconds and minutes ticking away. Claude Diamond, a top business consultant, uses an egg timer when a prospect calls him.

Claude turns the three-minute hourglass over and tries to qualify the prospect in the time it takes the sand to run to the bottom. By three minutes, both parties should know if they want to work together. It helps both the buyer and the seller by not wasting anyone's time.

Manage Your To-Do List

To-do lists are great, but most people are using them incorrectly. For instance, if one of your tasks is to make a call to a potential customer named Sally and you leave a message with Sally's assistant, that task is not yet completed. The task can only be crossed off your to-do list when Sally returns your call. Don't cross off tasks on your to-do list until a connection is made. It feels great to cross things off the list, but don't check off calls unless you make contact with the human behind the phone number. If you leave an email or voice mail, but there has been no reply, the task has not been completed.

Another way to manage your to-do list effectively is to prioritize your tasks. Does getting a manicure have the same priority as revising your sales and marketing plan? You can assign letters to your tasks such as A, B, and C projects, or you can prioritize the events with numbers such as 1 through 5.

Buy Time

Unless you find the likes of housework and yard work rejuvenating, consider hiring people to clean your house, mow the lawn, and water the grass. Housekeepers and gardeners are relatively inexpensive. You can also hire a personal assistant to run those pesky little errands that devour your time. There is a proliferation of service companies that even offer to take back library books, pick up dry cleaning, and do your grocery shopping.

> *The most popular labor-saving device is money.*
> —Phyllis George, sportscaster and entrepreneur

TAKE RISKS, STAY PROTECTED

Being a business owner makes you vulnerable to many possible hazards. The entrepreneur must courageously walk an obstacle course filled with pitfalls. Taking risks is part of entrepreneurship, but to preserve your peace of mind you need to be smart about what risks you take and to protect yourself whenever you can.

Insurance

Buying insurance is the best way to protect your business from a real tragedy. Your property could experience a fire, flood, or earthquake that might destroy inventory and cause thousands of dollars' worth of damage. You could be the victim of a robbery or a lawsuit from a customer. You can't eliminate risk, but you can diminish it with the proper insurance.

The basic types of business insurance include:

- **General liability and property coverage.** Liability insurance protects you if someone gets hurt while using your product or is injured while on your premises. Property insurance covers your physical assets: the building, equipment, furnishings, fixtures, and inventory.

- **Automobile insurance.** If your business operates commercial vehicles or company cars, these vehicles need to be properly insured. If business use of your car is minimal, the necessary coverage can probably be included in your personal policy.

- **Professional liability policy.** This covers professional practices such as accountants, lawyers, doctors, dentists, pharmacists, and consultants for negligence claims.

- **Life insurance.** Key-man insurance (I vote for changing the name) pays the company upon the death of a key person, usually the owner or senior executive, to help the company deal financially with the loss and replacement of the owner.

- **Disability insurance.** This is a policy most people forget. If one of the key partners in a business is injured or incapacitated, this worthy individual still needs to collect her income. An additional outside person will also need to be hired as a temporary replacement for the services provided by the key partner. Disability is important because the odds of a temporary disability are higher than the death of a key partner.

- **Workers' compensation.** This coverage pays an employee's medical expenses and provides some income replacement when a worker is injured on the job. It is required by law in all fifty states. If you have employees, you need workers' comp.

- **Business interruption insurance.** If an insurable event befalls the business, such as fire or water damage, business interruption insurance will replace lost income, take care of ongoing expenses, and even pay to get you set up in a temporary facility.

- **Renter's and homeowner's insurance.** These policies are important for home business owners, because your computer, business records, and valuable information are all in your home. Be sure you have adequate coverage. To decrease liability, never meet customers in your home.

- **Flood and earthquake coverage.** This is usually not covered in standard homeowner and commercial policies. In flood- and earthquake-prone areas, this insurance can be relatively costly.

- **Umbrella policy.** These policies provide an additional layer of protection, covering payments and liability after the limits of your other policies have been reached.

Computer Defense

As marvelous as computers are, they also carry potential risks. Email attachments can contain viruses that can poison your system or worms that allow the sender to spy on your company. To protect yourself against computer viruses, get a good virus program like McAfee, Norton, or Panda Software. Scrutinize each email attachment before opening it. Some people only open email attachments from people they know. If they have never heard of you, the message is deleted, babe.

> *To think big and achieve big, you have to take risks. There's no way to be safe and reach high at the same time.*
>
> —Georgette Mosbacher, entrepreneur and author

Computers also have the nasty tendency to swallow data when you least expect it. The value is not in the hardware that sits on your desk. The gold is in the data that's stored in your computer. A treasure trove of documents, files, and information on your business resides on your hard drive. Back up your data every day on removable disks. As the victim of many computer crashes, I implore you to protect your data at all costs.

It's also a good idea to put financial information on removable disks rather than storing it on your hard drive. If financials don't reside on your computer, hackers can't embezzle the information. Take the disks off the premises and store them in a combination safe or fireproof box. Password-protect all confidential and sensitive information on your computer so that only the key partners have the right of entry.

Seamless Client Relations

To protect yourself in business transactions with clients, discuss all charges, lead times, and important clauses at the beginning of the assignment. Make sure your clients understand important facts about the way your company does business and what they can expect. Put all the project details in a written contract that is signed and dated by your client. If you're doing custom work, have the client sign off on proofs.

If you extend credit, keep a customer's personal credit card number or corporate card on file as a backup source of funds in case of a payment default. Protect yourself by faxing the customer a form for them to sign that authorizes your company to use the credit card if the payment is not sent. Be up front with your customers from the beginning and tell them it's standard company policy to keep a credit card number on file. They will not only understand, they will respect your policy. This little tip has saved many businesses from financial ruin and numerous collection headaches.

Additional Precautions

If people call your business and start asking too many questions, trying to glean confidential information, ask why they need to know those details. Just because they are asking for company details doesn't mean you have to comply and spill the beans. Be wary of security companies that call you and ask about your alarm system. Do not provide any particulars. Just say you are happy with your current security system and hang up.

Never volunteer your social security number. Giving your social security number is tantamount to giving someone the combination to a safe that holds your most precious belongings. If someone needs your social security number for identification, provide only the last four digits.

To prevent check fraud, shred or tear all unused checks before throwing them in the trash. Also shred important correspondence, credit card statements, and documents with account numbers and other vital information.

PROTECT YOUR IDEAS

There is always a conflict between broadcasting your business to everyone and making yourself vulnerable to people stealing your ideas. I teach a lot of women who don't even want to reveal the nature of their business for fear of having their trade secrets appropriated. This is fear mentality. Ken Kerr, a creative director for Disney, supervised a talented pool of artists who had hundreds of ideas coming off their drawing boards every day. Obviously, the artistic talent could not file a copyright for every one of these sketches. They needed the free flow of creativity to bring their company to greatness.

It's highly unlikely that someone will deliberately steal your ideas, but patents, trademarks, and copyrights can minimize the risk even further.

Patents

A patent is a grant of protection for an invention or a process. It is obtained through the U.S. Patent and Trademark Office (USPTO) for a term of fourteen to twenty years. Owning a patent gives you the legal right to stop someone else from making, using, or selling your invention without your express permission. Only an inventor can apply for a patent. An investor or anyone who did not directly invent the product cannot apply. An invention can be patented if it is new, original, and useful. The invention's novelty must be obvious to someone of ordinary skill.

Before you register a patent you need to do a search to be sure no one else has patented the idea. The nearest public library, the USPTO's website (www. uspto.gov), or IBM's site (www.patents.ibm.com) can help you in your search. You can also hire a professional patent searcher.

The downside to patents is that they require patience and lots of cash. Your costs for a patent can run as high as $10,000. While you are going through the patent process, you can write "patent pending" as a forewarning to anyone who is even thinking about stealing your invention.

Copyrights

A copyright is legal protection for authors, artists, composers, and software programmers. Creative works such as books, music, screenplays, catalogs, photographs, computer programs, advertising, graphics, and recordings can be protected by copyrights. However, book titles, slogans, lettering, ideas, forms, facts, mailing lists, directories, and U.S. government publications cannot be copyrighted. Any budding author can write another book called *Gone with the Wind.* Some private businesses will even take government publications, reproduce them, and sell them to the public. It's perfectly legal because there is no copyright protection for government pamphlets.

Anytime you create a work for mass publication, display the © symbol as a warning that it is protected intellectual property. Put the words "All rights reserved" as an extra safeguard. This gives you worldwide licensing rights to reproduce any or all of the work with the copyright. Filing with the U.S. Copyright Office gives you extra added protection because it establishes a public record of your copyright claim. The easiest way to file your copyright is to go to the website www.uspto.gov, print out the form, fill it out, and then send it in with a small payment.

When you send your copyright form to the government office, don't send it by regular mail. Send it registered mail with a return receipt requested. This way, someone has to sign for it and you have the name and signature on file. This saved an author friend of mine a lot of mental anguish. When she caught someone flagrantly plagiarizing her book, she called the U.S. Copyright Office and asked for a copy of her filing, but they couldn't find her paperwork. Fortunately, she sent the copyright form return receipt requested and kept the proof of receipt. The author merely took out the return receipt card and found the name of the government employee who registered her copyright. With this information, they were able to retrieve the public record of her copyright claim.

Trademarks

A trademark is like a brand name. It is any words or symbols that represent a product to identify and distinguish it from other products in the marketplace. The ™ mark can be used immediately next to your trademark. The ® register symbol can only be used when the trademark is registered with the USPTO. The more distinctive the trademark is, the easier it is to enforce.

CHAPTER 7

Packaging Your Image

$\mathcal{P}$ackaging is everything. Your personal brand includes your visual look, attitude, and core values. Your company image encompasses everything from the friendliness of the person who answers the phone to the look of your facility and your printed materials.

Rainforest Cafe is famous for its elaborately decorated restaurants. Eager consumers bought Fossil watches for the collectible tins. The lovable Pillsbury Dough Boy has sold millions of slice-and-bake cookies. Fluorescent colors with splash designs sell loads of laundry detergent, but they would be unappealing on food products. Great packaging is about truth and authenticity. It does not disguise, it reveals. According to Estée Lauder, "Packaging design should be called packaging communications. You're telling someone about [your company] through the package. Of course, if the product is inferior, no bottle, box, or bag in the world will cause the customer to come back for more."

Even if you don't have megabucks to spend on your image, like the big corporations, you can use some of their secrets and strategies.

YOUR PERSONAL BRAND

Robin Fisher Roffer, author of *Make a Name for Yourself: Eight Steps Every Woman Needs to Create a Personal Brand Strategy for Success,* talks about how to create your personal brand. To illustrate personal branding, she talks about two "brand goddesses": Oprah Winfrey and Madonna. Each of these women has meticulously developed her "package." Oprah is attractive and approachable, with arms that were made to hug. Madonna is physical, shocking, and sexually empowered (though her image has softened somewhat since she has become a mother). Think of these two brand goddesses when you set out to create your own personal brand.

Your clothes are a uniform. You want to dress similarly to others in your industry but differently enough to stand out and be noticed. Many business books advise you to dress for success with suits, high heels, and a structured corporate look, but clearly this depends on the work you do. If you own a recording studio and work with creative talent, jeans and T-shirts may be appropriate. If you own a health club, body-conscious active wear is your visual brand. If you own a daycare center, you need to create an approachable, down-to-earth look to build trust and rapport with parents who are entrusting you with the care of their child.

> *'Good enough never is'*
> *has become the motto*
> *of this company.*
> —Debbi Fields,
> cookie
> entrepreneur

Your personal brand is more than just your visual look. It is also your attitudes, values, talents, passions, and purpose. Think of some personal attributes that represent your authentic self, such as energy, integrity, humor, risk taking, empathy, and vision. Then think about how to project these characteristics and core values to your customers.

Great companies have wonderful tag lines. Apple's "Think different" and Nike's "Just do it!" are classics. When you're in business for yourself, your tag line is part of your personal brand. It can be descriptive or inspirational. One of my consulting business tag lines is descriptive, "Wealthy Bag Lady: Small Business Success for Women." The other is inspirational, "Wealthy Bag Lady: Your Power, Your Success . . . Your Way."

BRAND YOUR PLACE OF BUSINESS

Every business has a personality, and yours is visible the moment people walk through the door. First impressions are important and indelible. Whether your business is a notary service or a party supply store, your clients should feel as if they've come to the right place. This does not mean you need to spend megabucks on image. You can buy used furniture and fixtures, as long as your place of business is clean, professional, inviting, and creates the proper visual brand.

One of my favorite experiences was making a presentation at the Society for the Prevention of Cruelty to Animals (SPCA). The meeting was remarkable. While I was conversing with the three buyers, one woman had a beautiful tabby cat on her lap, another had a cockatiel on her shoulder nibbling her ear, and the man was holding a precious little pug. The working environment clearly reflected the purpose and values of the SPCA, and the animal lover in me felt proud to be doing good work for such a wonderful organization.

The Friendliness Factor

If you have an office or storefront location, make it as friendly as possible. If you get walk-in business, be sure your customers are greeted cheerfully. Monitor the person that personally greets clients on the friendliness scale.

An Unforgettable Ambiance

Colette Morgan was a buyer for B. Dalton Bookseller. When the company was acquired and she lost her job, she decided to open her own children's bookstore called the Wild Rumpus in Minneapolis, Minnesota.

The minute you enter the store, you know you're somewhere very special. Wild rabbits scamper freely through the book shelves, dodging the feet of happy adults and delighted children. A big fluffy cat is snuggled on a rocking chair. The music is playful and whimsical. At the back of the shop is an old wooden shed. With trepidation, you enter the shed, ducking under creepy cob webs. When you look through a glass on the creaky wood floorboards, you see live mice scurrying around under your feet. What an experience!

Colette has great low-cost events in her store. While spotlighting the *Sheep in the Jeep* book series by Nancy Shaw, Colette had a local farmer bring in a live sheep for a sheep shearing. Her store was written up in the local newspapers and people traveled for miles for a memorable experience.

A corporate megamall has been begging Colette to open a second bookstore in their shopping center, but she has politely refused their invitation because it is not part of her vision of providing personal service and creating a unique ambiance.

Train yourself and your team to "give good phone." The person answering the phone creates the client's first impression of your business. Be sure that they are smiling when they talk. Even on the phone, people can tell if you're smiling.

I'm surprised at how many companies spend tons of money on radio and television advertising to get you to call and place an order. Then, when you call you get a surly person who makes you feel like a gigantic intrusion to her day. Remember that customers who want to place orders or ask questions are not an interruption. These people are pure gold. They pay for your lifestyle and are your reason for being.

Music

One of my pet peeves is walking into a business that feels stark and barren because there is no music. Every step of my heels can be heard. I feel like I'm going to be scolded and told to be quiet by a librarian with blue hair in a tight bun.

Music affects moods, emotions, heart rates, breath rates, and attitude. Syncopated music with a strong beat increases adrenaline, cortisol, and other stress hormones. Calming melodies ease the strain of a challenging activity and make a difficult task much easier. Music stimulates the sales process because it affects emotions and makes people bolder. Think about a night club: when music is playing, people walk across the room to ask total strangers to dance, but then the music stops and everyone feels awkward and uncomfortable.

Even an office should have some music in the background to create a pleasant working atmosphere. Retail businesses should always have a soundtrack running to

SCRIMPING ON VISUAL BRANDING

Robin Fisher Roffer, author of *Make a Name for Yourself* and CEO of Big Fish Marketing is a branding expert. Her visual identity was so important to her that when she started her business with $10,000, she spent $3,000 on her printed marketing materials. The investment paid off well. Now she deals with top clients like Turner Classic Movies, Discovery Channel, Lifetime Television, and America Online.

make customers comfortable while browsing and willing to fire up the cash register. Just don't turn the music up too loud. Music that's too loud will force your customers to a quick exodus as predictably as no music at all.

LOOK GOOD IN PRINT

Dynamic imagery will brand your company and position it at the head of the pack. All your printed materials should be first-rate quality. A well-designed and -printed one-color piece is better than a shoddy four-color piece that calls attention to itself. Keep the message simple and try not to make your printed materials too busy.

It's important to keep a consistent corporate identity. Use the same graphic imagery on all your printed materials: business cards, stationery, brochures, website, catalogs, bags, and other promotional items. Make up pins and wear one on your lapel. It could even say something provocative; I have one that says, "Ask me about Wealthy Bag Lady."

Graphic Designers and Artists

Unless you have extensive design experience, you'll want to hire professionals to help you brand your image. Ask friends and business associates with great logos or marketing pieces to recommend the artist they used. Art and graphic departments of your local college, university, or art school are great sources for finding new up-and-coming young talent eager for experience.

In the digital age, finding a great artist or graphic designer is easier than ever. Try entering "artist services" or "graphic designers" into your favorite Internet search engine. Most professional artists and designers have their own websites where you can view samples of their work. These talented people can also work up some preliminary sketches for your project and email them to you. A good designer should ask you a lot of questions, and you should tell him or her as much as possible about your business and your target market.

Most artists are paid on a per-project basis. Make sure that you own the copyright and all rights to reproducing the work. Artists will go the extra mile for you and give you great quality and service if you offer to write them a glowing letter of recommendation and make yourself available as a future reference.

Logos

Your logo is your company identity. This is your visual personality. It can be corporate, friendly, humorous, authoritative, or whimsical. Spend some time and money to get it right. The logo should look good on your stationery, envelopes, business cards, and other small items as well as large billboards and eventually your corporate jet. (Hey, why not think big?) Pick colors that are high contrast and easy to reproduce. Black and white have the most contrast and make a strong statement. Send your designer examples of other company logos you like.

Test, test, and then test again. At one time, focus groups were expensive testing clusters for large organizations, not for small business. Now with email transmission, anyone can create her own focus group. Narrow the possible designs down to a few top contenders and show them to your potential customers, friends, family, and your success team. The great designs will filter out from the mediocre.

Variety is the spice of life, but once you've settled on a great logo, resist the temptation to change it unless you want to change it on all your printed materials.

Business Cards

There's no law that says a business card can only list your name, rank, and serial number. Put yourself in your customers' shoes and ask yourself what they want to know. If you own a closet-organizing business, you could print some tips for eliminating clutter right on your business card. If you run a dating service, you could list the most common dating mistakes and how to avoid them. Your business card has now been transformed into a valuable miniature information source, which establishes you as an expert and heightens your credibility.

The back of the business card is a great place to print these tips. You can also use inspirational quotes or testimonials from satisfied customers. Most people only use the front of their business cards and waste the prime space on the back. Turn up your creativity and think of ways that you can turn your business card into a powerful sales tool.

Stand out from the crowd. Don't blend in. You are a peacock, not a chameleon. Use shocking colors like fluorescent green and road-worker orange. Die cut a shape in the card. Punch a hole in it and write, "I fill the holes in your [career, business, life]." Create a "sticky" business card that people will keep, not throw in the trash.

Nancy Michaels and Debbi J. Karpowicz, authors of *Off-the-Wall Marketing Ideas,* suggest using creative edging. A tailor could alter her card with pinking shears. Leave room in the design to attach real objects. A doctor could attach a bandage. A seamstress could attach a button. Cut the card in an interesting shape. The managers of the Rainforest Cafe have beautifully colored business cards in the shape of a smiling tropical macaw. One of the most amusing business cards I ever saw was a smaller-than-normal card that said, "If you give me more business, I can afford a bigger card."

Explain any acronyms or industry buzzwords on your card. Many highly educated people find it necessary to list the entire alphabet after their names. Most people know what a Ph.D. is, but lay people don't know what an MFT (Marriage and Family Therapist) or a CSP (Certified Speaking Professional) is. If you print these accreditations on your card, include a line explaining their significance. A real estate firm may specialize in "multifamily residential," but most people know this term as "apartment buildings."

In the previous chapter, "Operating Smoothly," I discussed the importance of not putting your home address on business cards or other printed material. Some women omit the address portion of their business cards rather than investing in a mail box rental. This brands your business as an undersized concern and diminishes your credibility.

> *Big shots are only little shots who keep shooting.*
> —Christopher Morley, novelist, journalist, and poet

Photographs give you more believability and the prices of four-color photographic cards are becoming more affordable. A professional photograph of your smiling face lets people know they are dealing with a real person, not a faceless corporation. Some businesses, such as makeup studios, print dramatic before and after photos of their clients on their cards.

Once you've got your business cards, use them! Hand them out whenever you get the chance. A great way to make sure your business card is saved is to write a lead on it. This is the "give, then receive" philosophy of business. Let's say you meet a woman named Ruth who has an insurance agency. You happen to know of a business associate named Tina who is looking for insurance. Instead of taking out a piece of note paper, take out your business card and write Tina's name and

93

contact information on it. Then hand your business card to Ruth so that she can use the lead for her insurance agency. Do you think that Ruth will keep your business card? You bet she will!

Marketing Pieces

Your marketing pieces—brochures, flyers, advertisements, catalogs—must all reflect your company image and coordinate with your other branding efforts. Depending on your business, more people will be seeing your marketing efforts than any other aspect of your company. I'll go into detail about marketing pieces in chapter 14, "The Lure of Marketing."

LOOK BIGGER THAN YOU ARE

Just because you're a small business owner doesn't mean you can't act big. The bigger you appear to your customers and clients, the more you'll create a sense of stability and credibility. This is especially true if you work out of your home. Technology has freed us to be home business owners and telecommuters, but there is a good deal of

SUPERLATIVES SELL

Jennifer Kushell is the CEO of the Young Entrepreneurs Network. While still a student at Boston University, she and two partners founded the *International Directory of Young Entrepreneurs* (available online at www.youngandsuccessful.com). "We were three kids who started an international company. We had to come up with a lot of tricks to make our company look more substantial than it was," says Jennifer.

The partners invested a lot in the beginning on marketing materials. They did everything they could to look impressive, such as creating foil-embossed brochures. The reaction was amazing. "People gave us respect instantly. They expected that we were older and had more experience."

The network brochures contain the tag line "The #1 Resource in the World for Young Entrepreneurs." "People really liked that," says Jennifer. "It made us sound really big."

mistrust in the business world after the demise of the dot coms. To combat this wariness of home-based businesses, you need to look bigger than you are.

Don't underestimate the royal "we." Even if you're only a one-person operation, there's no reason you can't say, "I'm from the XYZ Company. Our corporate offices are in Los Angeles, California." Don't be afraid to use superlatives. You can call yourself "The Nation's Leader in . . . " or "The World's #1 Resource in the World for . . . " as long as it isn't a blatant lie.

If you work at home or your offices are exceedingly modest, choose a local restaurant, hotel lobby, or executive suite (see the "Location, Location, Location" section of chapter 4) where you can hold client meetings. If you take a prospect or a client out to lunch or dinner, always pick up the check.

Many of the tips from chapter 6, "Operating Smoothly," will contribute to your company's stature. Invest in that separate fax line. Utilize a box rental service so that your company has a street address and even a suite number. Act professional and always be impeccable with your word.

GIFTS AND PROMOTIONAL ITEMS

Promotional gifts—which could be as simple as a ball-point pen with your company name and logo—are a wonderful way to break through and brand your company.

There is a psychological phenomenon called the norm of reciprocity. This edict of human behavior states that if someone gives you something, you feel more obligated to give something in return. A free gift makes a person more likely to reciprocate by purchasing goods and services from your business. The value of the reciprocation does not necessarily match the value of the free gift. Giving a prospect a $5 calculator may result in a sale worth thousands of dollars.

Some popular promotional items are wearables such as T-shirts, caps, buttons, or sunglasses. When ordering promotional products, be sure to get the most advertising value for your money. Some items, such as bags and license-plate holders, have a billboard effect and a lot of public exposure. Other items, such as magnets and mugs, are usually confined to the home or office.

Another marvelous giveaway is a small sample of your product. Estée Lauder pioneered the gift-with-purchase. When she first started her business, she would give away a small gift to every customer. It might be a few teaspoonfuls of powder in a wax envelope, or a small piece of lipstick the woman could apply with her fingertips. No woman left empty-handed. If they liked the quality of the sample, they usually came back and bought the real thing. Today, Estée Lauder still gives gifts with purchases.

Customers who receive free company gifts are more likely to order, place orders more often, feel better about your company, and refer other customers. Pretty good, huh?

BLOOMINGDALE'S BIG BROWN BAG

In 1961 Bloomingdale's gave birth to one of the first designer shopping bags. Their wildly successful bag campaign was brilliant in its simplicity and economy. Bloomingdale's took the same ordinary brown paper bag that you get at the grocery store, made it bigger, and added some shopping-bag handles. Then they printed the words "Big Brown Bag" on the front and the Bloomingdale's name on the side gussets. It cost them only pennies per bag.

Women flocked in droves to the famous department store on Lexington Avenue to walk away with their purchases in the Bloomingdale's Big Brown Bag. The plain brown bag was transformed into a coveted fashion accessory. It also became a series of minibillboards for Bloomingdale's. The success of the Bloomindale's Big Brown Bag was a business owner's dream. Instead of throwing the bags away when they got home, women would save the bag and reuse it, maximizing the advertising value for Bloomingdale's. The shopping bag industry exploded. Other retailers excitedly jumped on the bandwagon. Tour buses even took eager sightseers on shopping trips to Bloomingdale's, telling vacationers that no trip to New York was complete without taking their purchases home in a Bloomingdale's Big Brown Bag.

CHAPTER 8

Bringing in Employees

Deciding whether to add staff to your business can be both difficult and exciting. Some women start businesses because they want to work alone, blaze their own trail, and make their own choices. Some have children and lots of responsibilities. The last thing they want to do is baby-sit employees. In contrast, other women enjoy the daily interaction with their support staff. They even credit the success of their business to their magnificent team of talented people.

For the first years of our business, my partner Sheryl and I did everything. We were the receptionists, printers, account managers, packers, and shippers. We even did the really glamorous work of filling the holes where the mice got into our warehouse. We knew our business inside and out, but if we wanted to grow we had to delegate some of these jobs to other people. In the years since then, our staff has varied according to our needs, and it's been both challenging and fun.

Once you hire employees, many things change. The paperwork can be complicated and time-consuming. Your budget becomes much more challenging; for most small companies, paying staff is the biggest expenditure you have, and you need to pay them whether business is booming or not. You also have the responsibility to treat your employees the best you possibly can. At the same time, the very fact that you're adding employees means that your company is growing, and that's great news.

ASSESS YOUR NEEDS AND RESOURCES

Even if you're overwhelmed with work, don't rush and hire the first person you find. First you must assess both your requirements and your budget. What will you require of your employees? How much can you afford to pay them? Do you really need to bring someone on full-time?

Job Description

Your first step is to write a description of the job you want to fill. It may take a few drafts to get this right. If you're a small company adding your first employees, think about different approaches. Where are your special talents most needed, and what duties could you delegate most effectively? Don't be afraid to bring someone in with talents you lack. If your business relies heavily on cold calling, and you just don't have the knack for it, consider hiring a natural. If you love interacting with customers, but hate filling out paperwork and processing orders, be willing to hand the administrative tasks to a capable member of your staff.

What specialized skills do you need in an employee? What kind of education? How many hours of help a week will the job require? Be sure to answer these questions before you write a help-wanted ad.

Budget and Logistics

Think carefully about how much you will pay your employees, and how much you expect to gain in return. Clearly, you want to offer enough that your staff will stay with you, but you can't pay so much that you cut into company profits. Do some research to determine the salaries of people doing similar work, and remember that the cost to your business will be more than just the salary of the employee. You also

An Artful Workforce

Ellen Daigle of Ellen's Silkscreening started her T-shirt printing business in her garage with the trusted help of her three daughters. Now Ellen runs a $2-million-a-year business and credits her success to the dedication of her employees. All of her salespeople are college graduates with art degrees, so they understand art, fashion, and style. Inspired by such incentives as good wages, health insurance, and profit sharing, her workers take responsibility for a good job as a team. "I work very hard to keep people," says Ellen. "I spend a lot of time and energy looking for the right people, training them, and making sure they are aware of how important they are."

need to account for employer taxes, employee benefits, and any new equipment your employees will need.

A lot of paperwork comes along with expanding your staff. To satisfy Uncle Sam, your employees must complete Form W-4 to indicate filing status and withholding allowances, and Form I-9 to verify eligibility to work in the United States. You won't just write a check for the agreed-on hourly wage. You must first deduct Social Security and Medicare taxes, and then turn that money over to the Internal Revenue Service. And that's just the beginning of the rules and regulations. Safety standards, overtime issues, minimum wage—it goes on and on. If your business is small, you might consider hiring a human resources consultant and using a payroll tax service to be sure you're doing everything right, or at least have a good long talk with your trusted accountant.

> *Success is not a doorway, it's a staircase.*
> —Dottie Walters,
> coauthor, *Speak and Grow Rich*

Alternatives to Full-Time Employees

If the logistics of hiring and administering full-time help sound overwhelming, here are some alternatives that might save you money, hassles, or both:

- **Temporary employees.** If your need for extra help is unpredictable or seasonal, temporary staff retained through a staffing firm might be an excellent solution. You'll pay a higher hourly wage than you would pay your own employee, but the firm takes care of recruiting efforts and all taxes and benefits. Temp workers are becoming increasingly more professional. Often, their talents and skills will surprise you. Today's temp may be tomorrow's full-timer.

- **Independent contractors.** Another solution is to hire an independent contractor to work on specific projects. Once you agree on the project, the contractor determines when, where, and how the work will be done. You pay only the fee, and the contractor is responsible for dealing with Uncle Sam on issues such as Social Security. Be sure, however, that the person doing your project qualifies as an independent contractor. Otherwise you might be responsible for taxes and other penalties. Consult your accountant if in doubt.

- **Part-time employees.** Flexibility and lower overhead are the two primary advantages of hiring part-time rather than full-time employees. You do need to deduct employment-related taxes, but you aren't required to provide medical benefits to employees who work fewer than forty hours a week. Sometimes good part-time help is hard to find, since many people can't survive without a full-time income. Students are a typical source of part-time help. Young people are refreshing and bring a great energy to the workplace, but they sometimes lack skills and staying power. Seniors and parents can also make wonderful part-time employees, particularly if they have medical benefits from other sources.

- **Leased employees.** This is a good option if you need full-time help but would like to avoid administrative hassles. Unlike a temporary agency, a professional employer organization (PEO) will often handle all the employment needs of a small business. They are able to provide better medical benefits for employees than a small business could, and they take care of all wages, taxes, and benefits. You pay the PEO, and they do the rest.

- **Interns.** Find a high school, trade school, community college, or university in your area and post a job listing for an intern. If there is an internship program, the students may be able to get course credit rather than your precious cash for working in your firm. The lure of interning is that their hours are flexible and they get real-world experience in a growing business. Interns are your angels on earth. Treat them well and make them feel special. Show an interest in their development and experiences that will help them grow. Make up business cards for them with a great work title, such as director of operations. Acknowledge their contributions and make them feel important. After you've groomed these wonderful young dynamos, you can always pay them a salary, so they stick around full-time.

CREATE A POSITIVE WORK ENVIRONMENT

Michael E. Gerber, author of *The E-Myth Revisited,* says people are continually asking him, "How do I get people to do what I want?" His answer is that you can't get people to do what you want. People are going to do what they want to do. According to Michael, "If you want it done, you're going to have to create an environment in which 'doing it' is more important than not doing it. Where 'doing it well' becomes a way of life for them."

There are so many ways to create a positive work environment. Put together a top-notch staff and offer them the incentives to stay. Make your business a fun place to work, a home away from home. Loyalty and trust should move both ways, from employer to employee and back again. Trust means that they know you are their ally. Be their friend and back them when they need it. Let your employees know that if they confide in you, you will respect their privacy and not use any confidential information against them.

Be humble. Accept the blame when you make a mistake. It makes you more human, but it also makes your employees trust you enough to admit when they've made a mistake. They know that one mistake won't terminate their job.

LEAD AND GET OUT OF THE WAY

General Electric has held the top spot on *Fortune* magazine's list of the "Most Admired Companies" for five years in a row. Jack Welch, GE's charismatic CEO, believes in leading people and then getting out of their way. Jack once heard an employee say, "They used our hands and feet for years, but the dummies at the top never realized they could have had our brains for free." Now at GE every brain counts. The opinions of the line workers are just as important as the big shots in top management. GE's "Work Out," a process for creating ideas without bosses around to dampen them, has become part of everyday life at the company.

Jack believes in tearing down bureaucracy, getting rid of slumbering businesses within the company, and bringing out the highest and best potential in his employees. His focus on developing talented people is legendary, and he rewards his star performers profusely.

Jack is also humble. He never pretends to know it all but instead listens to those who actually do the work. He rolls up his sleeves and helps them stretch their goals and propel their accomplishments.

Finding and Hiring the Best

Hire the best people you can afford. Long-term employees create a sense of confidence for your clients. Returning customers like to see the same staff. It gives them a feeling of continuity and makes it seem like family.

The best way to fill a job opening is to put the word out and tap into your own circle of influence. If you tell people you know that you're looking for top talent, they may just know the perfect candidate. Most business owners think first about placing a classified ad in the local newspaper. This is good as a part of your overall hiring strategy, but it may not give you a high caliber of top-notch aspirants. You can also contact college placement offices, senior centers, job banks, and employment agencies.

Always be on the lookout. If a business similar to yours is closing or moving, their employees may be in need of another job. Ask other business owners how they find top talent. Every industry has an association. As a member of this association, you can usually publish job openings and take advantage of their labor pool. Finally, you can post your job listings in places your prospective employees frequent. For instance, if you are looking for a printing press operator, post your listing in a shop that sells printing supplies.

Clear Expectations

Many business owners complain about how hard it is to find good help, but they may be failing to give their employees a sense of direction and clear job descriptions. Create a printed manual that shows everyone on your staff how you conduct business. Show them your mission statement to make them a partner in your success. Have employees sign a written contract with noncompete and confidentiality clauses.

Try to resist the temptation to micromanage employees. Hire capable people and step aside, so that they can contribute. Linda Ellerbee, CEO of Lucky Duck Productions, says her company did just fine when she was being treated for cancer. It made her realize she had not trusted her employees to do their jobs well. If you baby-sit your employees, they will come to depend on you too much, rather than take responsibility for their projects and creatively solve problems by themselves.

Respect

Let me spell that out: R - E - S - P - E - C - T. Because I was treated disrespectfully by my bosses, I vowed that if I ever became an employer, I would treat people with the respect they deserved. Money and incentives are great, but alone they don't give self-esteem. Remember, most employees want to do good work. They just need some direction and approval. Praise employees often. Ask for their ideas and input. Employees get a feeling of self-worth because they are contributing to the business as part of a team.

Learn your employees' needs and temperaments. Treat them the way they want to be treated, not necessarily the way you would want to be treated. Recognize that they have a life outside of the company, with an inner circle of people they love. Always ask about your employees' families. When an employee has a new baby, anniversary, or birthday, honor the event with a gift.

OPEN-DOOR MANAGEMENT

Rhoda Goldie, my "other mother" and mentor, knows more about employees than anyone I know. She was an amazing director of a hotel. The hotel industry is known for high turnover, but she kept a devoted staff who was with her for more than twenty-five years. Rhoda always maintained an open-door policy in which her staff could approach her anytime with problems and concerns.

One employee, Danny, told her that he was saving up to give his wife a diamond ring for their twenty-fifth wedding anniversary. Rhoda gave Danny a generous cash gift to add to the money he had already saved. He was elated. Now he could finally buy a beautiful keepsake for his wife. Many bosses would have just given Danny the money, but Rhoda went above and beyond the call of duty to make the couple feel special. She insisted that Danny bring his wife in, and Rhoda admired the ring and told them both how lucky they were to have each other.

Great Benefits

Certain benefits are required by law, such as providing workers' compensation coverage and allowing employees time off to vote, perform military service, or serve on a jury. It's the benefits that aren't required that will attract star performers. In economic prosperity and downturns alike, you need to offer perks to draw and retain talent. Even though you don't have the budget of a Fortune 500 company, you can still offer benefits that magnetize top people.

First on the list are retirement and health benefits. Retirement plans and health insurance plans take research, but they're worth it. A great insurance agent can be a lifesaver in choosing the best health coverage. A good brokerage firm, accountant, or financial planner will explain the different retirement programs and help you evaluate which one is best for you.

You'll also want to provide paid time off for vacations, personal and sick days, holidays, religious observances, bereavement leave, and maternity and paternity leave. Flexible hours for letting your team members leave work early to pick up a child from school, take care of an elderly parent, or attend a family event are easy to accommodate in a small firm, and the rewards are tremendous. You may also want to reimburse employees who want to get off-the-job training to improve their job performance.

If your company is incorporated, you may be able to offer stock options as part of your compensation plan. The amount of ownership offered to employees does not need to be large. William Dotson, president of Northwest Business Group, a management consulting firm, says "Usually a 1 or 2 percent ownership share will provide many employees with adequate motivation."

Don't forget creative perks and nonfinancial incentives. Celebrations such as parties, dinners, and company picnics are great for company morale. Casual dress is a real plus for many employees. Consider providing free food on a certain day of the week or month or arranging for quarterly outings to a matinee movie. MBNA, one of the largest credit card issuers, gives each employee a $500 check and a limo on their wedding day.

Finally, dignity and respect are the biggest benefits a company can offer. Just talking to people and acknowledging their importance and special contributions makes all the difference.

Generous Praise, Constructive Criticism

Employees want to do good work, but sometimes their good work is ignored while mistakes are criticized. Focus on the positives when managing your employees as well as correcting the negatives. When you give praise, tell the employee verbally and also write it down in the form of a note, memo, or email. You can also praise employees in the company newsletter or have a formal recognition and award ceremony for your superstars.

When giving criticism, soften it by first giving praise, and don't forget to offer insight on how performance could be improved. Most people take pride in their work. They are not looking for a confrontation with the boss. Never criticize a staff member in front of anyone else. This brings the criticism to the level of humiliation. Never, never say bad things about one employee to another. If you cause your staff members to wonder what you say about them behind their backs, the trust between you is broken forever.

There is no excuse for losing your temper in front of an employee. If you feel like you're going to lose your temper, talk to yourself or leave the room. Do a self-examination. The employee's mistake was probably because you didn't communicate your instructions clearly. Ask yourself what you may have not made clear instead of blaming your employees for their performance.

KNOW WHEN TO LET GO

Occasionally, you will have to let employees go, either because they aren't working out or simply because you no longer have enough work for them. If your relationship with a key person deteriorates and there is no hope for recovery, you cannot afford the luxury of keeping that person around.

THE NONPRODUCTIVE EMPLOYEE

An employee who is resentful, angry, confrontational, or just plain incompetent isn't simply unpleasant to have around. He or she will impact the profitability of your company. Laying off an unpleasant employee is not a pleasant task, but it's crucial to your bottom line as well as to the productivity of your remaining staff.

When you let him or her go, do it as decisively, cleanly, and courteously as possible. Avoiding unnecessary animosity is important for many reasons. It's an energy drain. It can block sensible negotiation and settlement. Biting your lip until it bleeds for a few days while getting the person out is infinitely preferable to bleeding for years from vengeful negative attacks. If there's anything reasonable you can do to diffuse the other person's anger, do it. But if bloody battle is unavoidable, make it quick. Above all, do what you must do to protect your business.

Letting go an employee because there is not enough work is hard for most women. Every business has peaks and valleys and there may be times when people need to be let go during the slow times. You can offer the employee a severance package of reduced pay for a few months while they find new employment and a glowing reference for their next employer. You can also make the termination gradual by keeping this person on call as a consultant.

A Woman's Yardstick Is Different Than a Man's

Remember the popular bumper sticker, "The one who dies with the most toys wins"? Men tend to have more of a checkbook mentality than women and measure success in terms of money and accumulated toys. Their personal lives become glorified balance sheets. They manifest an outward display of success. In contrast, women internalize success. Their ultimate victory is the ability to live life on their terms. Some women even make less money in their own business than they did as an employee but consider it a great trade-off for freedom and fulfillment.

Follow your fortune but don't go into business just for the money. My worst business decisions were made when I was motivated by the twin demons of greed and fear. Don't let these demons poison your psyche.

It is right and desirable to honor your femininity when measuring business success. Treat your staff like your extended family. Making sure an employee has the time off and the mental clarity to care for a sick child—then seeing that employee productively back at work and the child healthy—is as much a business success as a good quarterly report. In fact, it will probably have a positive impact on the quarterly report that a male boss might never imagine.

Many women believe that true wealth is the ability to run their business from their home and have more time with their family. You can work where you want, when you want. Some women business owners are also motivated by the need to express their creativity. Others are driven by emotional rewards and the desire to make a difference. Opening a day care center may not put you on the cover of *Forbes* magazine, but it will satisfy your need to shape the lives of the children who will be tomorrow's leaders.

PART III

BROWN BAGS TO MONEY BAGS

Controlling Your Finances

Wealth Only Corrupts the Corruptible

Wealth doesn't corrupt, it exposes. It makes you more of what you are. If you are greedy and selfish, acquiring wealth will only magnify the avarice inside you. If you are honest and giving, wealth helps you channel your compassion to truly make a difference in the world.

I've met many women who were scared by wealth and prosperity. They thought that people who were near and dear to them would resent their success. One woman even told me that if she was successful in her business, she would have to move out of her home. But if you make friends and family a part of your success team, they will not be alienated. Wealth gives you choices, not commands.

The media is full of stories about corporate greed, high-profile divorces, and celebrities who achieved fame and riches only to crash and burn in their personal lives. In the movies, business owners and wealthy people are portrayed as scoundrels. While watching *It's a Wonderful Life*, we root for poor George Bailey, not the evil Mr. Potter. In the movie *Norma Rae*, we root for Sally Field to organize her union and defeat the vile bean counters that run the factory. All of these images have an effect on our subconscious. We don't want to be the evil villain, so we may choose to put limits on our success.

Your beliefs are the difference between a lifetime of joyous contribution and one of subtle corruption. If you build your business ethically, and create wealth with accountability, everyone will come out ahead. Your relationships will be strong. Your life will be in balance. You can plan for your children's futures or use your wealth to better the world. You will have a life force that is positively infectious.

CHAPTER 9

The Money's in Your Hands

Women start their own businesses for many different reasons, including independence, flexibility, and self-expression. Gaining wealth is certainly a goal for most small business owners, but managing the finances is rarely high on the list. Your relationship with your money is likely to be one of the first things that changes when you go into business for yourself.

So much is handled for you when you work for someone else. Taxes are automatically deducted from your paycheck, even though you don't much like it. As an employee, you are usually insulated from cash flow issues. You can order and waste supplies, make long-distance calls at will, excessively use express mail, frivolously make photocopies, or spend everything in your management budget without much thought as to whether you're making the most cost-effective decisions. Chances are your behavior isn't any different from your coworkers.

Most great people have attained their greatest success just one step beyond their greatest failure.
—Napoleon Hill, author, *Think and Grow Rich*

Once you strike out on your own, you'll need to start thinking about how your actions will impact your company's bottom line. The survival of your business may depend on your ability to distinguish between your needs, your wants, and your absolutes. You'll need to monitor your own taxes and keep an eye on your own books.

SOUND ACCOUNTING

Did you hate math in school? I sure did. But when I went into business, I faced the fact that I'd have to be keeping track of my finances. Your bookkeeping system will help you manage a range of financial matters, including expenses, available cash and inventory, profitability, assets and liabilities, and accounts payable and receivable.

Accounting Methods

Most small businesses use one of two kinds of common accounting systems to track expenses and revenue: cash or accrual. Your choice will depend on your business structure, your sales volume, and whether you sell on credit.

- **Cash accounting.** This is the simplest method of accounting. If someone writes you a check, you record it when you receive it—not necessarily when it clears the bank. If you have an expense, you record it when you write the check—not necessarily when you incurred the expense.
- **Accrual accounting.** This method gets a bit more complicated. Income and expenses are recorded when they occur, not necessarily when cash exchanges hands. For example, if someone orders on credit, you enter the sale into the books when you write the invoice, not when you receive the payment.

Most new entrepreneurs, particularly sole proprietors, opt for cash accounting because of its simplicity. If you have inventory, however, you'll need to use the accrual method. Accrual is also a good idea if you sell on credit. Ask your accountant to help you decide on your method of accounting.

Who Keeps the Books?

Accounting has gotten easier in the age of technology. Lots of good computer programs are available to help you with your bookkeeping. If your business is fairly simple, you may be able to buy the software that best suits your industry and simply take it from there.

More likely, you'll want to hire a professional to help you out, at least for the first couple of years. A good middle ground is to hire an accountant to help you make decisions about your bookkeeping, set up your system, and teach you the computer program. Even if you decide to hand the reins over to someone else, you should be knowledgeable enough about your financial operations to be sure the bookkeeper or accountant is doing a good job.

TAMING THE TAX BEAST

One of the primary money scenarios that will change when you start your own business is the tax picture. When you work at a typical job, your employer deducts taxes from your salary. You groan at the cut in your paycheck, but you deal with it, and at the end of the year you dutifully send in your W-2, not a particularly complex procedure. You might even get a refund.

> *Don't stay in bed . . . unless you can make money in bed.*
> —George Burns, comedian

When you work for yourself, you need to deduct taxes from your own paycheck, which can hurt even more than when someone else takes the bite. As every welcomed payment comes in from a client or customer, you need to set aside a piece of it for Uncle Sam and Auntie State. You'll want to minimize your tax burden however you can, but it also helps to remind yourself how much you appreciate the smooth roads and good schools your taxes pay for (and make sure you vote for politicians who will handle your tax dollars responsibly!).

Different Forms for Different Folks

Your taxation obligations will depend largely on your legal structure, which I discussed in chapter 5, "Starting Off Right." If you're a sole proprietor, your business earnings are taxed as part of your personal income. You file a Schedule C (Profit or Loss from Business) and Schedule SC (Self-Employment Tax) right along with your Form 1040. It's pretty simple. You're also required to pay estimated quarterly taxes, which is mostly just a matter of remembering to send the check to the Treasury Department.

Taxes for partnerships, corporations, and LLCs get more complicated. You file both a personal tax return and a tax return for the company. If you're a sole proprietor, or very handy with math, you could probably do your own taxes. Otherwise, you'll probably want to get help from your accountant.

Tracking Your Expenses

Whatever legal form your business follows, and whether you do your taxes yourself or hand them over to a professional, the government allows you to deduct any and all business expenses from your taxable income, so you'll want to keep track of the cost of every paper clip and business-related phone call. This doesn't mean that you don't pay for these expenses, only that you don't pay taxes on the money you spend on them. Still, the deductions can really add up to big tax savings.

Any seminars you take on business or to learn about your particular industry can be a deduction. Trade shows, business meetings, travel, and entertainment of clients are also legitimate expenses that can be deducted. If you work from home, you can even deduct a portion of your home expenses—including mortgage or rent, utilities, and maintenance—though the portion of your house you're writing off can't be used for anything but your business.

It would be great if you could write off your dog as your roving security patrol, your cat as your rodent infestation service, and your children as your product beta testers, but stringent rules govern what can and can't be written off as a business expense, so don't push the envelope. Small business owners, particularly those who claim a home-office deduction, are far more likely to be singled out for an audit than the typical W-2 employee. Be sure to talk to your accountant or pore over the government publications before you claim anything as a deduction.

Get organized early on to track your expenses. Keep all bills and receipts. A good strategy is to have separate file folders for the various accepted deduction categories—advertising, legal services, repairs and maintenance, and so on—and put each receipt in the correct folder so that you don't have to organize them at the end of the year.

RUNNING LEAN AND MEAN

Your dream is to gain wealth through your business and put that wealth to wonderful use, preferably sooner rather than later. Realistically, however, you'll probably need to run a tight ship at least for the first few years. Even if your business is going swimmingly, it's smart to keep your overhead as low as possible. The ultimate task is to create a cost-conscious culture—to become Ben Franklin so that you never have to be Ebenezer Scrooge.

What does a brand new baby business need? Customers. The Bag Ladies was no exception. We had no money to rent mailing lists, so we created our own proprietary list of prospects. We scoured the business journals for new business listings, and entered the data ourselves. We even licked our own envelopes for the initial mailings and stamped each letter by hand. We attended local networking meetings, chambers of commerce, and mixers. Business liquidation sales were fertile ground for buying specialty office products and used furniture.

A friend of mine, Shelly, started a small boutique advertising agency in New York. She and her partner, Beth, invested a large part of their start-up capital in a beautiful office with plenty of designer furniture, state-of-the-art computers, and a tony uptown location. Unfortunately, they ran into a cash crunch and lost their business. Her advice to business owners is to buy the cheapest furniture and office space possible.

Our business looks like a Home Depot warehouse—concrete floors instead of carpeting, used desks, and so on. But the atmosphere is always inviting and friendly, music is always in the air, and you are always greeted with a smile. We do most of our business over the phone, but our walk-in customers know they are getting a good deal because we aren't spending all our money on a ritzy façade.

Cost Cutting at Southwest Airlines

As the rest of the airline industry was laying off about a hundred thousand employees in the wake of the September 11, 2001, terror attacks, Southwest Airlines sought savings everywhere but in layoffs. It switched to nonbleached paper towels for a savings of $75,000 a year. It put off the installation of new phone systems. Because of the high morale engendered by avoiding layoffs, Southwest was able to institute a voluntary program in which employees could give up as much as eight hour's pay every two weeks (by mid-December the program had saved Southwest $1.3 million). At Southwest's reservation center in San Antonio, workers even volunteered to mow the lawn.

Look for creative ways to run lean and mean until your feet are on the ground. Minimize luxuries such as travel and entertainment. Carefully research the best deals on expenses such as telephone and insurance. Get your staff involved. They're likely to come up with great ideas for cost cutting you'd never even think of.

Strong Vendor Relationships

Vendors are your partners in business. Work with them to keep your overhead low. Negotiate special pricing and be smart about your buying. Put your vendors on your team and ask how they can help you out. You'll be astounded at what they will do for you if you make it clear you're looking for a long-term relationship. They may lower prices, split costs with you, or arrange special payment terms.

When negotiating with vendors, never mention price first. The first one to state a price is the loser. Instead, ask open-ended questions like, "What is the best deal you can give me?" Then shut up and let them talk. Their discounted prices may be even lower than what you would have asked them for, and they may think of more creative solutions than you did. They are acutely aware of their competition. Remind them that you will remain loyal to their company if they can work with you.

Write out written purchase orders with pricing for vendors and check the statements when they come in. If you are overcharged, give your supplier a call. This due diligence in checking bills for overcharging has saved businesses lots of money and sometimes meant the difference between survival and failure in lean times.

If you've paid your vendors well in the past and you're feeling a cash crunch, you can request special terms, so that you can buy now and pay later. Even when your cash flow may be sluggish, don't ignore bills and late notices from vendors. Call them and explain why the payments will be late. If you have laid the proper groundwork and established yourself as someone with integrity, vendors will understand your situation. They will show their gratitude in spades if you call them before they have to call you to ask for a late payment.

To Fran Greene, the founder and president of Sun State Electronics Inc., in Winter Springs, Florida, strong vendor relationships are the key to growth. "Your cash flow is a circle, and you've got to keep everybody in the circle informed—especially your vendors." According to *Inc.* magazine, Fran makes sure that vendors understand that her company sells to large, slower-paying government agencies and so ends up with a sixty-day collection cycle. "Now, we could pretend to our vendors that we'll pay them in thirty days, but in many cases, that's not a possibility. So instead, we're honest with them up front, and that way, we build credibility," She explains. "Then, if something goes wrong and we need to stretch out our own payments a little longer, the vendors already know and understand our company."

Cash Is King

When you're first starting out, you'll want as much cash on hand as possible. Give your customers plenty of incentive to pay on time or early. Make the payment terms crystal clear. Talk to your customers when they make the initial purchase. Be a vigilant watchdog over your accounts receivable—be sure your credit-and-collection system operates at peak efficiency and can identify problems early. Call as soon as a payment is late, usually after thirty days, with a few days' grace period.

If you're launching a new product line, consider preselling your products from a prototype. Produce a small quantity of samples before committing your precious working capital into cash-intensive production. This is a highly leveraged, low-cost way of streamlining your business. When you see the late-night infomercials on a great collection of dance music, notice that delivery takes six to eight weeks. Did you ever wonder why it takes so long? It's because the CDs have not been produced yet. The music company waits until it gets enough orders and then goes into production and delivery. Smart, very smart!

The Marvel of Barter

Whole economies used to flourish on the barter system, so there's no reason you can't make bartering work for you today. Both products and services can be bartered for other products and services.

When Sheryl and I were first starting out, we wanted to exhibit at a trade show, but didn't have the cash for the booth space. We struck a miraculous deal with the trade show producer. The Bag Ladies would provide custom-printed bags for the entire trade show in exchange for booth space. It was a true win-win transaction. The trade show got terrific bags for their attendees and we were able to show our bag line and collect a multitude of leads.

Bartering is also a creative way to solve your accounts receivable problems. A good customer of ours, Jeannie, was going through a terrible cash crunch and couldn't pay her balances. We went to her store, which carried beautiful blown-glass gifts, and did all our holiday shopping there as a trade for the money she owed us. Incidentally, if you work with a customer during hard times, she will remember your kindness when good times roll around. Jeannie still buys from our business, refers other customers, and will always be extremely loyal to our business because we helped her out.

TURBULENT ECONOMIC TIMES

In some ways an economic downturn is a great time to start a business. You develop great business habits of keeping your overhead low, not being wasteful, and cranking up your creative problem solving.

We started The Bag Ladies during the recession of 1988. The negaholics and naysayers told us that our timing was really lousy. There was a recession and the economy was sluggish. They were right. It was really stinkeroo! Many other custom packaging companies were laying off employees and closing their doors for good. We were young and had no experience or contacts. But sometimes ignorance is bliss. We charged forth like the running of the bulls in Pamplona, Spain, with 110 percent of our energy and commitment. (No innocent bystanders were gored in the process.)

Some companies automatically get a boost in turbulent economic times because of the nature of the industry they're in. Collection agencies and makers and sellers of automotive replacement parts, for example, may do well in a recession. Fast food and discount stores have traditionally done well in a slower economy.

Customers hold onto their money longer in a recession. You'll probably find your clients waiting until the last minute to place orders. Lead times get much tighter. If your product takes time to produce, you may want to add an extra charge for rush service. In any case, your company has to be set up to move quickly to fill last-minute orders.

Don't wait for customers to tell you your prices are too high. By then you've already become part of the problem. You need to approach them first, right when they're beginning to panic. Anticipating slower sales, companies stop hiring.

Projects are put on hold. People don't pay their bills as quickly as they used to. Everyone becomes more conscious of cash.

Get back to the basics of business when the economy is slow. Remember that people buy from other people, not from companies. Hit the streets and do more relationship selling. Call your customers and say, "I know times are hard, and we've figured out how we can save you some money." You can become the hero to your customers. Customers will feel better knowing that you're on their team.

Turbulent economic times call for an aggressive marketing approach. Tell your customers that you understand that times are hard and you have special programs to help them. Keep your good salespeople and increase their incentives to sell volume. Create a sense of urgency with sales and promotions.

CUTTING MARKETING IN LEAN TIMES

In an economic slowdown, most business owners panic and cut their marketing budget. Big mistake! Marketing is the life blood of your business. In lean times, marketing is more important than ever. All you have to do is change your marketing message. Address the turbulent economic times and let your customers know that you understand what they're going through. Now that you've addressed the problem, it's time to offer a solution. People will listen to anyone who will offer compassionate solutions to their crucial problems.

When Kmart's revenues took a hit, its CEO, Chuck Conaway, decided to slash the marketing budget. But by the late fall of 2001, the company had lost far more in sales than it had saved in marketing costs. Kmart was getting its blue lights punched out by Wal-Mart and Target. "There's no doubt we made a mistake by cutting too much advertising too fast," Chuck later said.

In contrast, the online broker E-trade didn't like watching its revenues decline, so it scrapped its budgeting rules and increased its spending in marketing. The result? E-trade signed up sixty-six thousand new customers in 2001, up 17 percent from the previous year.

Get creative about how you let your customers know about your services. Orkin Pest Control knew that homeowners scrimp on maintenance services such as pest control during lean times. It also knew that the more consumers know about bugs, the more likely they are to buy their services. Orkin teamed with the Smithsonian Institution on "Insect Safari," a traveling exhibit designed to teach people about the pesky little critters. It was the most efficient marketing campaign the company had ever run.

CHAPTER 10

Getting the Financing You Need

*D*on't let a lack of money hold you back from your dreams. Contrary to the perception that new businesses require megabucks to launch, most entrepreneurs start their companies with as little as $5,000. There's a good chance you'll find your start-up capital close to home. As your company grows, have the confidence that further funds will be available. The source could be anything from a creative arrangement with a vendor to a multimillion-dollar infusion from a venture capitalist.

This is not to say that women don't have trouble getting financing. They do. Here are some of the reasons:

- Women lack awareness of the sources of capital.
- Women are often unprepared when meeting with investors and loan officers.
- Women still face barriers because of gender. Most financial institutions don't intentionally discriminate against women, but old habits and the status quo are hard to break.
- Women are more risk-averse than men.
- Women may not have as much collateral and hard assets as men do.
- Many women business owners exhibit less self-confidence than their male counterparts, which can impact the presentation of their ideas.
- Women are starting businesses in record numbers. Although this is admirable, start-up ventures are considered risky.
- Women start smaller businesses. From a lender's perspective, it's just as hard

to get a $50,000 loan as a $500,000 loan. It's more cost-effective for the bank to service the $500,000 loan.

- Women start service-based rather than asset-based businesses.
- Women lack female mentors and role models to show them how to move ahead with their businesses.

Still, women entrepreneurs are accessing capital in a range of ways. Bootstrapping is high on the list. Next comes debt financing, in which a financial institution or individual gives you money you will later repay. With equity financing, though, an investor provides capital in return for equity in your company. I'll go into more detail on all of these in the pages that follow.

Remember the "Hobby, Lifestyle, or Growth?" section in chapter 4? The kind of capital you'll need, and where you'll find it, will depend on the nature of your business. Owners of hobby businesses usually do just fine with bootstrapping. Lifestyle businesses will probably seek out some debt financing. Women owners of fast-growing businesses—firms that achieved revenue or employee growth of 30 percent or more over the past three years—have a larger appetite for capital than those who own slower-growing firms. They are more likely than women who own slower-growing firms to access a wide range of credit sources and to borrow to finance their businesses, but they access this capital much differently than their male counterparts. Fast-growth women entrepreneurs are more likely than fast-growth men entrepreneurs to depend on their business earnings and personal debt for business financing. Men are more likely to seek out a business or a commercial bank loan.

Some women entrepreneurs go straight to the top, accessing capital through angel investors, venture capitalists, and public offerings. These women are the "gazelles" of the business world. They also are risk takers. Always assess your risk tolerance when you make decisions about financing. If you seek out capital aggressively, and your business doesn't meet expectations, you could end up deeply in debt or losing control of your company. If you have confidence in the potential of your business—go for it!

> *Spending money you haven't earned yet is like using up years you haven't lived yet.*
> —The Motley Fool, authors, *Money Guide*

WHAT LENDERS AND INVESTORS WANT TO SEE

Anyone who gives you money—whether it's your college roommate or a top-tier venture capitalist—wants to be assured that you understand your business. Before you look to anyone else to help you out, be sure you have a crystal-clear vision of where you're going and how you plan to get there. You need to know not only your company but your industry as well, inside and out.

In chapter 5, "Starting off Right," I discussed business plans. Now's the time to be sure you have a *wow* of a plan. Make it stand out! The executive summary must be a knockout for a potential lender or investor to read further. Projections must be realistic. Paint word pictures so that your business is a story that hooks the reader. Mock up articles about the meteoric success of your business in three years. Include photos, lots of color, and dynamite graphics.

Lead with your passion. Investors see too many lackluster proposals. They look for passion and drive. The most successful entrepreneurs are also good storytellers. Your passion for business should bust out and grab 'em.

BOOTSTRAPPING

Most women-owned businesses are financed by bootstrapping—personal assets, loans from family and friends, credit cards, and lots of creative maneuvering. According to Kimberly Stansell, author of *Bootstrapper's Success Secrets,* a bootstrapper is a person who starts a business with inadequate capital and manages to build it up relying more on resourcefulness than a checkbook balance and outside help. Kimberly interviewed hundreds of bootstrapping veterans across the country and found that "the start-up capital 'amount' isn't our common denominator. It's our ability to maneuver successfully through the challenges that working with a little or no money poses."

Greg Gianforte is the CEO of RightNow Technologies, an Internet software company started out of a spare bedroom in his house. RightNow technologies now has 230 employees and grosses $30 million in sales. According to Greg, "Lack of money, employees, equipment, even lack of product, is actually a huge advantage, because it forces the bootstrapper to concentrate on selling to bring cash into the business."

Grants

You may think that "free money" in the form of grants would be a great way to boot-strap your business, but truth be told, free money is the hardest kind of financing to get. Most grant money goes to nonprofit organizations involved in activities such as community revitalization or research, with a few grants awarded to individuals for artistic activities or fellowships. The time you spend chasing grant money would be better spent drumming up work or seeking financing from more promising sources.

Personal Assets

The first place to go for bootstrapped funds is right at home. Using your own assets rather than looking for outside help may limit the speed at which your company grows, but it allows you to maintain the freedom that may have drawn you to entrepreneurship in the first place.

Your savings account, of course, is the first place to look for start-up funds for your business, but don't stop there. Do you really need that BMW you indulged in a couple of years back? What if you sold it and bought yourself a used Honda Civic? If you own stocks or bonds, consider liquidating some of these assets to get your business on its feet. Another option is a margin loan, in which your brokerage firm lends you a portion of the value of your securities. The interest is reasonable, but the danger is that if the value of the stocks and bonds decline, you'll get a margin call requesting you to supply more collateral.

If you start your business part-time while still working full-time, you may be able to borrow against your retirement account. Interest for this kind of loan is also quite reasonable. If you own your own home and have a lot of equity—that is, the value of the home is substantially higher than the mortgage—you may be eligible for a low-interest home equity loan or line of credit. Assess your risk tolerance and have a definite plan to pay off the loan. For many women, the risk of losing their home may cause sleepless nights. Refinancing is another way your home can supply cash for your business.

Friends and Family

Many small businesses have gotten off the ground through the help of friends and family. These people know you, care about you, and often would love to see you succeed. If you don't want to be barred from your family reunions, however, be sure to treat Aunt Tilly or Uncle Manny with the same professionalism and respect as you would a venture capitalist.

Let friends and family know about your business in an informal manner before you ask for money. A good approach is to give them your business proposal and ask for their input. Tell them that you respect their opinion and you want their feedback on your business. They will be flattered that you asked them for advice and not feel pressured. Once a friend or family member expresses interest in helping you financially, make an appointment and meet in a formal atmosphere. Show them your polished business plan if you haven't already done so. Explain your goals for your business and let your excitement shine through—it's likely to be contagious. Discuss options. Your "investor" could loan you money that you will repay with interest, or take equity in your company. Make every attempt to keep the meeting professional rather than personal. The friend or family member is making a business decision, not an emotional decision. If you get turned down, accept gracefully.

Any time a friend or family member decides to put money into your business, put your agreement in writing. Specify the interest rate of a loan and when payments are due. If your investor will have equity in your company, specify the terms and his or her involvement. You'll probably want to bring in your accountant or lawyer to help you with the written agreement. Uncle Sam gets involved in all kinds of ways with the transaction of money from one hand to another, and you want to be sure to protect both yourself and your investor.

Be conscientious about the people in your inner circle that you would normally treat informally. Provide them with updates and progress reports in writing. They will appreciate being a partner in your business and being a part of your team. Treat these generous souls well and you will reap the rewards in spades. You can even show your face at family reunions. If you need to approach them for more bridge financing in the future, or if you need to change the terms of your agreement, they will be receptive.

Credit Cards

Credit cards are one of the most frequently used sources of start-up capital for women, but their interest rates are extremely high and they should be used with great care. Credit card loans do nothing to establish your track record with business lenders. They are personal unsecured loans and put you in danger of damaging your credit history and FICO score (Fair, Isaac, and Company's credit score) if you fail to repay them. Credit card collectors are generally much tougher and less negotiable than commercial loan collectors. If a bank has given you a loan and you get in a financial tight spot, it is likely to stick with you for as long as it can. Credit card companies are quick to put derogatory items on your personal credit report.

However, many successful businesses have been started with the owner's credit cards and cash advances. Credit card financing can be a viable tool in certain situations, such as when you have a purchase contract from a client in place and you have a specific plan of how to repay the credit card loan in a short period of time.

When you get credit card solicitations and special offers in the mail, put them in a special credit card reference file. Credit cards often offer attractive specials with

A MOTHER'S HELPING HAND

Sherpa, a little dog that could fit easily in a bag, was the inspiration for an innovation in pet portability. This Lhasa apso needed a stylish tote that would allow her to ride in the passenger cabins of commercial airliners. Her owner, former flight attendant Gayle Martz, obliged by creating soft-sided carriers and launching Sherpa's Pet Trading Co. in 1989. Her totes meet airline regulations while providing a safe and comfortable way for small pets to travel with their owners. The carriers, recommended by the American Society for the Prevention of Cruelty to Animals (ASPCA) and the Humane Society, are used by jet setters, including Brooke Shields, Tony Bennett, and Joan Rivers.

A great story, to be sure, and even better when you look at the humble beginnings of the New York–based company. Born of passion and market need, the business that now does more than $4 million in sales annually was launched with just $5,000 in start-up capital that Gayle Martz borrowed from her mother.

When asked what it takes to start a business with nominal funds, Gayle says, "Dreams plus no action equal fantasy. Dreams plus action equal reality."

125

low interest for a limited time. Many intrepid women entrepreneurs play the credit card shuffle game, moving money and refinancing one credit card with another card that has a lower interest rate. Watch out for hidden fees and transaction costs. Be a watchdog and check your credit card statement every month for annual percentage rate increases. Read the notices about changes in terms that most people throw in the trash.

EQUITY FINANCING

The concept of equity financing sounds too good to be true. Wow! Someone gives you money—sometimes *lots* of money—and doesn't expect to be paid back. In fact, however, it's a lot more complicated.

Basically, what happens with equity financing is that you gain capital, but you lose control. The investor expects to become partial owner of your company—typically anywhere from 20 percent to 80 percent—and often to have a say in management. If the investment is large, the investor may insist on a controlling share of the company. This means that down the road, if the investor doesn't like what you're doing, you could get booted out of the business you brought to life.

On the hobby-lifestyle-growth scale, it's definitely the growth companies that attract equity financing. Venture capitalists in particular are looking for fast growth and big returns on their investment. Realistically, a small percentage of women's small businesses will get equity funding. Here are the basics:

Angel Investors

An "angel" is an individual investor who can help bring a company to life in its early stages. The term originated on Broadway, where angels step forward to fund the production of theater shows.

CREDIT CARDS

Credit cards are easy and tempting, but the interest rates are exorbitant. Explore other options before you turn to credit cards, and be sure to pay them off as soon as you can.

Most angels give six-figure loans, as opposed to the millions lent by venture capitalists. You may be able to find an angel investor in your circle of influence. Professionals such as doctors or lawyers often have discretionary income to invest. Perhaps you know a business associate who thinks you have a great idea and would like to help you get it off the ground.

To help match entrepreneurs in need of capital with angels willing to invest, groups of individual investors known as angel networks have sprung up around the country. You may have to present your business plan before the angel network before you can connect with individual investors. The Small Business Administration has launched an online network called the Angel Capital Electronic Network. Go to www.sba.gov for more information.

Venture Capital

Venture capital is the big leagues of business financing. Though venture capital firms still invest primarily in high-tech companies, many firms now target a wide range of industries.

You can find venture capitalists by referrals, on the Internet, and through venture fairs. The best way to land a meeting with a venture capitalist is through the kind of "quality introduction" I discussed in chapter 3 under "Your Circle of Influence." A banker, lawyer, accountant, or other entrepreneur who has a contact with the firm may be able to offer the introduction. Having an intermediary does not guarantee that you receive funding, but it improves your chances of getting a fair and careful review.

Venture fairs give you the opportunity to present to many key influencers in the venture capital marketplace at one time. A word of caution: Don't go to a venture fair until you are ready. The investors in the venture capital market know each other and word spreads quickly about companies that are unprepared.

If you're lucky enough to land a meeting with a venture capitalist, you will need a flawless business plan and a polished PowerPoint presentation with slides. Develop your presentation down to sound bites and be prepared to "bottom line it." In the "Organizations" section of chapter 3, I mentioned Springboard Enterprises. This is definitely an organization you should check out if you're seeking venture capital; they offer great guidance for venturing into this high-power world. Once you've made the initial contact, continue with patient and consistent follow up. Be persistent. You could easily make presentations to a dozen venture capitalists before you find one eager to invest.

Are you intimidated yet? If you're gutsy, patient, and professional, and you have the kind of fast-growth company attractive to venture capital, this may be a great way to launch your company quickly.

> *I have a lot of things to prove to myself. One is that I can live my life fearlessly.*
> —Oprah Winfrey, talk show host and CEO Harpo Productions

DEBT FINANCING

A far more likely route for most women entrepreneurs will be debt financing. You borrow money and later you repay it. Bank loans, lines of credit, and microloans are the most common forms of debt financing. Armed with the right information, you can speak the banker's language, understand what they require, and get the money you need.

Bank Loans

At one time, bank loans were known as "inside-the-box financing." These traditional funding sources required at least three years in business, positive net worth, tax and financial statements, and conservative underwriting. The borrower needed to demonstrate business cash flow and collateral to repay the loan. Bankers wanted to minimize their risk, so they looked for the company's accounts receivables, personal and commercial real estate, business inventory, and equipment that could be easily converted to cash to pay back the loan.

Women business owners often found their paths blocked when trying to secure traditional bank funding and credit. Marilyn Bushey, president of the National Association of Women Business Owners (NAWBO), Dallas–Fort Worth chapter, knew the frustration all too well. She remembers searching for funding when starting her first business. It wasn't until her husband cosigned her bank loan that Marilyn was able to move forward. Now the president of Power PACT Training and Facilitation, she is watching other women owners following in her footsteps.

The problem is that banks and financial institutions feel more comfortable with midsize companies with strong financial statements. Roseanne Hart, president of The Hart Agency and education committee head for the Dallas–Fort Worth NAWBO chapter, says several factors impede a meeting of minds between financiers and women owners: "Women in business often don't have the financial base and documents the financial institutions require," she says. "Most financial institutions are targeting companies grossing $2 million to $5 million, but 72 percent of women-owned companies gross under $1 million."

In recent years, banks have finally started to court women borrowers. Some large banks are offering the kind of relationship banking that was, at one time, the exclusive bailiwick of small banks. Wells Fargo, Bank of America, and Wachovia, for example, have made huge cash commitments to women-owned businesses. Many banks now even have special women's lending departments. Wachovia has committed to lend $5 billion in a five-year period to women-owned businesses. According to Gigi Dixon, senior vice president and manager of commercial bank marketing at Wachovia, "The commitment is necessary because it is simply good business. The bank believes that doing business with women and minorities is not just the right thing to do—it's a business imperative in a changing marketplace." They provided more than $400 million in loans to women-owned businesses in their first year of the program.

The best place to start when you're looking for a loan is probably with the bank where you've already established a relationship. Loans will vary greatly. Sometimes you pay just the interest at regular intervals, and the actual amount of the loan in a "balloon" payment at the end of the loan period. Other times the interest and principal are combined in a single payment spaced out over time. The application process can sometimes be daunting. Your lender will help you decide what kind of loan best suits your needs.

A typical first loan for a small business is a line of credit, which extends the available cash in your business checking account. In a way, a line of credit is similar to a credit card—the money is available for your use, but you only take it when you need it. Lines of credit can be established in advance of your needing them, and the application process is simpler than for a term loan. It is a good strategy to borrow small amounts of money then repay it quickly, so that you have a track record with the bank.

Here are some suggestions for securing debt financing with your bank:

- **Lenders focus on weaknesses.** Admit the weaknesses in your business, explain them quickly, and move on to the positives.

- **Remember that your relationship is not with the bank, it is with the loan officer.** If this individual moves to another bank, show your loyalty and move your account along with him or her.

- **Make your lender a partner in your business.** Make it a point to say hello to him or her when making your deposits. Take him or her to lunch and give your lender small gifts. Update him or her with progress reports and visit your lender at least once a quarter.

- **If you're turned down for a loan, ask why.** Maybe you can change something in your package and resubmit.

Microloans

Microloans are small loans, often under $25,000, created with wonderful intentions—to help those members of society who are underserved by traditional financing institutions. The application process is usually much simpler than for traditional loans. The most common source of microloans is through the Small Business Administration, which I'll discuss in the next section. A number of independent organizations also offer microloans to small businesses.

One of the most impressive is Count Me In for Women's Economic Independence (www.count-me-in.org). Nell Merlino, founder of Take Our Daughters to Work Day, and media specialist Iris Burnett founded this innovative nonprofit organization. In a burst of creativity, these women revolutionized the microloan industry for women. Rather than seeking contributions solely from private and government foundations, Count Me In asks individual women to contribute $5, $25, $100—whatever they can—to a giant empowerment program for emerging businesswomen. If you get a loan from Count Me In, the money could have come from your next-door neighbor, the supermarket checker, even your third-grade teacher.

Count Me In for Women's Economic Independence offers an extremely user-friendly application that's very forgiving of applicants' credit problems that may have arisen from divorce or other personal situations. The group serves as an online lending institution, giving small business microloans (under $10,000) to women who've had trouble securing funding from traditional sources. Many of Count Me In's loan recipients have annual incomes hovering around $20,000—hardly the typical small business clients that banks tend to work with.

GOVERNMENT LOANS

When you think of dealing with the government, what comes to mind? Lots of bureaucracy, stupid outdated rules, hacks with minimal intelligence, red tape, and frustration? Dealing with government loan programs is much less taxing (every pun intended) than you may think. You see, the government, both federal and local, wants you to go into business for yourself. They are totally supportive, because they can be your silent partner. A portion of your business revenues will go to the government in the form of taxes. You may also create jobs, help revi-

> *"Come to the edge,"* he said. *They* said, *"We are afraid."* *"Come to the edge,"* he said. *They came. He pushed them . . . and they flew.*
>
> —Guillaume Apollinaire, French novelist and critic

talize certain areas of your city, and benefit your community in a very positive way. Believe it or not, the government can't wait to help you.

Small Business Administration

In addition to the marvelous business development centers I mentioned in chapter 3, "Your Supporting Cast," the Small Business Association (SBA) also helps facilitate loans to small businesses:

- **SBA Guaranteed Loans.** This is the most popular and widely used government loan. The SBA usually does not lend money directly to businesses. Instead, SBA loans are obtained through intermediaries. Participating banks will give you the loan and the SBA guarantees 75 to 80 percent of the bank loan. The bank is at risk for only 20 to 25 percent. This turns a marginal loan applicant into a great candidate. In most cases, the maximum loan guaranty is $1 million. SBA loans are attractive because they are for a longer payment period than traditional bank financing and rates are better than credit card interest.

- **SBA Microloans.** The Microloan Program provides very small loans to start-up, newly established, or growing small business concerns. Under this program, the SBA makes funds available to nonprofit community-based lenders or intermediaries, which in turn make loans to eligible borrowers in amounts up to a maximum of $35,000, with some loans as low as $100. The average loan size is about $10,500. Applications are submitted to the local intermediary and all credit decisions are made on the local level. To be eligible in many cases, a good reputation in the community will be enough to get the money. The criteria are set by the individual nonprofit agencies.

- **Small Business Investment Companies (SBICs).** SBICs are privately owned, for-profit companies licensed by the SBA. They provide both loans and equity to start-up businesses. Many business experts credit SBICs for starting the venture capital revolution. They operate like most other venture capital firms, but the appeal of the SBIC to the organizers and borrowers is the government leverage on the funds provided. SBICs were original investors in both Intel and Apple Computers, so if you obtain funds from these firms, you'll be in very good company.

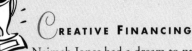

CREATIVE FINANCING

Naimah Jones had a dream to produce a line of cosmetics for women of color. She took her idea to a major Southern California department store and secured a tentative order. The problem was, she had no samples to show the department store buyers at their next meeting, and certainly no product—or the money to produce it—if a big order were placed. Her solution was to turn to suppliers and professionals who could benefit from being a part of a groundfloor opportunity.

Naimah persuaded a manufacturer who wanted to expand his market base to produce the samples to take to the buyers' meeting. A photographer and graphic designer also lent their talents. The department store placed the order! The manufacturer then agreed to produce $80,000 worth of cosmetics and wait six months for payment until Naimah received payment from the store. With a viable dream and creative financing, Naimah Cosmetics was up and running.

State and Local Government Programs

Many wonderful state, county, and city government programs exist for women and minority entrepreneurs. Most communities have special incentives for establishing businesses in disadvantaged areas of the city to renovate those enterprise zones. They are also receptive to businesses that create jobs and revitalize the area's economy. There are even loans for business owners who have been turned down by a bank. These special programs are constantly changing. To find out about them, call your local government offices, check their websites for postings, consult special firms that help you procure government funds, and read the local business journals.

OTHER FINANCING OPTIONS

Debt and equity financing aren't the only ways to get the funds you need to jump-start your business. Another option, if you need quick cash and have a signed purchase order for major bucks from an established business, is to go to a factoring company. The factoring company will pay you cash for your purchase order or invoice and take over the collection of payment from your customer. The catch is that the factoring company pays you substantially less than the amount of the invoice. Factoring can be an expensive form of financing, but it frequently helps new businesses get out of a cash-flow bind.

A more creative place to look for financing is from your suppliers. Particularly if you've established a good working relationship, your suppliers may be willing to give you extended terms for payment. This will allow you to collect payment from your customers before you pay your own bills for a particular project. Suppliers may also be good candidates for investment in your company if they've seen your business grow. They know the industry, and their involvement in your company could be a great source of not only capital but advice as well.

CHAPTER 11

Multiple Streams of Income

To achieve true economic freedom, make it a goal to develop multiple streams of income that flow into your life. Some of this income will come from passive sources such as investments or royalties. Some will be the result of old-fashioned hard work.

INTERNAL PROFIT CENTERS

As an employee, your primary source of cash is the paycheck from your employer. As an entrepreneur, you have marvelous opportunities for multiple sources of income. Let's take a typical retail business, a women's apparel shop. Most shop owners are content to spend their days selling some outfits and then going home. But the free enterpriser on steroids will not stop there. She will do private consultations to the local women who want more fashion sense, develop her own fragrance, write books and articles on how to achieve effortless beauty, give seminars, design her own line of clothing, and even organize her own fashion shows. She can team up with other businesses, such as shoe stores, and refer clients to them for a commission on the sales. She can even license her own designs to other manufacturers. Internet and mail-order clothing sales are other profitable arms of her business.

Here are some other ideas for profit centers in your business:
- **Personalization and customization.** Customers will pay more for products with their company name for promotion and advertising value. Individual consumers will pay extra for personalized items.

- **Rush charges.** If a customer needs to expedite the production of an item, charge a fee for the privilege.
- **Tag sales.** Suggest an additional item with the customer's regular order. An example is the classic, "Do you want fries with that?"
- **Rental of storage space.** If you have a warehouse with extra space, consider renting a portion of it to a business or individual in need of storage.

LICENSING AND ROYALTIES

More than $100 billion in retail sales arises every year from licensing, which carries the potential of creating true lifetime royalty income. In simple terms, you as the licensor are the owner of a unique product, character, idea, system, name, or design. You may have created the intellectual property or obtained the rights to it. An agreement is reached between you and the licensee, who is the manufacturer of the product. The manufacturer and their salespeople do all the work and you col-

ONE SMART COOKIE

One of our customers in the early days of The Bag Ladies stands out lovingly in my mind. Her name was Kendra. She was a single mom who baked cookies out of her home, working on a shoestring. She only needed a few bags and had been turned down by all the other packaging companies because her orders were too small. Could I help her? I liked what she was doing, so I agreed. Hey, I was the boss now. I had the freedom to make decisions.

Then Kendra expanded her cookie business into catering. At first she catered small parties, but eventually she became a coveted caterer for television and movie sets. She went from ordering hundreds of bags to ordering thousands.

One day I was driving in Los Angeles and I found myself in a traffic jam. Weird, huh? While sitting idly in my car, I saw a billboard for the "Banking on America" campaign to stimulate small business lending. The familiar woman in an apron had a smile on her face as big as a Cheshire cat. It was Kendra in her kitchen. She was absolutely radiant. Her small business was big now. She was doing a major partnership with Bank of America.

lect fees and royalties. The average royalty fee is 6 percent of the wholesale price. Licensing is a highly leveraged activity. The licensor bears no up-front costs of manufacturing, sales, or marketing but maintains all the control over product quality. The licensee takes all the risks.

Designer Diane von Furstenberg came across licensing by accident. A couple approached her to license her designs on scarves. Diane would get an up-front fee and a royalty on all the scarves sold. It was wonderful. She didn't have to be a watchdog at the factory, find storage for the inventory, hire a sales force, or do the marketing. The ambitious couple did all of the work for her. She just gave final approval over the merchandise and collected the checks.

Licensing started in 1904, when the Buster Brown comic strip license was acquired and used for children's shoes. Richard Outcault, the creator of the Buster Brown character, was paid a percentage royalty on every pair of shoes. Several decades later, licensing catapulted to the big time when an enterprising businessman, trying to ride the coattails of the Mickey Mouse phenomenon, approached Walt Disney and asked permission to silk-screen the image of Mickey on some wooden pencil boxes for kids. These pencil boxes quickly sold through the initial print run of ten thousand. This licensing deal changed the entire Disney company forever. The Licensing and Merchandising Division eventually became Disney's most profitable division, bringing in even more revenue than their movies.

Jared Silver of Executive Portrait Specialists took his first photograph when he was five years old. That experience sparked his lifetime love of photography. He became a commercial photographer specializing in executive portraits and developed a proprietary system of On-the-Spot Retouching.

His clients, high-powered business executives, are extremely strapped for time. Silver's photography studio comes to their office, takes their photo, and develops it pronto! As an added bonus, he performs his retouching magic with the skill of Michelangelo on speed, making his clients look instantly younger and thinner. Women don't have to be on a crash diet before their sitting. Men experience the removal of one or more chins. Voilà! A beautiful no-hassle finished portrait. Executive Portrait Specialists is a perfect licensing vehicle because it is a ready-made business for other portrait photographers. Jared is the licensor because he owns the proprietary system. Other photographers are the licensees, who pay him a licensing fee and a royalty on all their sales. After the initial training, all Jared does is collect the checks.

If you have created a product that can be effectively replicated, you might be a great candidate for licensing income. A seminar or educational opportunity can also be licensed. If you become an expert in your chosen field, you can license the idea to people who will teach it around the country and pay you an up-front fee and a royalty on all their sales.

In chapter 6, "Operating Smoothly," I discussed patents, trademarks, and copyrights. Be sure to protect your idea before you license it.

> *Success doesn't suck.*
> —Darius Rucker, lead singer of the rock band Hootie and the Blowfish

COACHING

Can you imagine a dream business of helping other people improve their lives? A great way to build on your core business is to share your valuable expertise and knowledge with others. Your unique business and life experiences can be parlayed into a lucrative coaching career. Whatever business you're in, consider doing consulting as an added stream of income. A coach or consultant is someone who provides a specialized expertise, content, behavior, skill, or other resource to a client. This intervention usually focuses on a specific client need.

If you run a restaurant, you could coach emerging restaurateurs about the food service business. Why not help others avoid trial and error, which is expensive in both money and time? If you have managed employees, you could coach corporations on how to maximize their employee relationships and avoid costly liability and turnover.

Coaching is a transportable, flexible business. You are not tied to a specific location or set business hours. Flexibility to your client's needs and schedule is the key to your coaching success. You could begin by coaching in the client's place of business or your own, then grow your business nationally and even globally by coaching over the phone. Coaching will also help get more clients into your core business and establish you as the leading expert in your field.

To add yet another income stream, consider expanding your coaching practice with proprietary products. Books, seminars, special reports, audio tapes, and video programs are easy to create, and they increase the value of your coaching package. Remember, people don't need information. There is enough free information on the Internet. People need solutions. Super coaches get inside the hearts and souls of their clients and know their needs intimately so that they can come up with extraordinary solutions.

Remember to run your coaching practice as a business. Many women have trouble asking high fees for their time and expertise. Practice your presentation and state your rates with confidence.

INVESTMENTS

Perhaps the best way for your business to supply additional streams of income is to invest a portion of your profits. Sure, at first you're excited to make any profit at all, but as soon as your business is up and running, be sure you put it to work toward the future.

Maria Nemeth, author of *The Energy of Money,* had a client who was the first one in her family to live without welfare subsidies. This woman's goal was to have an investment account. As a cleaning woman, she cleaned one extra house a month and invested the $50 in her dream account. Even on a cleaning woman's income, she had an investment portfolio of stocks and mutual funds and had increased her net worth by thousands in a very short time.

My advice is that you set aside at least 10 percent of your earnings for investments. Ironically, many people can live better on 90 percent of their income. If you become a consistent saver, you'll be financially ahead of most people. About 5 percent of Americans are consistent savers. Only 5 percent of Americans control the wealth of the entire country. Coincidence? I think not.

In chapter 9, "The Money's in Your Hands," I discussed running your business lean and mean. The same principle holds for your life outside your business. Sure, it's exciting when the checks start coming in, but take a good look at the big picture and tighten the belt to meet your investment goals.

The key to wise investment is diversification. The scope of your outside investments is limitless, and the best choices change with changing times. I'll briefly discuss two of the most common investment vehicles—securities and real estate—in a moment. You'll want to consult your financial adviser or real estate broker before you make any decisions. Whatever your investments, once they begin to grow, you will have an increased sense of accomplishment and well-being.

Pay Off Your Debts

If you find yourself with some surplus cash, or have proudly set aside that 10 percent of your income and are ready to invest, the first and most important investment you can make is to pay off your debts. If your bumper sticker reads, "I owe, I owe, so off to work I go," it's time to start turning that around.

Not all debt is created equal. Debt on appreciating assets—the loan on your business, the mortgage on your home—can be considered good debt. Consumer debt such as credit card bills or car loans are the debts you should pay off as soon as you can.

Securities

Securities include investment vehicles such as stocks, bonds, mutual funds, and options. The shelves of bookstores are filled with advice about investing, and you should do plenty of research or consult with a financial planner before you make your final decision on where to invest. The best advice is to pick good stocks, bonds, and mutual funds that have performed well in the long run. If you have a good tolerance for risks, and enough cushion in your investment budget, you can go for larger returns on your money.

Real Estate

The government encourages the great American dream of home ownership. If you own your own home, you can take advantage of the eighth wonder of the world: mortgage interest deduction. The interest you pay on your mortgage can be deducted from your

> *You only have to do a very few things right in your life as long as you don't do too many things wrong.*
> —Warren Buffett, American investment entrepreneur

income taxes. It may actually cost you less money to own your home than renting it because of these marvelous deductions. And your investment will be increasing in value at the same time.

A friend of mine, Ella, lived in an apartment. She desperately wanted to own her own home, but everyone had told her not to make the move because her rent was really low. Despite that, she ended up finding a great house with creative financing. The owner had been transferred to another city for her job and she needed to sell fast. Ella didn't even need a down payment. When she calculated what she was paying each year, to her amazement she was actually paying $100 less each month—$1,200 a year—to own her home rather than renting.

Another great real estate investment is the building in which your business is located. If you buy a multitenant building, the other businesses help you pay the mortgage and your particular space may even be free. In the best scenario, you are profiting every month by your tenants' lease payments and the building becomes more than walls and a roof. It is another source of cash flow that will appreciate every year. Management of a commercial building is extremely time-consuming, and you'll probably want to consider hiring a professional management company so that you don't end up taking on another full-time job.

The same is true with residential rental property. You purchase a residence and somebody else pays you for the right to live in it. It's your own personal monopoly board. As with commercial property, always try to build in the cost of a professional manager when determining profitability. If you have to fix toilets and leaky faucets and become the property's handywoman, you are relegating yourself to minimum wage work.

Retirement Plans

As much as possible of your investment budget should go into a retirement account such as an Individual Retirement Account (IRA) or Simplified Employee Pension (SEP). These accounts usually consist of investment vehicles such as stocks, bonds, and mutual funds, but you won't pay income tax on any interest or dividends generated until you retire. What's even better is that you can deduct the amount you put into your retirement account from your income taxes (with some complicated exceptions), with the maximum amount you can put in depending on the plan. With a regular IRA, you can only put in $3,000 a year. With a SEP-IRA, you can put in up to 13 percent of your self-employed income.

Talk to your accountant or brokerage firm about these and other retirement account options. A good place to start is with IRS Publication 560, *Retirement Plans for Small Business*. You can get it free by calling (800) TAX-FORM or logging onto www.irs.ustreas.gov.

Invest in Yourself

This is where women can learn from men. To achieve your true greatness, you must invest in yourself. When I approach men with the prospect of success coaching, they are quicker than women to see the benefits. They view spending money on coaches and consultants as an investment that will have an infinite return. If they spend $10,000 a year on a consultant, they will be armed with enough information to make an extra $50,000—and 500 percent is an excellent return on investment.

Because of self-worth issues, many women are slow to invest in themselves. Don't fall into this trap. Look for ways to spend money on yourself that will pay off in the future.

PART IV

BAG OF TRICKS

Attracting Your Ideal Customers

Selling Is Nurturing

Many women entrepreneurs say to me, "I'm not a salesperson. I'm not comfortable with selling." Because they don't want to be perceived as aggressive, selling turns them into jelly. They become timid and angst-ridden. The meek may inherit the earth, but they sure won't make the sale. You don't need to be obnoxious to be a good salesperson. You just need confidence, passion, and a sincere desire to help.

Do you remember the times in your life when you gave a family member needed advice, bandaged your kid's skinned knee, or spent hours on the phone with a girl-friend, lending a sympathetic ear? As a woman, part of your role as a nurturer involves alleviating pain, giving advice, and solving problems. As a business owner, your customers need a salve for their pain and are seeking your guidance. They look to you as a trusted adviser who can offer brilliant solutions. Experienced women entrepreneurs have learned that selling is really about nurturing relationships. You do not need to push and pester until the prospect is bullied into buying. Instead of think-ing of yourself as a salesperson, think of yourself as a nurturer and confidant.

There is no better euphoria than to close a sale. It's the ultimate high. People vote with their wallets and they just voted for you. A sale is an affirmation of your excel-lence—the culmination of your hard work, skills, and talents. As the sales nurturer, you are truly impassioned. You are besotted by the value of your product or service. You know that people's lives will be better if they take advantage of your wonderful offerings. All you have to do is tell the story, demonstrate the benefits, and offer real solutions.

CHAPTER 12

Communicating Your Passion

*Y*our business is up and running. Now it's time to launch into the brave new world of sales and marketing, to match your product or service with the people who need what you have to offer. What this really boils down to is communication, which for many of us is easier said than done, especially when it means communicating with strangers.

CONQUERING SHYNESS

Studies show that more than 90 percent of people identify themselves as shy. There is even a Shyness Institute in Palo Alto, California. Conquering your shyness is the first step to effective communication. Practice shyness control by talking to strangers on a regular basis. One of the best places is the supermarket line. Instead of being grouchy, smile and make eye contact with the people in line with you and find something to talk about. It makes the waiting go faster, and you may learn something interesting.

Great conversationalists listen more than they talk, so encourage the person you're conversing with to open up. Ask about her favorite recipes, restaurants, and what the good bargains are at the market. When I travel, I always talk to the people on the airport lines. I've found some great points of interest for sightseeing and some of my favorite restaurants by talking to strangers. The locals can give you the best advice about where to go when you're traveling.

I've always been extremely shy. In fact, when a friend of mine from high school read an article about me—public speaking to large groups, media tours, interviewing multimillionaires and celebrities—he said, "That must be another Linda Hollander. The Linda Hollander I knew wouldn't even open her mouth."

COMMUNICATING FACE TO FACE

All those pointers you learned in chapter 2—"Attitude Is (Almost) Everything"— will come into play when you set out to communicate your business to the world. Keep your goals and visions in mind. Use sensory anchoring. Listen to your inner hero, not your inner beast.

Don't focus solely on language when trying to build rapport. Some people hardly notice the words you use. They remember nonverbal cues such as your friendliness, confidence, body language, use of eye contact, mannerisms, and tone of voice. People experience the world through sensory information, and most individuals favor one sense over another. Some people are primarily visual; others are

A REEL WOMAN

Audrey Hope is a woman on a mission. Her purpose is to "bring light into darkness," and she is motivated by a true calling to help women. Audrey saw that women and girls suffer from low self-esteem. She didn't just dwell on the problem. She created a solution. Audrey broke down many barriers to create her award-winning television show, *Reel Women,* which presents positive images of strong women with profound thoughts and feelings.

Reel Women has showcased prominent women in the media like Betty Friedan, author of the *Feminine Mystique* and founder of the National Organization for Women; Callie Khouri, screenwriter of *Thelma and Louise;* and Terry McMillan, author of *Waiting to Exhale.* The guests on Audrey's show have also included women who have pointed out the myths in our history books that have damaged women and spiritual leaders who have illuminated feminine power.

Women need more champions like Audrey Hope. I am honored to know her and to be touched by her greatness. She has that rare mix of intelligence, beauty, and humanity. She has touched so many women on a deep level and changed so many lives.

auditory or sensory. By watching where people direct their eyes, you can tell what sense they favor. If they look up they're more visual, if they look to the side they're more auditory, and if they look down they're more touch oriented.

Mirroring is another technique for bonding and gaining rapport. This involves delicate matching of the body language and mannerisms of the person you're talking to. If she crosses her legs, you cross yours. If she puts her hand under her chin in a thinking position, match this posture. If done subtly, you will make a human connection and the prospect will not even be aware of the mirroring.

To improve your conversational skills, read newspapers, books, and magazines. Log onto Internet news sites, watch the television news, or listen to talk radio. It only takes minutes a day, but you will have infinite subjects to talk about and be perceived as well-read and in the know. Susan RoAne, author of *How to Work a Room,* even suggests reading the sports section of the paper. Speaking in sports lingo is the entry code to many desirable circles of influence. Many people are extremely impressed by women who know sports. This may give you the advantage on a plate.

COMMUNICATING ON THE PHONE

A good deal of your business will be conducted over the telephone, particularly if you're starting small or operating out of your home. Clearly, any time you make a business-related call, you should have the content of your message down pat. You want to get the words right. But there's plenty of evidence that your tone of voice and manner of speaking is even more important than your words.

Smile when you talk on the phone. This may sound silly, especially if you're sitting in an otherwise empty room, but you'd be amazed how much a smile affects your tone of voice. A professional trick is to put a mirror in front of you to check out your smile. Another is to look at a photo of your family, friends, or favorite pet. Speak a bit more slowly than normal. Fast talkers can seem nervous and unprofessional.

Any time you make an unscheduled phone call, ask the person you're calling if they have time to talk. This courtesy will be appreciated and will help your information get through. If the person has an urgent call coming in, a meeting in the next minute, or some other time distraction, they will not be paying attention to your presentation. You want the full attention of the person you're calling, and you want them to think of you as considerate.

When speaking on the phone, be focused and concise. Unless you're dealing with a schmoozer, don't run off at the mouth or make trite small talk. People are usually too busy for this, and will appreciate a straight-to-the-point but friendly approach. Create a positive impression and control the process of information transfer.

Gatekeepers

Frequently, you won't get straight through to the person you want to talk to on the phone. Instead, you'll need to deal with a gatekeeper. Many people feel that they can bulldoze their way past the assistant or whoever screens the calls for their prospect. They think that the support people aren't powerful enough to take seriously or treat respectfully. Big mistake! Gatekeepers are major influencers. According to Michael A. Boylan, author of *The Power to Get In,* "Secretaries and assistants—particularly executive assistants—can wield almost as much power as the people they work for. This can make them formidable opponents—or invaluable allies."

If the gatekeeper dislikes you, you will be blackballed. Gatekeepers make preliminary judgments on their boss's behalf, are knowledgeable about how the organization works, and are keenly aware the power centers in their company. They can also be an invaluable source of information. Most important, they decide which communications their boss actually sees and have a significant say in who gets to see their boss.

When you first talk with a gatekeeper, find out his or her full name with the correct spelling, but use the first name and the boss's first name to establish rapport. Never, never be rude or try to bully the assistant; it will get back to the boss and you'll be shooting yourself in the foot. If anyone was rude to an assistant of mine, it would be a big red flag about that person's character and lack of human decency. Acknowledge the gatekeeper's power and assist her by providing the information she needs. Humanize the interaction by being direct, honest, straightforward, and very clear about the purpose of your call.

If you're lucky, you won't even need to get past the gatekeepers. Deal with them respectfully, and they will often give you exactly what you want. You may not need to talk to their boss at all.

Voice Mail

Today, most businesses have erected virtual fortresses around themselves through the use of technology: fax machines, personal computers, cellular phones, online services, caller ID, email, and the dreaded voice mail. Gatekeepers can be frustrating, but at least you're talking to a human being.

When answering machines first came on the market, many people flatly refused to "talk to a machine." With the proliferation of voice mail, no one can get away with this anymore. People have a love-hate relationship with voice mail. Prospects love it because it is the ultimate screening device. Salespeople hate it because it is the ultimate screening device.

Voice mail "phone tag" can certainly slow down communication. Let's say you manufacture sportswear. Your customer left you a voice mail saying he wanted to order some T-shirts, but he didn't specify the color of the shirts. If you have to keep leaving each other messages to straighten things out, a situation that could have been handled in five minutes may drag out to five days. On the positive side, voice mail makes communications more efficient, allowing you to state the reason for your call or leave important information directly, rather than through an assistant. With voice mail, you can communicate your passion for your product. Don't, however, try to sell anything on voice mail. For that, you need to talk one-on-one.

Voice mail is part of doing business. Since you have to live with it, consider giving yourself a voice mail makeover. As annoying as voice mail can be, make every effort not to sound annoyed when you leave your message. I'm surprised that so many people leave a voice mail such as, "This is Gina. Call me at 555-5555"— click! It sounds like Gina was sucking a lemon when she left this message. How can you improve on this picture? First, start with "Hi" or some other friendly greeting. Lastly, end the message by being cordial and upbeat: "Please give me a call. I look forward to talking with you soon. Bye!" Leave your phone number twice. There are times when you can bypass the company voice mail by pressing zero and getting a live operator. The live person can then page or locate your prospect. If you need to leave a voice mail message, just leave one or two messages. If you leave more, you will be perceived as a pest.

PUBLIC SPEAKING—OH NO!

Most people are shy, prefer anonymity, and are afraid of being judged. That's why fear of public speaking is so huge. According to Peter Desberg, author of *No More Butterflies: Overcoming Stagefright, Shyness, Interview Anxiety, and Fear of Public Speaking,* "Everyone likes to look good in front of an audience. If you think they will evaluate you negatively, you will become anxious and experience tension and fear." The ego is a fragile thing, and public speaking combines many human fears.

> *The number one fear of most people is public speaking. The number two fear is death. Do you know what this means? At a funeral, most people would rather be the guy in the box than the guy giving the eulogy.*
> —Jerry Seinfeld, comedian

Stop being selfish! Shyness and fear of public speaking are the ultimate forms of selfishness. Don't give your own anxieties priority over helping others. You have wonderful gifts that you can impart to others by teaching and public speaking. To deny them of these unique gifts would be self-centered and egocentric.

The good news is that fear of public speaking can be unlearned. After a while, you'll really enjoy talking to groups of people. It's a blast!

The Elevator Speech

Imagine yourself in the elevator on the tenth floor of an office building. In walks your perfect customer, she just doesn't know it yet. Your mission, should you choose to accept it, is to tell this person the benefits of your business and get her salivating to give you money by the time the elevator hits the ground floor. That's the elevator speech. It's also called the four-line pitch. It may not be as challenging as speaking for an hour in front of a packed auditorium, but it's a start.

In your elevator speech, don't define yourself by your title. When Susan RoAne, author of *How to Work a Room,* is asked what she does, she could tell people she's a networking consultant and author. How boring! Instead she says, "I teach people how to work a room and be a networking maven." A great elevator speech like this one prompts the listener to ask, "That sounds interesting. What's a networking maven? Tell me more."

Start working on your elevator speech as soon as you start your business. Practice in front of the mirror, and then in front of your friends. Once you step in that elevator, you'll be ready to go.

Seminars and Presentations

Teaching seminars and giving speeches gives you credibility as an expert in your field. It's challenging at first, but you have plenty of tools in your arsenal to get you through the tough parts.

Remember sensory anchoring? There's no better time to use it than on the day of a big presentation. The first few times I was asked to speak to a group of women business owners I was terrified, but I used sensory anchoring to get past my fear. I arrived at the meeting place early. Wearing royal blue—my power color—I went methodically to each of the four corners of the room, did my victory dance with my arms in a "V" over my head, and exclaimed, "Yes!" Those four corners of the room became my power centers. I owned the room. During the speech, if I felt scared or anxious, I looked over at each corner that I had claimed, and a feeling of calm and confidence washed over me. Now, if you ever see me speak, you'll probably come early to see me do my victory dance. It's quite comical, but it works.

> *Expert: One who doesn't know more than you but uses slides.*
>
> —The Toastmaster's Treasure Chest

Here are some additional tips to help you give dynamite presentations:

- **Prepare and practice.** Run through your entire presentation as often as you can before you have to get up in front of an audience. Write a loose outline rather than writing the speech out word for word and then reading it. It's a good idea, however, to write out and memorize your introduction and conclusion. A strong introduction launches you with confidence into your presentation. If you stand up and speak from the heart it will be more real than if you read from notes. Conclusions are also extremely important. This is your chance to wrap up the talk and leave people thinking you're wonderful.
- **Arrive early.** Many times the meeting room does not have what you need to do a good presentation, such as a large writing board, microphone, hook-up for your laptop computer, or water to soothe your throat as you speak. One

time I arrived early at a hotel to set up for a seminar and found out that the air-conditioning was on the fritz. The room was as hot as an oven. Frantically, I went to the front desk and begged for a room fan. Luckily they found one and it made the climate of the room tolerable.

- **Take away empty chairs.** This tip is from Malcolm Kushner, author of *Public Speaking for Dummies: Tried and True Tips for Dazzling Speeches and Presentations.* Find out how many people are expected to show up for your presentation and take away the extra chairs. People feel very uncomfortable showing up for a class or a speech that looks like it isn't popular. Taking away empty chairs also eradicates apathy. It also forces people to sit close together, creates a group synergy, and stimulates participation.

- **Greet your audience.** Another advantage of arriving early is it allows you to greet people. Introduce yourself, shake hands, offer name tags, and ask questions that will help with your presentation.

- **Always get contact information.** Contact information is crucial, but having people put their business cards in a hat isn't the best strategy. Many people don't even carry business cards. A better bet is to place a short information form on the desk or chair of each audience member before they arrive. I even provide a Wealthy Bag Lady pen. Then I collect the forms and use them in drawings for free prize giveaways.

- **Get your adrenaline going.** If you can, do an aerobic activity such as running or low-impact exercises before your talk. Popular speakers' tricks are to push against a wall lightly or to run up on stage. If there are other speakers before you, you can tense up your muscles in your chair and relax them while you wait your turn.

- **Breathe slowly.** Your breathing is accelerated when you're nervous. Develop a consciousness about your breathing and take deep slow breaths. Your entire body will relax.

- **Use affirmations.** Choose something specific, such as "Everyone in this room is a friend that I haven't met yet," or "Everyone in this room wants me to succeed."

- **Visualize a positive outcome.** Imagine being treated like a rock star. After your presentation, the audience members leap to their feet, cheering, applauding, turning on the flames in their cigarette lighters, requesting an encore, and giving you a standing ovation. It works every time.

- **Speak from the heart.** Don't get up there and only tell your audience how great you are. To endear yourself to people, reveal mistakes you have made and things you regret, and admit to your human frailties. This creates a strong emotional connection with your audience.

- **Use humor.** Think of funny stories from your own life experience that you can share with people. These stories reinforce your humanity and show the audience that you don't take yourself seriously. If you have a good time on the podium, the audience can have a good time with you. Humor is the ultimate tension reducer.

- **Make eye contact.** Establish eye contact with as many people in the room as possible, especially at the end of a thought or story. Don't concentrate solely on the "heroes" in the audience, the friendly faces who are really into your talk. They'll wonder why you're staring at them.

- **Give prizes to audience members.** Use those information forms in a drawing and give away promotional items. Everyone loves to be a winner, and they also like to see other people win. When I'm teaching, I start by giving a prize away. I ask the audience, "Is it okay if I give something away now?" They always say yes and then pay more attention to the presentation. After all, they might be one of the lucky winners at a later drawing.

- **Ask for evaluations and testimonials.** Stop your presentation about fifteen minutes early and ask the audience members to fill out a speaker evaluation. Include open-ended questions such as, "What were the most important things for you to learn?" "How well did the speaker cover these subjects?" "If you could change one thing about the presentation, what would it be?" Use the answers to improve your presentation. Also provide space for the audience members to write a brief testimonial. These wonderful testimonials can be used in your marketing materials and will help you get future speaking engagements.

NETWORKING POWER

Every time you meet someone who might need your goods or services—or even someone who knows someone who fits that description—is an opportunity to network. Stay alert for great ways to network spontaneously, and also actively seek out networking opportunities. When you first start your business, consider joining at least two organizations, one that focuses on your chosen field and the other a more general organization such as the Rotary Club or a local businesswomen's group.

Going into a room of complete strangers, meeting them one or two at a time, and telling them about you and your business can be even scarier than public speaking, but networking events offer such great bonuses that it's really worth breaking through your fear and shyness.

Great Places to Network

In chapter 3, "Your Supporting Cast," I discussed women's organizations such as the National Association of Women Business Owners (NAWBO), the National Association of Female Executives (NAFE), and eWomenNetwork.com. These are wonderful places to network, but don't fall into the trap of going exclusively to women-only events. Mixed-gender events offer great opportunities, too. Aldonna Ambler, an entrepreneur, venture capitalist, and growth strategist in Hammonton, New Jersey, articulates, "I grew my businesses through sponsorships, but I never would have had the sponsors if I had worked only with women."

NEGLECTING TO COLLECT LEADS

You give an inspiring, brilliant talk. You create instant fans in your audience, people who would be glad to receive information about your business products, books, future classes, or speaking events. But you neglect to get the names and contact information of your audience members so that you can contact them in the future. Don't miss a great opportunity for future sales. You could easily double your business by collecting contact information on information forms from your audience. Loyal supporters are always glad to hear from you.

Here are some other great places to network:

- **Industry meetings.** Every industry has some kind of association. These associations meet at regular intervals or once a year. Industry meetings are a great place to learn about trends and changes in your trade. They also provide fertile networking ground.

- **Chambers of commerce.** Chambers of commerce are regional entities that provide arenas to make contacts and exchange ideas. Regular meetings encourage networking and address local community issues.

- **Seminars and conferences.** People with similar interests congregate at seminars and conferences. Between the keynote addresses, speeches, and breakout sessions there will usually be breaks when you can network with the other attendees. In a full day or multiday conference, there is always a lunch break during which you can network to your heart's content.

- **Trade shows and conventions.** Whether you're attending or exhibiting, these are highly concentrated arenas for networking. People have come from all over the country and even the world to glean knowledge, exchange ideas, and make contacts. Trade shows and conventions have cocktail parties, dinners, entertainment, and sightseeing events. Participating in these events allows you to establish rapport by meeting people in a more relaxed atmosphere than the trade show floor. I'll discuss trade shows in more detail in the chapter 14, "The Lure of Marketing."

- **Leisure activities.** For years, we heard about the "old boys' network" and how great deals were made by men on the golf course. Now women are getting into golf, tennis, running, and skiing. These pastimes provide great arenas for making power contacts and building your million-dollar Rolodex. And don't forget nail and hair salons. These institutions are to some women what golf courses are to men. Many lasting business relationships have been forged in beauty salons. If you meet a woman you want to network with, ask where she gets her hair and nails done. Then ask her to introduce you to the best stylist or manicurist in the joint. Of course, you'll have to meet her at the salon. While you're there, you can create some serious female bonding over the shampoo and drying nail polish.

Tips for Successful Networking

Your first step for successful networking is to walk up to an approachable person, make eye contact, and smile. Your smile is the welcome sign for your face. Introduce yourself with your name, company, and elevator speech. Always carry plenty of business cards. This advice may seem obvious, but I've met plenty of business people at networking events who didn't even bring their business cards. If possible, wear an outfit with pockets. Keep your business cards in your left pocket. When you reach out your right hand to shake theirs, reach your left hand into the left pocket, pull out a business card, and hand it to them. Put the business cards you collect at the event in your right pocket.

Don't be stingy about those business cards! Recently I met a great promoter, DeLyn Patrick of DLP Career Coaching. When we exchanged cards, she didn't just give me one of her business cards, she forked over a whole stack so that I could pass them out to friends and associates. Smart lady!

Here are some other strategies for effective networking:

- **Get to the event early.** This way you can get a good seat and save your place. If there is a speaker, you can claim a prime seat to see the speaker without obstructions of big heads and hairdos. The front tables at events tend to be power tables. By arriving early, you can assure yourself a seat in these influential circles. Getting there early also eases the nervousness you may be feeling.

- **Concentrate on quality, not quantity.** According to Jacqueline Jones, former southwest regional coordinator of NAFE, for most people the number of business cards they collect becomes the barometer of their networking success. Instead of just collecting business cards, concentrate on the quality of the contacts you are making. On the back of each card, jot down the date, event, and any important information about that person or their company.

- **Work the room counterclockwise.** Most networkers traverse the room in a clockwise manner. To stand out from the crowd, take the road less traveled and go counterclockwise.

- **Break into conversation circles.** This is probably the most intimidating part about networking. It's best to break into groups of three or more people. If two people are talking, they may be discussing something personal or doing important business. Plant yourself near the group so that you can hear what they're talking about. Then position yourself in the group, introduce yourself, and add a comment that relates to the topic being discussed. You can also compliment something a person is wearing or remark on his or her keen insights, intelligence, or storytelling. Everyone loves compliments.

- **Make eye contact with everyone in the circle.** At a recent networking event, I was having a conversation with a man named Bill when Bill's friend Steve came over and joined us. Steve talked only to Bill and never even looked at me. Was I invisible? After Steve left, Bill apologized for his friend's boorish behavior, explaining that Steve was probably shy and uncomfortable. I didn't buy it. You cannot disguise shyness with rudeness. If you're talking to a group of people, make sure you introduce yourself and make eye contact with everyone in the group, not just a select few. Even if you're lucky enough to meet a key influencer, don't ignore his or her associate. If you're talking to a husband and a wife, make sure to look at both of them.

- **Extricate yourself from a bore.** Eventually you will come in contact with a bore. The bore has no idea how dull he or she really is. If you're monopolized by the mind-numbing chatter of the bore, politely excuse yourself or say that you need to say hi to someone else in the room.

- **Network as a team.** I got this little gem from my friends Susan RoAne and Patricia Fripp. These two women have different businesses. They attend networking events together, but when they arrive at the room, they split up. Patricia will be in a conversation with someone. Then Susan will join them. Patricia will say, "This is my friend Susan. She's probably too humble to tell you, but she is a great speaker, consultant, and a best-selling author." It's the ultimate live testimonial system.

- **Follow up.** Consider writing quick emails to the people you met at the event, or calling the key influencers to see if you can arrange a meeting. Thank-you cards and e-greetings are wonderful ways of acknowledging a person's importance.

Don't be afraid to network! It's a great way to meet interesting people, broaden your knowledge, and help your business grow.

CHAPTER 13

Pricing for Profit

$\mathcal{P}$ricing is an art, but an elusive one. The art of pricing means achieving what you need by delivering the goods and services your customers want. One of the trickiest decisions for women business owners is determining what to charge for their products or services. Women notoriously undercharge because issues of self-worth become embroiled in pricing. Some women (gasp!) even give away valuable products and services.

In figuring their pricing some entrepreneurs use elaborate computations. Others just guess. But if you calculate or guess wrong, you'll soon be out of business. According to Edith Quick, partner with her husband, Roy, in Quick Tax & Accounting Service in Saint Louis, the art of pricing is in "striking a balance between the money you need to stay in business and the customer's perception of what your product or service is worth."

When some women first start their businesses, they are shocked and delighted that anyone would pay them to do what they love. They ignore the basic laws of pricing and building in a profit and practically give their goods and services away to establish a customer base. Although I recommend giving away low-cost items with high perceived value, such as free reports, trial samples, books, how-to information, and gifts, you need to price your main product or service for profit.

KNOW YOUR COSTS

Many women, when I meet with them and ask if they are priced for profit, honestly don't know. When we break down the numbers, they are angry and surprised to find out that they are only making minimum wage. A business owner making only minimum wage? What's wrong with this picture?

Before you decide on your pricing, you need to take a close look at your costs. If you're offering a service from a home-based business, your costs include administrative expenses such as telephone, travel, and office supplies. If you're offering a product, you need to take into account hard costs such as the expense of buying or manufacturing your product. There are also fixed and variable costs to consider. An example of a fixed cost is the lease payment on your store or office. It is the same every month. A variable expense would be postage because it fluctuates every month.

Acknowledge Your Worth

Women's decisions about pricing are frequently wrapped up in self-worth and status quo. Women are accustomed to making less money than their male counter-

Don't Give It Away, Honey!

Remember when you started dating and your mother (maybe even your grandmother) gave you advice about men and what they value? She probably said something like, "Why buy the cow if you can get the milk for free?" This same ageless wisdom applies to your business.

When Jan Brogniez, coauthor of *Attracting Perfect Customers,* was first in business as a consultant to leading-edge firms on increasing company revenues, she hoped she could build a customer base by offering complimentary first sessions. She did her proprietary strategic design process with the display board for a woman named Patty. It took three hours, and at the end Patty said, "You mean to tell me that you're giving this away?" Jan said, "Yes. That was our agreement." Patty told Jan that the three hours they spent together was the most valuable thing that she had ever done. She accomplished more in three hours than she did with other highly paid consultants in six months. Then Patty went over to her personal checkbook and wrote out a check for $500, because she did not want to wait to run the cost through her company. As Patty was giving Jan the check, she admonished her, "Don't let me ever hear that you're giving this process away." Jan never did a complimentary session again.

parts. Being paid less may not be desirable, but it sure is familiar. It takes guts to put a high price on your products and services.

The first step to pricing for profit is to acknowledge your worth. This doesn't mean you should overvalue your product or service, but you shouldn't undervalue it, either. According to Georgette Mosbacher, former CEO of La Prairie Cosmetics and author of *It Takes Money, Honey,* "Although we represent 49 percent of the workforce, figuring out what to charge is a lot harder for women than for men. Instead of being a measure of the value of our work and key benefits, fees get all tangled up with questions of self-worth—and I have to tell you, this is a problem for a lot of women."

THE PERILS OF PRICING TOO LOW

It is extremely difficult to compete on price alone. If you choose to make price a key selling point, be prepared for fierce competition. Customers who come to you strictly for price will leave you for a better price. There is always a sneaky competitor licking his chops at the chance to undercut your prices. And believe me, your worthy competitors make it their business to find out your prices. Fierce competitors have even been known to lose money on a first order, just to sign up a new account. If you sell your dependability, quality, knowledge, and reputation, it will be harder for others to compete with your unique selling proposition. Give your customers more than price as a reason to buy from you.

Ironically, if you price your products high, you will get a better caliber of clients. The clients who put in the smallest orders are the most high maintenance. They will try to whittle down your profits, nitpick about prices, and complain the loudest. The large volume customers are far less trouble. They pay on time, don't quibble about prices, and are appreciative of the value you provide. They will also refer their affluent business colleagues and associates to you.

Building a Customer Base

Many entrepreneurs—and women in particular—think they can build a customer base when they first go into business by pricing their products and services artificially low. This is a good strategy, but if you later drastically increase prices, your customers will get royally ticked off. Clients understand gradual price increases, but a drastic price increase will cause anger and resentment.

Instead, I would offer a low introductory special when you first start your business, but make it clear when your prices will increase. Tell your prospective customers what the real value of the widgets are. Let Cathy Customer know that your widgets sell for $100, but she can get a low introductory price of only $75 until a certain date. That gives her an incentive to try your business now and to increase the volume of her orders to save money for a limited time.

> *What women want is what men want. They want respect.*
>
> —Marilyn vos Savant, columnist and writer

You do want to build your customer base, but there's a good chance you can do it more effectively by honoring your worth.

Perceived Value

"There is a direct and strong relationship between the prices you charge and the image of your company," says Erin O'Donnell of Pepper, O'Donnell & Co. Inc., a marketing and public relations firm in Winter Park, Florida. "For example, do you want to be viewed as a no-frills, low-cost operation, or as a high-end, full-service company? What is important is that your pricing structure be compatible with the image you want to create."

Service businesses in particular need to focus on value. O'Donnell recalls a client whose sales rose dramatically when he increased his prices. "He was a consultant, and his product was information," she says. "In the lower price range, it had a lower perceived value—that is, his clients thought that what he had to offer couldn't be worth much if he was charging so little for it. But when he started charging more, the perceived value went up, too—and so did his sales."

When testing your pricing, start with a price that is higher than you're comfortable charging. Sometimes high pricing works better than low pricing, because of the perceived value. A well-known example is a celebrity skin care cream by Tova Borgnine, the beautiful wife of actor Ernest Borgnine. The Tova Company sent out two mailings. One priced the skin cream at $30 and one priced it at $18. The higher-priced skin cream outsold the lower priced cream because of the snob appeal.

Loss Leaders Are Risky Business

In essence, extremely low prices are a good strategy only if you sell products or services in extremely high volume—not a likely scenario for a small business owner—or if the low-cost item represents only a fraction of your total income. Loss leaders—merchandise that is advertised and sold at a price representing a loss of profit for the retailer—is a great strategy for the major retailers. Giant discount stores and major grocery stores have used this strategy for years to draw the customers into the store in the hope that they will buy the low-priced item and then make additional purchases. But there is too much risk and not enough reward in this strategy for most small businesses.

If you offer specials to get customers through the door, make sure you are making some profit on each sale item and that your other merchandise is likely to sell as well.

PRICING STRATEGIES

So now that you've been admonished not to set your prices too low, you're probably thinking, "How do I set them just right?" Here are some strategies.

Check Out Your Competition

Find out what your competitors are charging for products and services similar to yours. Collect their sales information and catalogs. Go to trade shows where they're

A VALUABLE WORKSHOP

When Stacey Hall, coauthor of *Attracting Perfect Customers,* started giving her workshops about a unique system for pumping up your customer database, she charged only $25, and there were hardly any takers. At the end of one of her workshops, a student told her she should be charging more for the tremendous value of her information. Stacey said, "Nobody is coming at $25. How can I charge more?" The woman told Stacey, "People will come when you honor the value of what you have." After that, Stacey charged $100 for the workshop and attendance shot through the roof. There was so much demand for her workshops that she had to raise prices again to $250, a tenfold increase from her original price of only $25.

exhibiting and visit their websites. Study their pricing and make sure you're in the ballpark. Your prospects will also give you information on what your competitors are charging. You don't need to be the lowest price in the market, but you can't be twice the price of everyone else in your industry.

Don't just look at your competitors' prices—look at their value-added services. For example, Shahid Kinnare's Timezone store in Memphis, Tennessee, has numerous watch and jewelry retailer competitors nearby. "So I look at what services they don't have," Shahid explains. "I give free jewelry cleaning for a lifetime. I give a lifetime guarantee on all my watches."

To determine standard prices for your industry, ask trade associations, chambers of commerce, or other industry groups for pricing studies, surveys, or related information. Many industries have helpful pricing books about the market.

Think Mathematically

A classic strategy for many industries is cost-plus pricing. You determine the total cost to produce an order, then add a standardized profit percentage to arrive at your price. A good way to determine industry-standard percentages is simply to ask your suppliers. When you purchase goods, ask the vendor what the standard markup is on that product.

A variation of cost-plus pricing is to create a "magic markup" formula. The owners of Huckleberry Mountain Co., a Jackson Hole, Wyoming–based specialty manufacturer of candies and preserves, determine wholesale prices by multiplying ingredient costs by two, then adding 20 percent, says Judy Johnson, co-owner with her husband, Doug. The 20 percent markup covers distribution and sales commissions; the doubling of ingredient costs covers labor and overhead.

Many entrepreneurs find such formulas easier than trying to figure out all their costs or surveying their customers. However, use any formula with caution. It may not cover all your actual costs—a quick path to financial disaster. Or you may cheat yourself out of some profits because customers may be willing to pay more than the formula dictates.

Another mathematical trick is to calculate your profit backward. Some service providers and consultants start with the annual income they want to make, then calculate how much they need to charge. The rule of thumb is that you will have one thousand billable hours a year. If you want to gross $100,000, you have to bill $100 an hour. If you're selling products rather than services, you can also use the backward calculations formula. Determine how many widgets you sell in a year. Then determine what profit you need on each widget to achieve your desired income.

No formula can substitute for the one number you must know: how much it costs to make a product or deliver a service. This is your break-even point and your price floor.

Think Psychologically

Psychology plays a role in pricing, and retailers are the masters of "magic number" pricing for moving merchandise. Many retail items are priced at a digit less than a round number, such as $9.99 instead of $10 or $999 instead of $1,000, because the mind tends to perceive the difference as much greater than just a penny or a dollar.

To find out the magic numbers, test different price points and see which numbers trigger buying signs in your customers. Be wary, however, of PFA (plucked from air) pricing. When you use the magic numbers formula of pricing, make sure you're making a profit. Many entrepreneurs just pick numbers that sound good and activate sales, but forget the basic tenet of business: profit.

> *Aerodynamically the bumble bee shouldn't be able to fly, but the bumble bee doesn't know it, so it goes on flying anyway.*
> —Mary Kay Ash, CEO of Mary Kay Cosmetics

Combine Strategies

You may find the most effective pricing method is a combination of two or more basic strategies. For example, Ernest J. Florestano used markup and competitive pricing when deciding what to charge for the magnetic water-treatment devices manufactured by his Norfolk, Virginia–based company, Descal-A-Matic. "We did market research to find out what our competitors were charging, then did [markup] calculations," Ernest explains, "and determined we could price our product in the midrange of the market and still achieve our profit goal."

Add Some Cushion

Pumping up your prices slightly gives you some bargaining room. Some customers always ask for a price discount as part of their buying strategy. Customers want to know that you will work with them and not hide behind a rigid pricing policy. If a desirable customer wants to negotiate a better price, adding some cushion gives you some room to create a true win-win situation.

It's a good idea for service providers to add a little to their hourly rate so that they don't nickel and dime their clients to death. If a client calls you with a question that takes five minutes, don't charge for it but do track those calls. Then if a client complains about the bill, you can point out all the free services you offered all year.

If yours is a business that includes making written bids and proposals, guarantee your prices for a specified time. On the bottom of your quotations, write: "This quotation valid for xx days." Raw material prices in some industries can be extremely volatile. Your business may be able to absorb small increases, but major cost jumps can wipe out your profits. Ask your suppliers how long they will guarantee their price levels, and then do the same for your customers.

WHEN IT'S TIME TO RAISE THE BAR

Don't be afraid to raise your prices. Remember that pricing is an ongoing process. Regularly evaluate your prices and be prepared to change them if necessary or appropriate. Some companies go for years without raising prices for fear of losing their customers. Then, when they finally raise their prices, their customers balk and bolt. It's far better to raise prices slightly every year, so you won't paint yourself into a corner and have to make a drastic increase that customers will resent.

Price increases can also be handled with finesse. A business coaching client of mine, Beverly, took over her father's accounting practice after his death. She raised prices on the existing clients and contacted them for their feedback. Surprisingly, most clients were very understanding and many of them even admitted to her, "We knew all those years that we weren't paying enough for the great services your company provided."

Robert Sher, CEO of Bentley Publishing Group based in Walnut Creek, California, knew he needed to raise prices on his framed art prints, but first he did a careful analysis of his product line. He didn't jack up prices across the board. By comparing his prices with those of his competitors, he found that he had fallen well below the industry average for his smallest prints. He raised those prices a hefty 40 percent. His large prints, he found, were already priced more in line with those of his competitors. He raised prices 5 percent for newly introduced large prints, while older ones stayed at the old prices. But his most important step was keeping the lines of communication open with his customers. He was even more willing to give volume discounts. Robert says of his sales force, "We presented it as, 'Yes, prices are going up, and here's why. But there's some flexibility.' That was really, really important."

You can also use price increases as a sales tool. Create a sense of urgency and pump up sales. One of my vendors sent out an announcement that said prices would be going up and gave my company, as a preferred customer, a chance to buy at their current prices for another thirty days. This savvy business encouraged volume pricing so that we could buy at better prices.

CHAPTER 14

The Lure of Marketing

Every company, no matter what it does, is a sales and marketing company. Or make that marketing and sales. The familiar expression you've heard so often is actually backward. Marketing—everything you do to attract customers—comes first. Then comes sales, which is everything you do to close the deal. The more effective your marketing, the easier your sales. Marketing is one of the noblest endeavors in the world. Your clients are out there searching for you, and marketing helps them find you and your product or service. The law of attraction says that what you are searching for is also trying to find you.

According to Nancy Michaels and Debbie Karpowicz, authors of *Off-the-Wall Marketing Ideas,* you should "put aside any tendencies to downplay your strengths for the sake of appearing modest when you are self-marketing, especially when your budget is small and the competition is fierce. Self-promotion does not mean bragging and boring others with how great you are. It simply means making others aware of your business and the services and advantages that it offers."

Small business experts say to spend anywhere from 20 to 50 percent of your time, at least in the early days, on drumming up business. It may just be a matter of working the phones to remind people that you're out there—calling your contacts, calling your contacts' contacts, and cold calling hot prospects. Your marketing will become more sophisticated as your business becomes more established.

Denise Michaels, author of *Testosterone-Free Marketing for Women: Seven Secrets Why Old Boys Marketing Doesn't Work for Women,* told me in an interview, "Many women get into the 'Field of Dreams' school of marketing, which is no marketing at all. Subconsciously, they think, 'If I build it, they will come.' Honey, the world is not waiting to beat a quick path to your door." Marketing cannot be just a one-shot deal. A successful campaign must include many coordinated exposures to current and potential customers. You need at least five hits—anything from a word-of-mouth referral to a splashy ad on TV—before a sale is made.

TARGET YOUR MARKET

Defining your target market is an important component of your business success. Your target market is the specific segment of the population who can use your product or service. Don't tell me your product is for everyone. It's not. You're actually better off if you narrowly identify your target market and niche your business. Your niche will make you rich. You can always expand a narrow niche to include more types of customers.

One way to look at your target market is in terms of demographics and psychographics. Demographics are external socioeconomic factors such as age, income, sex, occupation, education, and family size. These factors are easy to measure. Psychographics are internal factors—what makes people tick and how they view themselves in relation to the world. Both are essential in your marketing plan.

The women's lingerie business Victoria's Secret offers a marvelous example of a defined target market. Demographically, the typical Victoria's Secret customer is a twenty-six-year-old single female earning under $40,000 a year. She is a college graduate with a bachelor's degree. This woman drives a Toyota Camry and works at an advertising agency. She reads *Cosmopolitan, Vogue,* and *Glamour* magazines as well as romance novels.

Psychographically, the Victoria's Secret customer wants to be beautiful, sexy, desirable, and loved. This woman wants to be taken seriously in her career and to express her sensual side and playful spirit. She is in touch with her femininity but is also very strong and independent. Because the target customer for Victoria's Secret is a romantic who wants to be beautiful and desirable, the company uses fantasy imagery in its advertising.

Victoria's Secret is marketed to a younger demographic, so you won't find any control-top underwear in their line. Young women don't need to pull anything in or pick anything up off the floor. When Victoria's Secret came up with a line of cosmetics, they didn't include any line preventers, age-defying creams, or products for "mature skin." You're probably thinking, "But my sixty-year-old mother shops at Victoria's Secret," or "My fifteen-year-old niece buys lingerie at Victoria's Secret." This proves that target marketing really works. By tightly defining their market, they have broadened their appeal. Your mother or niece shops at Victoria's Secret because she wants to feel like the twenty-six-year-old woman with the glamorous lifestyle.

For effective marketing, you need to know the age, sex, ethnicity, income level, family size, geographic location, and education of your target market. More important, you need to know their motivations, challenges, problems, core values, and desires. Remember, people buy emotionally to eradicate their pain and solve their problems. What is the problem that you are the solution to? What makes your perfect customer get up in the morning? What makes their heart sing? Once you've targeted your market, you can start deciding how best to reach them.

WORD OF MOUTH

Most people are exposed to two hundred to one thousand sales communications a day and act on very few of them. They develop a "propaganda radar." Word of mouth is a way to break through this radar. Imagine that a friend calls you to recommend a movie, book, or product. You may not take every recommendation, but you'll probably take one or two out of five. In other words, you're much more likely to act on a recommendation from a friend, colleague, or trusted adviser than a commercial communication.

Absolutely nothing beats word of mouth as a marketing tool. It relies on the spoken word, rather than the premeditated sales strategy. Not only is it free of cost, but it's free of any perceived manipulation by the company offering the product or service. It's this independent credibility that gives word of mouth its awesome power.

Most people believe that word of mouth is pure happenstance, something they cannot control. In fact, there's a science to word of mouth marketing. As George Silverman says in *The Secrets of Word-of-Mouth Marketing,* "The idea that word of mouth cannot be harnessed is probably the most dangerous and costly marketing oversight."

Endorsements and testimonials from satisfied customers are one of the most persuasive forms of marketing. They enhance your credibility and make your message more believable. Your assignment is to become an avid collector of testimonials.

When clients give you compliments, ask them if they will put their kind words in writing or if you can quote them. When you have your collection of testimonials, you have a powerful arsenal. Key influencers who have high name recognition make the most compelling testimonials. If you have worked with people who are held in high esteem or represent highly respectable corporations, by all means quote them in your literature. Always use the person's full name, company (if appropriate), and where they are from. Don't use initials or an initial for the last name. The endorsement will lose power and credibility.

Here are some ways of harnessing word of mouth:

- Provide a superior product.
- Give speeches, teach seminars and workshops.
- Create a referral selling program.
- Reach key influencers in your marketplace.
- Provide a direct, low-risk experience with your product, such as a demo or trial sample.
- Provide an iron-clad guarantee.

Whenever someone does you the word-of-mouth favor of referring a new customer, call and thank him or her. Scott, the owner of a catalog-printing company, referred an excellent customer to me. I called Scott, thanked him personally, and told him that if I came across customers who need beautiful four-color brochures I

THE POWER OF WORD OF MOUTH

When Celestial Seasonings first began to sell herbal teas in 1969, the company was so small it couldn't afford to advertise. So the company president, 19-year-old Mo Siegel, enclosed a note in each box of tea asking people to tell their friends how good it was, or better yet, to serve it whenever they could.

Because Celestial Seasonings produces a quality product with marvelous packaging, its satisfied customers eagerly shared the news with their friends. Starting with word of mouth, the company has grown today into one of the largest distributors of herbal tea in America.

would send them his way. I even got an added bonus for making the call—Scott referred another prospect to me, named Helen. I called Helen and closed another sale. The payoff for the short thank-you call was thousands of dollars.

FREE PUBLICITY

Media coverage is one of the most powerful marketing tools available. Not only does it spread the word about your company, it also enhances your credibility, improves your image, and has the potential to boost your business. Positive press coverage may not guarantee fame and fortune, but it can offer swift passage from obscurity to prominence. No other medium carries the weight of the independent press.

> *Even those deaf to the bragging cries of the marketplace will listen to a friend.*
> —Paddi Lund, author, Building the Happiness-Centered Business

Publicity does have its drawbacks. You get immediate and long-term results, but you have very little control—you can't target your market. Exposure is directed toward a broad audience, who may not be your potential customers. You may also have to share the spotlight with a competitor or those with opposing views.

Look for the news value in your story, and don't confuse a news story with an advertisement. Do your homework on the target demographic. This is the audience for the radio show, magazine, or newspaper. Remember that the media like controversy. You could be part of a trend or antitrend. Community involvement can get you publicity. You can also be one of the experts whom they call on a particular story.

Whenever you pitch for media coverage, be sure to have a hook. Nancy Greystone, a radio producer in Los Angeles, the biggest radio market in the United States, recalls an accountant who called to pitch her. He obviously had never listened to the radio show or bothered to think of a hook. If this guy had any media savvy, he would have suggested that he could be on the show near April 15 to tell listeners how they could save on their taxes.

Radio and television interviews can be unnerving, but they are great free publicity. People who tune in to talk radio actively listen to the subjects being discussed. These listeners are good consumers, and talk radio is skewed to an audience older than thirty years. Radio is probably the most publicity-friendly medium. The host will usually let you mention your company name and contact information or, better yet, they can mention it for you.

Television appearances are considered the pinnacle of publicity, but in fact television has its drawbacks. If you appear on a popular morning show like *Today* or *Good Morning America,* good for you, though the producers may look askance at your mentioning the name and contact information of your company. They're looking for good consumer information and entertainment, not advertising. Also, the viewers who watch morning television are usually rushing to get started with their day and paying only selective attention. With radio or print advertising, the readers and listeners are more focused on you and your message.

When seeking out free publicity, start with your local newspapers. They are easier to break into than national newspapers like *USA Today,* or large metropolitan papers like the *New York Times.* For radio interviews, you can cut your teeth in small markets like the Midwest and then graduate to the large and crowded markets like Chicago, Los Angeles, and New York.

After you get publicity, promote it like crazy. Mention it when you pitch other media outlets. Include magazine and newspaper articles about your business with catalogs to prospective customers.

Debbie Hobar—founder of Precious Places, a shop-at-home children's room decorating service in Fairfax Station, Virginia—succeeded in getting a mention in *Glamour, Entrepreneur,* and *Home Office Computing.* "As soon as you're on one national publication, it snowballs," says Debbie. "As soon as you hit a national publication, your business takes a whole new approach."

Be ready to pounce on opportunities for publicity. If you can link your business to breaking news, call the media—quick! Joel Roberts is a former Los Angeles radio talk show host and media consultant par excellence. I attended a seminar of his in which he talked about working with Steven Covey, author of the *Seven Habits of Highly Effective People* and a college professor. Steven was uncomfortable with the media culture of hype and sound bites. Joel said, "A book is about light for all time, but the media is about the heat of the moment." I've never forgotten that. Your media message needs to contain heat and immediacy. If your energy and life force scream out at producers and editors—and the consumers they

171

serve—the sheer force of your power will be magnetic, and wonderful things will happen for you.

News Releases and Media Kits

A news release is a straightforward document you send to editors of print and online media to call their attention to a newsworthy aspect of your business. It should be two or three pages double-spaced, with your contact information in the upper right-hand corner. Your goal is not to write the story for them but to encourage them to write the story about you.

Another tool for gaining publicity is the media kit. Editors and producers get lots of media kits every day, so package yours in a provocative way and make it compelling. Your media kit could contain:

- A cover letter.
- A fact sheet about your business.
- News releases.
- Photocopies of articles that have been written about you.
- Photographs: black and white and glossy head shots.
- Brochures and other related materials.
- Biographical information.
- Product samples.
- Books you've written.
- Suggested interview questions.
- Audio tapes of radio interviews.
- Video tapes of television appearances.
- Wild promotional giveaways.

Be creative in sending and packaging your media kit. Most media seekers send their press kit in a folder. I send mine in a shopping bag with lots of goodies. Some publicity seekers put their media kit on their website and suggest that editors and producers log on. This cuts down on cost, phone tag and lag time, and may accelerate decisions.

Creative Events

Events are a great way of attracting media. This could be anything from a grand opening of your store to participating in a public charity fundraiser. Some companies do monthly events tied to holidays—Valentine's Day, St. Patrick's Day, Easter, Back to School days, Thanksgiving, and Christmas are great for promotions. Debbie Allen, author of *Confessions of Shameless Self-Promoters,* gave me an absolute gem. You can create special events such as conferences, award shows, luncheons, or parties and register them with Chase's Calendar of Events (www.chases.com). You can even register your own holiday.

The catchier your event is, the more likely it is to attract attention. At an animal rights' group event, for example, a young lady had her nude body painted like a tiger, complete with stripes and whiskers, and put herself inside a cage. The group was protesting the use of these magnificent big cats in the circus. Outrageous? Controversial? Gutsy? Sure it was, but the media was there in droves.

ADVERTISING

The main difference between advertising and publicity is that advertising is costly—often very costly—and publicity is free or low cost. In addition, free publicity is more believable; paid advertising doesn't always make it past people's

PUBLICITY VERSUS TRADE SECRETS

You may feel a conflict of interest between getting publicity and protecting your ideas. You want as many people as possible to know about your business, but you don't want them to steal your ideas or trade secrets. My partner Sheryl Felice and I were approached early in our entrepreneurial careers to be the subject of articles in newspapers and magazines. The story of our business, The Bag Ladies, was very newsworthy. Unfortunately, we were victims of fear mentality and worried that if we broadcast our business story other people would rip off our ideas. We also rationalized that ours was a business-to-business service and that the readers of the articles would not be our target market. Big mistake! By turning down free publicity, we left a lot of opportunities and money on the table.

"propaganda radar." With advertising, you control the content, target your audience, and you are the sole focus of the ad. The life span of an ad will depend on where it's placed; a yellow-pages ad lasts a year, while a TV spot is gone in fifteen or thirty seconds. Most advertising must be repeated to be effective. A onetime newspaper or radio ad is like throwing your money away.

> *Success is not to be pursued. It is to be attracted by the person you become.*
> —Jim Rohn,
> international speaker
> on success

The impact of your ad will depend, to a great extent, on its design. The best ads are brief and focused on special products or services. If you have design experience, you're in like Flint. If not, consider hiring a professional to help you; I discuss graphic designers and artists in the "Look Good in Print" section of chapter 7.

Print Advertising

With all print advertising—yellow pages, newspapers, magazines—contact the salespeople and inquire about the demographics. To compare apples with apples, figure out your "audience delivery" in cost per thousand, or CPM (yes, it seems like it should be CPT, but the "M" stands for the Roman numeral for one thousand). Always contact the publication you are thinking about and ask for a media kit. Remember that ad rates are negotiable, especially if you do repeat advertising.

MEDIA KIT WITH WIT

Debbie Karpowicz wrote a humorous dating book, *I Love Men in Tasseled Loafers*. She also created a special drink, the "Tasseled Loafer," which was served at her book-signing parties at hotels. Debbie sent her book, the recipe for the drink, and a shoehorn to the media in shoe boxes. Her news release was rolled up and tied with actual tasseled leather laces. She also concocted chocolate loafer lollipops and included them in her media kit.

In response, she received scores of calls from curious local and national media. Editors proclaimed that her presentation was one of the wittiest they had ever seen.

Consider the shelf life of the publication. If you buy enough print advertising, ask the publication to do an article on your business. Articles plus display ads are a powerful mix of exposure and believability. Here are the print options:

- **Yellow pages.** The yellow pages ad is usually the first type of display advertising a business purchases. The positive side is that it is highly directed to your target market. The negative side is that you are next to all your competitors. A display ad has more impact than an in-column listing. The yellow pages sales representative may even help you design the ad.

- **Business directories.** There are many excellent trade directories that your target customer may keep around for an entire year. Prospects consult directories whenever they need your product or service. Although you will be sharing the page with your competitors, these directories are powerful marketing tools.

- **Classified ads.** These ads are good for testing the demand for a new product. Many entrepreneurs advertise for a product, even before they have produced it or purchased it. If enough people show interest, they know they can make the investment in the new goods. Classified ads are also good for testing ad copy. You can put a few different ads in the same section of the paper with different verbiage and see which one pulls in the most responses.

- **Newspapers.** This form of print advertising is easy to get in quickly. However, newspapers usually have a shelf life of only twenty-four hours. With newspaper ads, you need to budget for repeat exposure. This helps build recognition and credibility.

- **Magazines.** The advantage of magazines is that they are aimed at special interests and easy to target. In addition, readers spend more time browsing magazines than newspapers. Magazines have a shelf life of one to six months, which helps justify the expense.

Broadcast Advertising

Most small business owners believe that radio and television advertising is way beyond their means and not really targeted to their customers, but you may find it's well worth the investment. Establish your target market and set a rough budget. Contact the salespeople and find out the CPM, but also get references and talk to

- **The PS.** Many people read the headline of a letter, then glance at the photograph, and then read the PS before committing to the body of the letter. This is your chance to summarize your message, create a sense of urgency, and draw your reader in.

Brochures, Flyers, and Catalogs

These printed marketing pieces are more polished and immediate than sales letters. The format is more visual and less text intensive, but the rules of good copy are the same. If you're mailing the brochure or flyer, you should also enclose a cover letter that has all the elements of the sales letter.

The winning formula for brochures and flyers is to state the problem, then tell the reader why your company is the solution. Make the solution simple and straightforward. Your company name and contact information should be prominent. But nobody cares about a company name until they're already interested in the product or service. And nobody is interested in a product or service until they have a sense that it can solve their problem and ease their pain.

As with print advertisements, you might want to hire a professional to help you polish the design, but you'll certainly want to offer some input, since you know your business better than anyone else. Here's how to get started:

- **Concept phase.** Start a design file. When you see a great advertising piece, cut it out and put it in a file. Print out good visuals from the Internet for inspiration. Bring in your success team for a brainstorming session.
- **Layout.** Sketch out layouts for your piece. The overall layout is what people will see first. People read from the top left of the page to the bottom right, so either of these quadrants would be good for your logo and ordering information. I like to lay out my designs on computer, but you can also do freehand drawings. Many publishing programs have style sheets that you can use. You choose the layout and then fill in your headlines, body copy, and graphics. These templates are good but should be used only as a starting-off point only. You don't want your layout to look like everyone else's.
- **Headline.** Headlines are extremely important with brochures and flyers. Make sure they communicate your most important message. Limit the

headline to three lines or fewer of text. Unless your headline is only a few words, caps and lowercase is easier to read than all capital letters.

- **Copy.** Usually less is more. The shorter the paragraph, the more likely it will be read. Limited bullets, good use of color, lots of white space—all these elements enhance your message by making the copy easy to read. A few strong, brief points are far more effective than dozens of weak ones or strong ones hampered by excess verbiage. Flush left and ragged right is the best paragraph style. This gives an informal look and doesn't create awkward spaces between the words.

- **Typefaces.** Serif fonts (such as Times New Roman) have little tails finishing off the main strokes of the letters. Sans serif fonts (such as Arial) do not. Sans serif type is best for headlines and subheads, and serif font is best for your

Barbie Pink

If you want to understand the importance of color in marketing, just look at the Barbie doll. Barbie was born in a small garage in Hawthorne, California, in 1959. (She really looks good for being over forty years old, doesn't she?)

Ruth Handler, Mattel's cofounder and Barbie's creator, saw her young daughter Barbara and her friends playing with teenage and adult cutout dolls rather than baby dolls. With the adult dolls, the girls could project their grown-up fantasies and try on roles for adulthood. Ruth created the curvy plastic statuette and named it Barbie after her daughter. "I believed it was important to a little girl's self-esteem," she has said, "to play with a doll that has breasts."

Pink is the most feminine and romantic color, and it was a natural for Barbie's marketing. Pink was part of her packaging, clothes, even her dream houses from the beginning. I've done bags for Mattel and mostly everything is in their signature Barbie pink.

Barbie has become a powerhouse that has changed the entire toy industry and generated millions of dollars worldwide. More than one billion Barbies have been sold, and the doll is the flagship of Mattel.

body copy. Decorative fonts are sometimes effective, but you don't want to use too many typefaces in a given marketing piece—it's not a ransom note!

- **Psychology of color.** Colors are everywhere. They affect our brains, our attitudes, even our nervous systems. The brighter the color, the stronger the emotional response. Green, brown, and red are the most popular food colors. Blue is an appetite suppressant, and it's also associated with business and success. IBM has been known as "Big Blue." Yellow is a thought color; that's why most Post-it notes are yellow. Black gives a feeling of authority and elegance. If your budget only allows you to print your advertising pieces in one color, black on white is usually your best bet. Color can be a great tool for bringing your marketing efforts to life.

If you sell by mail order, a catalog will be crucial to your business. This doesn't mean it has to be fancy. You could start with something as simple as a black-and-white four-page foldover and graduate to more sophisticated catalogs as your business grows. Look at catalogs you like to get an idea of how you want yours to look. As with brochures and print ads, you can come up with a lot of your own great ideas before you turn to a professional designer or printer.

If you produce expensive four-color catalogs, send them only to customers who you know want them. You can include a response card, your website address, or a fax-back sheet in a less expensive mailing and send catalogs when they're requested.

INTERNET MARKETING

Internet marketing is here to stay. Email allows you to communicate with people all over the world, sending not only written messages but complex "attached" graphics. A website allows your customers to learn about your products and services twenty-four hours a day. Even if you don't use the Internet directly for marketing purposes, it's an indispensable research tool for many aspects of your business.

The Internet is a multifaceted, fast-changing world, and I'll barely scratch the surface in the paragraphs that follow. In the end, the same rules apply to Internet marketing and low-tech marketing strategies. The Internet is just another outreach and communications tool for solving your customers' problems and alleviating their pain. Start with small steps to integrate the Internet into your marketing plans.

Internet Service Providers

I discussed the basics of computer choice in the "Systems and Equipment" section of chapter 6. The next step is to choose an Internet Service Provider (ISP). Different ISPs offer different services, but the basic idea behind all of them is to offer data transfer to and from the Internet and to allow you to access information and send and receive communications. Services are provided for a monthly fee, a rate based on use, or both.

Research a range of ISPs before you make your choice. Ask friends and business associates what service they use. An important function of an ISP is the storage and handling of your website, so your choice of an ISP will depend, among other considerations, on whether you have a website and how large it is. You'll also want to know if the ISP provides services such as email forwarding and "autoresponders" that automatically respond when people email you.

I highly recommend choosing an ISP that allows you to talk to a live human being. I'll gladly pay more for a provider with good customer support.

Your Website

A website allows you to present far more information to your potential clients and customers than any brochure or advertisement. With a website, you can describe your services, show your wares in glorious detail, and even sell online. As I mentioned in the "Make It Real" section of chapter 5, registering your domain name should one of the first steps you take in starting your business. Once you're ready to get your website up and running, you won't be disappointed to learn the name has been grabbed by someone else.

The best way to decide on the basic design and content of your website is to look at other websites. Notice their layouts. How many pages are included in the website, and how are the various pages linked? Is the site easy to navigate? Is it pleasing to the eye? If you sell a product, look at sites that sell products. If you offer a service, study the websites of similar businesses.

Numerous programs are now available for designing and maintaining your own website, with new ones appearing all the time. Large online services such as America Online also offer tools for website design and maintenance. If your website is at all complex, however, you'll probably want to bring in a professional. A good strategy is to hire a designer to give the website a professional look but insist on a program you can learn yourself so that you can update the site without professional assistance.

The look of your website should reflect your basic brand strategy and benefit statement. The design should be pleasing, but fancy bells and whistles are usually not necessary. The website is a branding device and marketing tool. The same basic rules of business communication are true here: It's not about you—it's about the benefits you can offer your customer.

Once your website is designed, executed, and on the Internet through your ISP, people all around the world will be able to access it. How exciting! Unfortunately, they can also access more than a billion other sites, so you'll need to put some effort into drawing "traffic."

Here are some keys:

- **Search engines.** The first step is to submit your site to search engines, navigational tools that allow Internet users to type in a word or phrase and get a list of websites containing that word or phrase. It is estimated that search engines bring 84 percent of traffic to most websites. The submission process can be a challenging and time-consuming task, so you might want to ask a pro to help you out.

- **Internet advertising.** There are a couple of ways you can alert Internet users to your Web presence. AOL, Yahoo!, and other large portals sell classified ads for under $20. The way to win with these ads is to have a killer headline and something that makes your ad stand out from the crowd. A more expensive proposition is to put a banner ad on a related site. The effectiveness of a banner ad will depend on how good the fit is between your company and the host site.

- **Links to related sites.** A win-win strategy is to trade links with other website owners. Find a complementary website and call the owner personally. Don't email them or you may be a victim of "delete, delete, delete." If someone emails you to do a link exchange, call them personally to see if it's a good fit. Ask them to write their own description of their site as they would like it explained to your web visitors. You could also do a web search for "linking services" to help you find a good match.

- **Low-tech tools.** Don't forget to use your low-tech marketing strategies to alert your potential clients and customers to your website. Be sure your website and email addresses are on all your correspondence and marketing pieces. Take out a classified ad. Send postcards mentioning that your site has just been launched or has some great new features.

Email Marketing

Even if you don't have a website, you can still make use of the Internet for marketing. You can send email sales letters much like those you send through the postal service. You can use email to distribute your newsletter, or inform people about special offerings. To get the most benefit from your email marketing pieces, encourage people to forward them to their friends.

The first element in a successful email marketing campaign is to collect the email address of every person you talk to. Train your staff to ask for email addresses along with the contact information of everyone who expresses an interest in your business. If you meet someone and she hands you her business card, write down her email address if it isn't listed.

Don't abuse your email privileges. Never even consider sending spam. Assure people that you will not slime them with too many messages. If you have a policy of never selling their names, let people know. Always provide a way for people to remove themselves from your email list. You can even preface the emails by telling people that they are receiving the email because they are a subscriber who requested the information.

Here are some considerations for drafting your email messages:

- **ALL CAPS.** When sending email, don't use all capital letters. It looks like you're shouting at the reader.
- **Emoticons.** "Emoticons" such as :-) give the message a friendly feeling. You can easily create them on your own keyboard. For more professional correspondence, you may want to leave them off.
- **Length.** The average line length is fifty-five to sixty-five characters. Longer lines of type create breaks in awkward places within the sentence.
- **White space.** Leave white space between the lines, so the message will be easy to read. Separating important thoughts and sections by using the

underline key will also heighten the visual appeal of your message.

- **"From" box.** Put your full name or the name or your business in the "from" box, rather than your email address. Most people would rather open up email from "Mary Jones" than "Mjones@earthlink.net."

Whenever you send email, put a "signature" on the bottom of the correspondence. The email signature is a minicommercial and can include elements such as your tag line or a reason to go to your website. Depending on your ISP, the email signature can also include a direct link to your website. Remember to write the words "click here"—when people get a directive, they're more likely to click through. Use the underline key to make a line before and after the signature to separate it from the body of the email.

Here's the signature I use on my emails:

Wealthy Bag Lady – Tel 888-286-0602
To Get Free Reports on Small Business Success for Women,
Click Here:
www.WealthyBagLady.com

A final tip: Once you register your domain name, use it in your email address. Instead of Joan@aol.com, use Joan@MyCompany.com. The last time I checked, America Online was not paying you to promote their company, and there are plenty of benefits to promoting your own business. You don't even need a website to do this. Most hosting companies and ISPs provide this service. All you need to do is register the domain name. You can even set up a forwarding system so that you don't need to get rid of your old email address.

Technology versus Humanity

I went from thinking that computers were for nerds with glasses and pocket protectors to embracing high-tech and becoming a female nerd (minus the glasses and pocket protector). I love technology, but I don't let it replace good old-fashioned human conversation. When someone emails me with a question, instead of emailing them a reply, I call them personally. If someone goes to my site and requests information, I call them and ask them what they are looking for and how they heard of my company. Websites and email communication are great, but people still buy, sell, and form relationships with other people.

TRADE SHOWS

Trade shows exist for essentially every industry and are a tremendous marketing resource. Some trade shows are ordering shows and others are informational. At informational shows, the exhibitors hand out literature, introduce new products, and give out product samples. At ordering shows, you can write orders on the spot; if you're exhibiting, this helps recoup your costs.

Whether you're attending or exhibiting, make sure the show is a good match for your product mix or services. The trade show organizer can give you information about the number of attendees from the previous year, who the exhibitors are, who the attendees are, and what they are looking for. Talk to other people who have attended and exhibited at the show.

Attending Trade Shows

Going to trade shows as an attendee is one of the best ways to learn about your industry, monitor trends, negotiate the best pricing, and form relationships. Attending is a piece of cake next to exhibiting. Have a plan of attack for the show. Set goals. Get the trade show information in advance and make notes on which exhibitors to talk to. Check out the networking events—seminars, dinners, and mixers are great for learning about industry trends and forming alliances and contacts. Bring a note pad, notebook computer, or portable tape recorder for notes. Take down the information on the people and companies you want to follow up with at the show. If you want to see a key influencer who isn't at the booth, get the contact information of the booth worker and use his or her name when asking for the key influencer in the company.

Don't forget to have fun. Being an entrepreneur is your passport to travel, meeting fascinating people, and experiencing life to its fullest. Plan a few fun tourist days at the show location. Traveling is an adventure. You should take the opportunity to experience the sounds and sights of every destination you visit for business. Go ahead and create some fabulous memories.

Exhibiting at Trade Shows

A great way to attract new customers, cement relationships with current customers, and monitor trends in your industry is to exhibit at a trade show. Most trade show exhibitors, however, need a course in Selling 101. If you have a great sales presentation, you will rise above the mediocrity. Exhibiting at a trade show can be expensive, so here are some helpful tips for getting the most out of your trade-show investment:

- **Stay in the hotel where you are exhibiting.** A great deal of trade show sales are made outside of the trade show floor. Being at the sponsor hotel puts you in the middle of a powerful arena, with admittance to all the action.

- **Make your booth friendly.** When designing the layout of your booth, try not to place tables at the front. These tables act as physical barriers, and people become reticent about actually walking into your booth. Make eye contact and greet people in the aisles, so that they feel comfortable about approaching you.

- **Have plenty of brochures and order forms.** I've attended trade shows where exhibitors ran out of literature on the first day. Bring more literature than you think you'll need so that you don't run out at the show. You can even ship your business cards, literature, order forms, samples, and company information to the show location so that you don't have to carry it in your luggage.

- **Prepare your presentation.** Better yet, prepare two different trade show specials. Instead of asking, "Can I help you?" ask, "Have you ordered from our company before?" When prospects say no, show them the line and offer them your trade show special for new customers. If they've ordered from you before, show them your new products and services and give them your trade show special for preferred VIP customers.

- **Have at least two people working the booth.** Unless the attendance of your show is low, it's very hard to work a booth with only one person. If you're a solo operator, you can bring a friend or family member. Some trade shows offer an option of hiring an additional salesperson to work your booth, or you can place a classified ad in a local newspaper before the trade show.

- **Give free gifts and promotional items.** Hand out branded gifts and advertising specialties with your business name on them. Customers who receive free company gifts are more likely to order, place orders more often, feel better about your company, and refer other customers.
- **Create a great trade show bag.** Go for the "billboard effect": Order a larger bag than you think you'll need and make the graphics as dynamic as possible. The way to win here is to have the other exhibitors' bags placed inside yours. Make the design of the bags universal and not show-specific, so that you can use any extra bags at another show or for your product literature, samples, and products.

The most important aspect of your trade show experience takes place when you get home. Many businesses exhibit at trade shows, collect names of interested people, and then don't follow up on those leads. If you do a trade show, make a full commitment. After the show, send out an email thanking the attendees for visiting your booth and put in some kind of special offer to them. Mail information to people who requested it. If you think follow-up mailings and offers are too expensive, you shouldn't be exhibiting at the show.

The best follow-up is by telephone. A few years ago, I went to a trade show where one of the exhibitors was a very enterprising young lady named Randi. She used the show as the ultimate lead generator. Her company personally called everyone who had visited their booth and asked if they could make a presentation in person. I accepted the offer, and when Randi showed me her line of corporate gifts, I saw many wonderful things that I didn't have time to notice during the hectic atmosphere of the trade show. Because Randi was a master at follow up, I placed many orders with her company.

MEASURE YOUR RESULTS

An important key to successful marketing is to keep track of what works and what doesn't. When people call to inquire about your products or place an order, always ask how they heard about your company. Find out where each and every lead comes from. Put a special code on each mailing and ad that you do. When people call to get information or to order, ask them to read the source code so that you can track which marketing pieces and ads are pulling better than others.

Other ways of source coding are special email addresses for different ads, special phone numbers or extensions, and special mailbox addresses or department codes. For example, if you have an ad running in *Health* magazine, encourage people to write to your address, Dept. H. Another way to track your ad responses is a special suffix pointer on your website. In the *Health* magazine example, readers could respond to the website address www.MyCompany.com/healthmagazine.

Most people with websites have no information about who has visited their site. Big mistake! Your website is a robust way to pump up your database. Always have email capture on your website. Don't just provide a guest book. Offer free stuff—such as a free report filled with valuable information—to get visitors to fill out forms and give their contact information.

Now that you've done all this marvelous marketing, you're ready to move on to sales.

CHAPTER 15

The Hook of Sales

My six favorite words in the world of business are, "I'd like to place an order." The phrase is all the sweeter if I've never given a sales presentation to the person who speaks those words. It means all my hard work at marketing has paid off—the customer has seen my marketing materials, or learned by word of mouth how great the company is, or heard me interviewed on a talk show. Marketing is everything that happens before the sale is made, and if it's done effectively, the sale is as easy as taking the order.

The art of sales is simpler with some businesses than others. You'll rarely need to give a sales presentation if you own a restaurant, unless you're waiting tables. If your marketing is effective, and your food and service first rate, the orders will take care of themselves. With most businesses, however, you'll have to go out and sell.

According to Barbara J. Winter, author of *Making a Living without a Job,* "Almost nobody starts a business because he or she loves sales and marketing. Only after the original idea for a business has been hatched do self-bossers realize that they rely on sales and marketing to make the idea work. At this point, the fear of selling often takes over and becomes a deterrent to many would-be owners."

Remind yourself that selling is nurturing. Think of yourself as a trusted adviser rather than a salesperson. Spend more time listening than talking. Offer solutions and make your client's life easier, not more difficult. Recommend other products and services to your clients that can help them, and never sell products they don't need. Refer them to other people and businesses that can also assist them. Call them periodically to see how they are doing.

Learning sales skills is not just a good thing, it's a necessary thing. It'll make you or break you. Sales is the life blood of your business. Get pumping. Nothing happens until a sale is made.

SET THE STAGE

You've already started setting the stage for sales by creating a great product or service, learning how to price for profit, and telling the world about your business through marketing. You've got a few more steps to go before you actually make your pitch to a prospective customer.

Research and Qualify Your Prospect

Sometimes prospects will come to you, requesting information about your product or service. Other times you are the one who will seek out the prospective customer.

> *I am the world's worst salesman, therefore, I must make it easy for people to buy.*
> —F. W. Woolworth, founder of Woolworth's discount department store chain

There's no point in trying to make a sale to a prospect who isn't a good match for your company. Do some research to learn as much as you can. Read articles about your industry and your prospect's business. Go to the library and look through business directories to discover companies that might be interested in your products. Research will take some time in the beginning, but it will save you countless hours of wasted time and disappointment. Research preserves your positive attitude, and after a while you can do it within minutes.

Part of qualifying the prospect is to make sure the person you deal with has decision-making power. It's important to deal with a "make-it-happen person"—someone who is empowered to give you a decision or affect a change for you. Try not to deal with someone who always has to consult his or her boss and then call you back.

Before you go into a presentation, ask what the client's budget is, or ask what he or she can spend on each widget you have to sell. If she says she doesn't know what the budget is, name prices and see if you can come to some kind of agreement. If you have an interior design firm, your services start at $5,000, and your prospect tells you she only has $500 to spent, it probably isn't a good match.

Research your competition as well as your prospect. Most salespeople are so concerned about product knowledge and looking good in front of a prospect that they forget about their competition. Know how your company is superior to the competition, but never trash your competitors. Give them honest credit for what they do well.

Watch for Opportunities

One of my greatest opportunities came from boredom on a cross-country plane flight. I needed something to stimulate my mind and keep me from falling asleep, so I listened to an audio interview of different business leaders and heard an intriguing woman. Her name was Sheila Cluff and she owned two very successful fitness retreats in California, The Oaks at Ojai and The Palms at Palm Springs. The interview was stimulating and I loved her energy and entrepreneurial spirit. When I got back to my office, I valiantly called Sheila Cluff to tell her what The Bag

A Niche to Fill

While working twelve- to fourteen-hour days for a staffing company, Victoria Lowe learned about the industry. Her husband told Victoria that she was so good in her job that she should start her own company. She started Alert Staffing in her living room.

One of her previous coworkers, Carin Maher, believed in Victoria's passion, commitment, and talent, and volunteered to work for no pay to help build the fledgling business. It was hard for Victoria to obtain financing, so she raised her early capital from family and friends, got a small loan and some advice from the Small Business Administration, and maxed out her credit cards.

In time, Victoria saw a niche that she could fill. Companies wanted staffing solutions that could offer diversity in the workplace. It was time for a national minority woman–owned company. Victoria saw a place that she could live in.

Victoria grew Alert Staffing by partnering with small and midsized companies and ultimately targeting the Fortune 500. Now she sits atop a staffing empire. Carin Maher, her first unpaid employee, is now vice president of operations support. Alert Staffing has sales of more than $200 million a year, with an annual growth rate of 30 percent. By recognizing the opportunity that fit her vision and strengths, Victoria Lowe is well on her way to building a $1 billion company.

Ladies had to offer. It must have been a sunny day in Ojai, because I got a warm reception and an appointment to see her.

When I met with Sheila, she was between her yoga workout and water aerobics class and wearing a leotard. This woman was radiant and her energy was boundless. I showed her the promotional bags and she placed a great order for both of her fitness retreats. She has been my customer for more than ten years—all because I heard her interview at thirty-five thousand feet and acted on my gut impulse to call and get the order.

Make Ordering Easy

According to George Silverman, author of *The Secrets of Word-of-Mouth Marketing*, "The best product doesn't always win. The product that is the easiest to decide on wins." If ordering from your company is too difficult, the prospect will buy from your competition.

Here are some suggestions to make ordering easy:

- **Don't offer too many choices.** Having too many things to choose from confuses people, and the confused mind says no. Even if you have an extensive line of products or services, choose one or two that will suit the potential customer's needs and sell them on those choices.

- **Be a "no problem" company.** You are there to remove your clients' hassles, not create them. Give clear answers to their questions. Don't tell them about all the problems in your company or about the trouble it takes to accommodate their requests. People like dealing with low-maintenance companies who alleviate their worries. If your answer to most customer requests is "no problem," they will be eating out of your hand and remain fiercely loyal.

- **Take credit cards.** Customers like the convenience of credit cards, and they can make your life easier as well. Plastic leaves a paper trail, which makes returns easier if there is a dispute.

- **Offer strong guarantees.** Guarantees take the risk out of ordering. The traditional thirty-day guarantee is too short for most people. People are busy and they fear that they won't even be able to try the product within thirty days. Smart businesses are offering six-month, one-year, and even lifetime guarantees. With longer guarantees, you'll get more orders and fewer returns. You are also standing behind your superior product or service.

PRESENT WITH CONFIDENCE

Before you make a sales presentation, you need to feel confident and be prepared. Practice, practice, practice. Practice in front of your mirror. Practice in front of your loved ones. It gets easier with time. Make your presentation quick, clear, and concise. Respect the prospect's time. Be good natured about the interruptions that are likely to occur, such as phone calls, the prospect's customers needing help, or coworkers needing information.

Most business owners are focused on their products and services when the focus should be on the needs of the client. People love to buy, but they hate to be sold. They do like to be guided and told about features and benefits, and they want a knowledgeable sales nurturer to answer questions for them. Don't push your customers. They will only push back.

Identify Your Prospect's Pain

People don't buy your products or services. People buy solutions. Potential customers are calling you because they have a problem that you can solve. Ask targeted questions that will allow your prospects to identify their own pain and problems. Once you uncover the prospect's pain, and you know money is available, you can tell the prospect about how your solutions will solve their problems and ease their pain.

A good way to help prospects identify their needs and recognize your solutions is to take a piece of paper and draw a line down the middle, creating two columns. Draw a plus sign at the top of one column and a minus sign on the other. With your prospect, make lists of the positives and negatives of purchasing your product. A negative is that it costs your client money. A positive could be that the money is an investment that will bring exponential rewards. Don't be hesitant to emphasize the negatives. Everyone expects negatives, and it gives you more credibility to acknowledge this. But make sure the negatives are closely followed by ways to deal with them.

Listen More Than You Talk

You have two ears and only one mouth for a reason. Many salespeople think they can impress prospects by spilling everything they know about their product or service. By asking questions, you get the prospect to do most of the talking. By listening, you shift the focus from you to the prospect, where it belongs. Being a good listener flatters the prospect and shows your interest. Learn to ask questions and then shut up. Questions enable you to obtain information that otherwise wouldn't be forthcoming.

> *The smartest person in the room is the one who listens more than they talk.*
> —Andrea Michaels, CEO of Extraordinary Events

Only one person has the know-how and the wherewithal to solve the prospect's objections. And that's the prospect. Questions help the prospect resolve his or her own opposition. Some people need to speak out loud to make sense of a situation.

Prospects hide their true motives as a built-in defense mechanism to thwart salespeople. By probing and listening, you can uncover the "real" issues. Questions, when handled in a nurturing manner, help prospects reveal their true motives without any pressure from you.

Admit When You Don't Know the Answer

Occasionally a customer will ask you a question that you don't have an answer for. Admit that you don't know the answer, but let the customer know that you will research it for them and get back to them with information they need. If you try to fake the knowledge and the customer finds out, your credibility is shot. The customer can no longer trust what you say and the relationship is over.

Warm Up to Cold Calling

When I first started my business, the telephone terrified me. It sat there mocking me. I knew I had to make business calls to try to get people to buy my products, but I didn't want to do it. It felt pushy. I thought about all the times I got calls from those annoying telemarketers.

First I made calls to friends whom I knew would be glad to hear from me. Then I called my current customers. Surprise! They were glad to hear from me too and some of them placed orders. Then came the hard part: cold calling. Even the words *cold calling* sent chills down my spine, but I pushed past the fear, made some cold calls, and—though it took a little longer than with established customers—I got some orders. I received huge rewards for doing my "feared thing first." One of my best customers today is the result of my cold calling.

In a way, my fears about cold calling were justified. Some people were definitely rude. But I wasn't as devastated as I thought I would be. After an encounter with a rude person, I didn't stop. I made more calls until I got a friendly voice on the other end of the line. I told myself I wouldn't stop until I talked to someone pleasant.

Because of the annoying people who invade our homes with their irritating solicitation calls, telemarketing has gotten a bad rap lately, but it's a powerful way to make a strong connection with new and existing customers. The most important elements of selling over the phone are enthusiasm, trust, product knowledge, and good listening skills. Be a welcomed guest rather than an annoying pest. Call satisfied customers and ask them why they like your product, why they do business with you, and what the benefits are. This follow-up technique will pump up your enthusiasm. Plus, you can use their answers in the next steps.

- **Ask a satisfied customer or mentor to grease the way.** This applies when the past customer and the new prospect are friends or business associates. What better way to turn up the heat on a cold call than to politely ask a satisfied customer to make a call to the prospect before you do?

- **Be sensitive to your prospect's moods and schedule.** Nothing is more annoying than an insensitive clod who dives into a canned speech. Making calls during dinner or too early or late in the day kills any chance of building a relationship. Monday and Friday are usually not the best days for telemarketing; Tuesday, Wednesday, and Thursday are better. Respect your prospect's time. If it's not a good time to talk, don't just go into your pitch by rote. Reschedule another time to talk and they will appreciate your sensitivity.

- **Get into the no-fear zone.** Visualize your prospect handing you a big fat check. Surround yourself with family photos, framed testimonial letters, and motivational quotes like "Do it now!" to put you in the mood. Use the sensory anchoring technique described in chapter 2, "Attitude Is (Almost) Everything." Get into your no-fear zone by recalling a confident winning moment. Wear your power color and lucky scent. Have your lucky coffee mug in front of you. Motivate yourself by playing music that excites your spirit. Stand up and make a victorious gesture and say a power phrase such as "Yes!" Say your affirmations before you start.

- **Watch your tone of voice.** You don't want to sound sheepish and embarrassed, nor do you want to be arrogant. The ideal tone is warm, businesslike, curious, and straight to the point. If you're in a bad mood, don't even bother making outbound calls.
- **Take note of your brilliance.** When you find yourself becoming so comfortable with phone dialogue that you are improvising—and your spontaneous dialogues are eliciting excellent responses—stop in your tracks after you hang up and write down your brilliant scripts for future use.

PERFECT YOUR FOLLOW-UP

The best kind of sales are those when your marketing is so effective the customer simply calls and places the order. What a pleasure! The next best are those when you wind up your sales presentation with a closing that leads to an order (I'll move on to closings in a moment). If neither type of order falls into place, follow-up is paramount.

In my twenty-plus years in business, I've only met a handful of people who were really good with follow up. At one time, I was looking for an accountant. I got referrals from other business associates, interviewed possible candidates on the phone, and drove across town and battled traffic to meet in person with five prospective accountants. How many of them do you think gave me a follow-up call? The answer is zero. These men and women were brilliant number crunchers, but they knew nothing about sales or growing their practices. They had a very qualified prospect (me) coming to them and willing to give them thousands of dollars. Because of ignorance and inactivity, they left a lot of money on the table.

Pass the Litmus Test

Many prospects use follow-up as a litmus test. They look at business relationships as a proving ground and the beginning of the relationship as a preview of coming attractions. They wait to see if you'll call them after the initial contact as proof of your performance. The honeymoon phase of the business relationship is like dating, when everyone is on their best behavior. Many prospects feel that if you aren't good at follow-up and communicating when you are courting them, then you will be inattentive after they have given you their money. In my experience of looking for an accountant, I did not choose any of the initial candidates that wouldn't even follow up with me after our initial meeting. I surmised that if they were neglectful and unresponsive at this prebusiness stage, they certainly would be sloppy about follow-up after I gave them my money.

> *Listen . . . everybody has a right to my opinion.*
> —Madonna, singer, songwriter, actor, and producer

Be impeccable with your word. If you can't close the prospect during a face-to-face meeting, follow up with a phone call and make a note to call again at another time. If you said you would send samples, a proposal, or more information, do so in a timely manner. If you can't fulfill a promise, don't just ignore the customer. Call them and let them know. Follow-ups are best done by telephone, but you can add direct mail, fax, and email to the mix. If you're faxing or emailing information, call before the transmission to let the recipient know the information is coming, then call after the communication to see if it was received and if they have any questions.

Reconsider the Maybes

Some sales gurus will stress the importance of not taking maybe for an answer. If the prospective client says yes, it's great. If he or she says no, you can at least move on to the next sale, but a maybe requires a lot of time that might be better spent pursuing other customers.

Use your feminine perception to determine which of the maybes are worth pursuing. Sometimes, because of company policy, a decision simply can't be reached at the time of your presentation. You certainly don't want to aggravate your prospect by pushing for the impossible. Wind up the presentation gracefully, then follow up with a thank-you note to the prospect for his or her time. Phone calls, emails, and faxes will remind your prospect that you are still interested in doing business.

CLOSE WITH APLOMB

After the presentation, it's time to go for the close. Many capable businesspeople are great at presentations and establishing rapport, but they fall short of asking for the commitment and making the sale.

Decode Your Prospect's Personality

There is no "one size fits all" in sales. People are different and they need to be sold in different ways. Creating rapport by talking about the prospect's family and the paintings in his or her office will inspire friendliness with some people but irritate others.

Sheryl Nicholson, entrepreneur, author, and certified speaking professional, talks in her seminars and workshops about the "People Puzzle," a great way to decode personalities and learn how to deal with different individuals. In the People Puzzle, there are four distinct personality types: drivers, influencers, steady supporters, and cautious conservatives (DISC). No personality type is better than another, just different.

- **Drivers.** Drivers are make-it-happen people. They are dominant, decisive, and direct. Their greatest fear is loss of control. Make your sales presentation quickly with a driver. Don't make small talk, and don't make physical contact. Back up your claims with hard facts.

- **Influencers.** Unlike drivers, influencers fear rejection. They love people and recognition. Your sales presentation with influencers will involve give and take. Ask for their opinions. Make friends with them, make eye contact with them, and touch them if appropriate.

- **Steady supporters.** Routine is comforting to steady supporters. They are team players but slow to change. Be patient when making a sales presentation to a steady supporter. Speak slowly and softly, with intermittent eye contact.

- **Cautious conservatives.** Cautious conservatives are intelligent, analytical, and possibly arrogant. They fear moving too quickly and tend to suffer from paralysis of overanalysis. For all you Star Trek fans, Mr. Spock is the classic cautious conservative. Be prepared when presenting to a cautious conservative. Stick to business and support their logical approach.

Closing Techniques

You've identified the personality of your prospect. You know you offer an excellent product or service. Your presentation has been clear, sensitive, and informative. It's time to close. Is your prospect hesitant? As with any nurturing relationship, there are times you may have to show a little firmness.

- **Assumption close.** If, at the end of your presentation, you ask, "Do you want to place the order?" you are giving the prospect an easy out. The assumption close is where you "assume" the sale and ask the prospect a strong closing question, such as, "What color would you like?" or "Would you like to pay with cash or a check?" This technique works well with the driver and the influencer.

- **Silent close.** People are uncomfortable with silences, and you can use them to establish a power base in selling. Rookie salespeople ramble on and on and don't know how to use silences effectively. Present your product, answer questions, and then tell your prospect the price. Now, here comes the hard part . . . Shut up! Resist the temptation to run off at the mouth. Your prospect will either agree to the sale or ask another question. Questions are great because they uncover the prospect's problems and pain and allow you to start the selling process all over again. A client of mine made a sale for a property worth millions of dollars to a client. When I asked her how she made the sale, she told me she used the silent close and it worked like a charm. The silent close is great for influencers because they are uncomfortable with silences.

- **Take-away close.** You've built up the benefits and features of your product or service. Then your prospect tells you your price is too high. Your next step is to say, "Do you mean that if I don't lower my price, we can't do business today?" By threatening to take away what the prospect wants, you maintain control. One of two things will happen. The customer will tell you that price is the main concern, which gives you the advantage because

199

you have uncovered his or her true objection. Or the customer will not want the product taken away and will start the selling process all over again, which gives you a great chance to close. The take-away close works well for the steady supporter and the cautious conservative.

- **Columbo close.** This technique is named after the fictional television character, Detective Columbo. This scattered, trench coat–wearing detective would interrogate a nervous, guilty murder suspect and then prepare to leave the room. Just as the suspect was beginning to relax, Columbo would turn around and say, "Can I ask just one more question before I leave?" Columbo's "one more question" was the most important question in his investigation, such as, "Where were you while the murder was taking place?" If you've tried other closing techniques, and the prospect still insists on thinking things over, prepare to leave the meeting, then turn around and say, "Can I ask you just one more question?" It doesn't really matter what the question is because it starts the sales process all over again. Unless the prospect is really pressed for time, the Columbo works with all personality types.

Collections

The salesperson should never be the person to call the customer and ask for payment on the invoice. Salespeople spend a lot of time and effort establishing rapport

BUYER'S REMORSE

As an entrepreneur, you know that the sale is not closed until the check clears the bank. You are elated to make a sale. But then you get back to your office, the customer calls and cancels the order, and you suffer the slings and arrows of someone else's buyer's remorse.

The way to minimize buyer's remorse is to get an agreement from your prospect up front during the initial sale. Relate to them how uncomfortable you were the last time a customer cancelled an order and make sure they understand everything about the price, product, benefits, and terms.

with their customers. If the salesperson causes the customer to be embarrassed and uncomfortable, it will hurt the trust relationship and may even cause the customer to go to a competitor. Asking for payment is essential to maintaining cash flow, but it can put the customer in a defensive and unpleasant position. Some customers may get insulted by collection calls. The reasons for late payments often are very personal, and revealing these details may be embarrassing for the customer.

Collections should be done by someone else in the company, not the person who interfaces with the customer. If you're a solo operator, hire someone else or ask a friend or family member to make the payment collection calls. It's always good to blame the accounting department. They can be the bad guys while the salesperson empathizes with the customer's problems.

LAND THE TROPHY CLIENT

The very concept seems daunting to many women, but your business will take a huge leap forward when you land your first trophy client. If you offer a quality product or service, don't be afraid to take it to big-name corporations. Once a Fortune 500 or blue-chip company does business with you, your credibility with smaller companies will grow exponentially.

Researching the trophy client is especially important. Study the organization to be sure it can genuinely benefit from your offer and is in a position to acquire what you're offering. The corporation may be in the midst of a merger, hostile takeover, lawsuit, or a rebranding campaign.

Go to the corporate website. Look up articles about the company on the Internet and at the library. Get hold of a copy of the corporate annual report. Read about key players in the *Biographical Directory of American Business Leaders* or *Who's Who in American Business.* Ask other business owners or the people on your success team about your trophy client. Maybe they can give you information or refer you to an information source. This is a great time to call into play your circle of influence. Getting a quality introduction from someone who knows a key influencer in your target company could make all the difference.

Don't make the mistake of using the bottom-up approach when trying to reach a major influencer. The rookie salesperson will call the company and talk to anyone who will listen to him. This is usually a low-ranking employee in the chain of command. If the salesperson is lucky enough to get in the door and make his presentation, and this low-level drone sees that he has something valuable to offer, the salesperson is rewarded with the opportunity to do it all over again to someone else.

Meanwhile, the competition comes along with a big difference. She has a connection, a referral, or some other "in." Her presentation is fine-tuned and convincing. She breezes her way in many levels above the rookie, makes the sale, and edges him out. The higher up someone is in an organization, the more people in that organization will listen to that person and care about what he thinks. If you can align yourself with someone influential and come in from the top down, you can actually borrow some of that person's power and authority to leverage open people's doors. This dramatically increases the possibility that people will pay attention to you.

> *Passion persuades and, by God, I was passionate about what I was selling.*
> —Anita Roddick, founder of The Body Shop

Once you get a coveted trophy client, leverage and parlay the experience to proliferate more corporate accounts. Landing a large corporate account lets you play at a higher level. It gets you into an elite club and gives you the keys to the corporate kingdom. There is pure power in gaining acceptance by a key influencer in the industry. Use it as your crowning glory.

One of our first trophy clients was Universal Studios. The Bag Ladies did an overprint of the Universal Studios bag. We then sent the extra Universal Studios bags off in a mailing to other film production houses and television and movie studios as samples of our work. The name recognition of the Universal Studios bag worked like a charm. We became known as specialists in the entertainment industry. Now our clients include most of the major film and television networks, film production houses, and major studios such as Columbia Tri Star, Disney, Fox, Sony, Warner Brothers, NBC, ABC, and CBS.

CHAPTER 16

Creating Lifetime Customers

*M*aking a major sale is a cause for celebration, but the business pros know that the first sale is not an end—it is only the beginning of the dance. Now you need to move on to establish an ongoing relationship. You'll make welcomed money on the first sale, but the real wealth in business comes from the cash flow created by your lifetime customers.

Most companies concentrate on the "front end"—the acquisition of new customers—but don't pay attention to keeping current customers satisfied and loyal to their business. According to JoAnna Brandi, known as the Customer Care Lady (www.CustomerRetention.com), "Companies who are not giving serious consideration to developing a strategy to keep their customers happy, satisfied, and loyal will not be thriving. In fact, they may barely be surviving." Why? Because getting new customers is far more expensive than keeping existing ones happy—up to ten times as expensive!

A long-held adage says that 20 percent of a business's customers account for up to 80 percent of the profits. With an increase of just 5 percent in the customer maintenance rate, a company can nearly double its profits.

> *Don't fall in love with your product or service. Fall in love with your client.*
>
> —Jay Abraham, marketing expert and author, *Getting Everything You Can Out of All You've Got*

Providing five-star customer service, doing consistent follow-up, handling dissatisfied customers gracefully, and designing loyalty programs are all great ways to create lifetime customers—the lifeblood of your business.

FIVE-STAR CUSTOMER SERVICE

Five-star customer service entails far more than filling orders and responding to inquiries and complaints. It's all about showing you care. People don't buy from companies. They buy from people. Your customers want a human relationship with you, not just a business relationship. They want to trust you, be respected by you, and feel good about doing business with you. Do everything you can to strengthen your relationship with your customers, for their sake and for yours.

Great companies view customer service as a profit center rather than a cost center, because serving customers' needs creates profit. Strive to consistently deliver a level of service that exceeds and even anticipates the customer's expectations and provides experiences that show you care. There is always something extra you can do that will give you the unfair advantage in business and set you ahead of the pack.

Responsiveness

The first key to five-star customer service is responsiveness. Your customers will put a lot of stock in the speed with which you respond to their concerns. If you respond quickly, customers will know you value their business. If you don't, you're suggesting you have more important things to deal with than their needs.

Allan Weiss, author of *Million Dollar Consulting* and an extremely busy consultant and speaker, returns phone calls whenever possible within ninety minutes. His clients have unlimited access to him, even on weekends. Yet he manages to live a balanced life with plenty of leisure time. How? He has learned to have efficient conversations. He goes from problem to solution quickly. These conversations are friendly, but they get straight to the point.

Respond promptly to all communications, whether they're phone calls, letters, or emails. This will engender trust and keep the lines of communication open with your customers.

Reliability

Customers want to know that when you say you'll deliver on Monday, it won't be Tuesday or Wednesday. They want to know they'll receive exactly what they order, not something "just as good."

With some businesses, reliability primarily entails keeping the quality of your product or service unwaveringly consistent. Many hotels and restaurants establish their customer base by a firm adherence to standardization. More often, your goal should be to underpromise and overdeliver. If you're working on deadlines, always overestimate lead times, then get the job done quickly so that you become a hero to your customer. Airlines have been doing this for years. They overestimate flight times so that they can say they have the most on-time flights or even get to the destination early to impress their passengers. Always give 110 percent to your customer service.

YOUR FORTUNE IS IN YOUR FOLLOW-UP

Your follow-up should begin as soon as a sale is completed. Pick up the phone, thank your new customer for his or her business, and make sure he or she is happy with your product or service. But don't stop there. The nurturing of relationships is the vanguard of women. In married couples, it's usually the woman who maintains the relationships with friends and family and schedules the get-togethers. Following up with your customer is the key to maintaining this crucial business relationship.

Show Your Appreciation

There are many ways to show your appreciation to your customers, and one of the best is with handwritten notes. This is where women can really excel in business relationships. In the technological age, the art of the handwritten thank-you note has become lost. Handwritten notes are personal and win hands down over form letters. Folks remember a caring person who took the time to write a personal note. The thank-you card may even be displayed in the customer's home or business.

Don't buy generic thank-you cards from the store. Make your own personalized cards branded with your company name. You can buy greeting card paper at the office supply store and print them on your color printer, or you can order them from an office supply catalog. Either way, be sure to handwrite a personalized message.

In chapter 7, "Packaging Your Image," I talked about the value of promotional gifts. There's no better recipient for gifts than your established customers. You don't have to spend a fortune to show you care. A simple gesture on your part will keep them placing orders and referring new customers.

Request Evaluations

After you've made a sale or provided a service, send a questionnaire to your customer to make sure he or she is pleased. Survey all your customers regularly and ask how you're doing. Let them know your goal is to provide ongoing service and meet their future needs. Installing a suggestion box in your store or office and setting up focus groups are other great ways to elicit evaluations from your customers. And be sure to remedy any problems these evaluations reveal.

Stay in Touch

A key ingredient of your customer follow-up is ongoing communication. Call from time to time, not necessarily to get the next order or referral but just to see how the customer is doing. Send email announcements of upcoming specials and solutions for your customer's business. Share information you think might be useful, recommend a good book, forward a relevant newspaper article. Women are masters at this.

A newsletter is a marvelous way to stay in touch with your regular customers. It could be a simple one-page sheet, a fancy newspaper-type document, or an email correspondence. The newsletter could contain updates of company operations, news about the customers themselves, and information about new products and services. This is also a great place for customer testimonials.

Send your regular customers birthday cards, anniversary cards, and holiday cards. These friendly greetings will ensure that your business remains in your customer's mind.

THE COST OF AN AUTO TIRE

An elderly lady came to the Nordstrom department store to return an automobile tire. She didn't have a sales receipt, but the clerk cheerfully inquired how much she had paid and gave her a full refund. Great customer-service policy, but here's the punch line: Nordstrom doesn't carry automobile tires!

The tire cost Nordstrom about $29. The story spread and was worth several million dollars in free publicity.

COURT THE DISSATISFIED CUSTOMER

It's a fact of business: Not every customer will be consistently thrilled with your product or service. In many cases, the biggest problem with dissatisfied customers is not that they make their unhappiness known, but that they stay quiet, at least to you. If their concerns are not addressed, they simply take their business elsewhere, and tell their friends about their woes. The classic statistic is that the average "wronged" customer will tell eight to sixteen people about a negative experience. That's a number derived before the electronic revolution—an Internet enthusiast, without much effort, could probably spread word of his dissatisfaction to thousands of your prospective customers. Not long ago, a website called IHateDunkinDoughnuts.com popped up on the Internet. It was created by an unhappy customer who asked for a refill of cream for his coffee at Dunkin Doughnuts and was treated disrespectfully by the clerks. You want your customers to find you when they search the Internet, but not like this!

Do everything you can to identify dissatisfied customers and solve whatever problems they might have. Keeping the lines of communication open is certainly the first step. If you have a good relationship with your customers, they'll feel comfortable about communicating their concerns.

> *The way I see it, if you want the rainbow, you gotta put up with the rain.*
> —Dolly Parton, singer and entertainer

Look at Complaints as Opportunities

The White House Office of Consumer Affairs says that for every customer who bothers to complain, twenty-six others remain silent. If a customer does complain, consider it an opportunity to improve your business. Customer complaints aren't fun, but they're a great way to learn about your weaknesses and remedy them.

If possible, give the person who handles customer complaints the power to handle the situation on the spot without consulting a supervisor. Be certain, however, that this person is qualified for the job. Never relegate customer complaints to a low-level employee.

Never argue with a customer. You'll never win the argument, and you'll very likely drive the customer away. If you have an irate customer on the phone, don't talk to her and try to resolve the situation when her anger and emotions are running high. Make an excuse to get off the phone and give her some cool-down time. This also gives you time to strategize how to handle her situation. Resume the conversation when you can both work reasonably toward a solution.

If you serve unhappy customers in extraordinary ways, they will come back to your business and tell others about you. In fact, the complaining customer may become one of your most loyal clients and a brand cheerleader for your business. By handling complaints promptly and resolving concerns, I have turned difficult customers into my biggest, most loyal fans.

Take Responsibility

We have become a society of victims. Nobody wants to take responsibility for his or her actions. When a customer complains, you can put yourself head and

$\mathscr{S}$KIN CARE FOR THE LONG RUN

Yona Lapin grew up in war-torn Israel, eventually advancing to the rank of sergeant in the Israeli army. Yona is both strong and feminine. Leaving Israel after the Six Day War in 1967, she came to the United States from Israel as a dancer, knowing nothing about business or the American economy and speaking very rudimentary English.

Many of her fellow dance performers piled on layers of thick stage makeup. The hot stage lights baked the makeup into their skin and clogged their pores. This wreaked havoc with their complexions and left them with damaged skin.

As a result of this experience, Yona became a pioneer in the skin care movement. In the 1970s, the focus was not on skin care but on makeup to cover up flaws in the complexion. Encouraging a routine to care for and replenish the skin was truly revolutionary. She started her own skin care line, Yona Skin Life Products, so that women could rehydrate and renew their skin. Makeup could now be an ongoing tool for enhancing a woman's natural beauty and radiance.

shoulders above the crowd by apologizing and taking responsibility for the situation. Listen patiently and try not to be defensive. Apologize, solve the problem, and take the time to say thank you. In business, you may need to apologize even if the faux pas wasn't technically your fault, so get ready to swallow your pride. If one of your employees or your vendors slip up, you're still responsible as the business owner. Don't make excuses. Assume responsibility, correct the situation, and make sure it doesn't happen again.

Give Refunds Cheerfully

This is your chance to stand out as a customer service superstar. If someone requests a refund, provide it without hassle and take the opportunity to get some important marketing information. Inquire why the customer is returning the product. Offer a substitute product if it's appropriate. Invite the customer to come back and order from your business anytime. You want a happy camper. An unhappy customer will tell far more people about a lousy experience with your company than a satisfied customer will tell about a good one. You can't afford to have unhappy people out there maligning your company.

LOYALTY AND REFERRAL PROGRAMS

It all started with the airlines. They came out with programs that encouraged passengers to be loyal and rack up those frequent-flyer miles to get free upgrades and flights. Business travelers thought they had gone to frequent-flyer heaven. By taking business trips to exotic destinations like Duluth—paid for by her company—the business traveler could pile up enough frequent-flyer miles to take her husband to Hawaii. This idea was so brilliant that before long, neighborhood businesses copied the concept. If you buy eleven submarine sandwiches at the local sandwich shop, the twelfth sandwich is free. All you have to do is get your frequent-buyer card punched. Pretty soon people's wallets were exploding with frequent-buyer cards, and they were loyal to the businesses with the special programs.

Customer loyalty programs work for small businesses as well as large. Develop a way for your heavy hitters who buy frequently to be rewarded. Depending on your business, providing free products or services as the bonus for frequent buyers could be more cost-effective than a cash discount. Create an inner circle of preferred customers. Provide these customers with benefits centered on word-of-mouth referrals. Membership in your "Tell a Friend" program could entitle customers to discounts on their orders, free gifts, or invitations to special events.

Send announcements to your current preferred customers about special offers and sales. Retailers can have special presale days for preferred customers. Business-to-business firms can send emails and direct mail solicitations for limited-time offers. On outgoing emails, encourage the recipient to forward the email to a friend. When asking for referrals, ask if you can use the contact person's name as an introduction. Offer a commission or member benefit if a contact results in a sale. You can also place postcards in your mailings that encourage word-of-mouth referrals with a special member benefit.

For the right kind of business, an autoship program is another great idea for creating customer loyalty and bringing in cash flow. If your company sells items that people use on a regular basis—such as beauty products or vitamin supplements—offer a program in which the product is shipped regularly and billed to a credit card, at a discount to "one-time sale" prices. Make it clear to your customers that they can cancel their autoship orders at any time.

The more committed you are to keeping your customers loyal, the faster your company will grow.

The Octopus Is Mightier Than the Elephant

The elephant uses her trunk to get what she wants, but she is clumsy, slow, and inefficient. Her skin also needs a good moisturizer, but that's another story. The octopus uses her many tentacles to get what she wants. She is able to do many things at one time. The octopus is streamlined, graceful, and competent.

Many women business owners, if they do any marketing at all, do elephant marketing. Elephant marketing is a weak, clumsy, one-prong approach to attracting customers. Grabbing peanuts one at a time is not an efficient way to sustain life. Elephant marketing is like a house of cards that can blow away with the slightest wind. If a hungry new competitor moves into your territory, you can be knocked out of the game. If the economy goes into a downturn, you have no backup methods of acquiring new accounts. With elephant marketing, you are not keeping up with business trends or technological advances. If you don't move ahead, you are left behind.

Octopus marketing, rather, is elegant and efficient. Just as the octopus uses her many tentacles to get what she wants, octopus marketing is a multipronged approach for acquiring and retaining customers. Octopus marketers do high-tech, low-tech, and no-tech marketing all at the same time. High-tech marketing includes your company website, email campaigns, newsgroup, and chat-group postings. Low-tech includes direct mail, display ads, directory listings, articles, news releases, information products, booklets, free reports, radio, and even television ads. No-tech marketing includes high-touch methods such as networking, trade shows, speeches, seminars, and promotional gifts.

Women, as natural multitaskers, are uniquely suited to octopus marketing. Put out those tentacles and watch your business grow!

PART V

BAG OF LOVE

Creating Your Legacy

The Heart Weighs More Than the Wallet

It happens. You're working on an important project when a friend calls and asks for your guidance. Your husband or significant other wants to go away for the weekend. Your son or daughter needs you to help with homework. It's tempting to put off their requests until your project is finished or you think you have more time. But there will always be urgent projects, deadlines, and impatient clients.

Your heart carries so much more value than your bank account ever could. It's an extraordinary organ, the origin of your life and your love. Listen to your heart. Connecting deeply with the people we love makes the tapestry of life a rich one. Taking time for others gives us priceless emotional rewards. Read to your child, share some meaningful conversation with your teenager, have a date with your husband, call a friend and invite her to lunch, rent "chick flicks" and make margaritas for a girls-only night. Your family and friends are not an interruption to your success journey—they are your touchstones and your reason for being.

No matter how much you give from the heart, it still remains full. You've sought out mentors and learned valuable tips, strategies, and insights. Now it's time to be a mentor and guide up-and-coming business mavericks. Use your experience to teach others lessons they could never learn in school. Don't give them a handout—give them a hand up.

Your business is the fulcrum that lets you make a huge impact on society. How do you want to make a difference? Ending world hunger? Eradicating illiteracy? Stamping out domestic violence? Cleaning up the environment? Making child abuse a thing of the past? Ending animal cruelty? Improving the condition of women in third-world countries?

Build your business with all your heart. Give power to your compassion. Value people more than money and dedicate yourself to giving back.

CHAPTER 17

Balance Your Mind, Body, and Spirit

Your business is thriving. You've fallen in love with your work and find yourself consumed by it. But at some point, you realize your life is no longer in balance.

Many Americans are willingly trading in prosperity in the form of fat paychecks for the kind of peace of mind that more free time offers. Demographers call this trend "downshifting," and women appear to be leading the way. For a healthy life and a thriving business, keep your focus on what really matters. Your family and community need you as much as your business does. Make it a priority to balance your mind, body, and spirit.

> It is imperative that a woman keep her sense of humor intact and at the ready. . . . It has been said that laughter is therapeutic and amiability lengthens the life span. Women should be tough, tender, laugh as much as possible, and live long lives.
>
> —Maya Angelou,
> award-winning
> author and poet

THE IMPORTANCE OF RELATIONSHIPS

We can't put a price on sitting in front of the fire with someone we love, having dinner with a great friend, feeling the purr of a cat or the nuzzle of a dog, or hearing "Mommy, I love you!" from our children. Why deny it, ladies? Our worlds are all about deep and important relationships. We thrive on connections. We nurture, we advise, we teach, we care. If our lives are to be in balance, our relationships are the first place to start.

Your Mate

If there is one important person at the core of your life, do everything you can to assure that your enthusiasm for your business doesn't undermine your primary relationship. Involve your husband or partner in key business decisions and always keep him or her in the loop. Keep your sense of humor and laugh about yourself and your lives together. If it's not life-threatening, it's probably not worth panicking over. Remember to express the specific things you love about your mate, and all the things you're grateful for.

Here are some suggestions for keeping your primary relationship strong:

- **Schedule ten minutes together at the end of each day.** Focus on each other totally. Tell each other about your day, your thoughts, your concerns, your hopes and dreams. Try not to interrupt each other or go off on a tangent. Make the environment safe for both of you to open up completely and trust each other with your feelings. Men have a tendency to try to solve problems. Sometimes women just want to vent and be heard. I know that when I tell my husband my problems, he likes to think of possible solutions. This is natural, and I love him for it. Whether you try to solve each other's problems is up to you, but never, never blame the other person for the problems in his or her life. This is the ultimate betrayal of trust.

CORPORATE FLEXIBILITY

Even large corporations are becoming more family-friendly and realizing the importance of employees balancing their lives. Stacy Reichert, director of product innovation at Pepsi Co, is married and has two beautiful children. Her husband, Jim is her biggest fan. She is a champion for women and men who want more flexible hours so that they can balance their careers and families. Stacy was instrumental in creating a revolutionary program that allowed Pepsi employees more flexible work hours so that they could attend parent-teacher conferences or their child's school play, or provide necessary care for their aging parents. You shouldn't have to check your soul at the door when you go to work in the morning.

At one time, the corporate culture at Pepsi was "Work Hard. Play Hard." Now it's "Work Hard. Live Hard."

- **Make a weekly date night.** Schedule one night a week to go on a date, especially if you're married. You did it when you were single, why not keep it up as an old married couple? Hire a babysitter for the kids and spend some time having fun (remember fun?), but don't let the fantasy of what date night is supposed to be put too much pressure on you. It doesn't have to be a candlelight dinner overlooking the ocean at sunset. It could be a simple dinner at home in front of the fireplace with the television off.

- **Plan time to travel together.** Take out those great gift calendars with the cute puppies and kittens on them and block out travel dates at the beginning of the year. Then call the airline or travel agent and book those great trips. Otherwise, you'll get too busy to do it.

Your Children

The best way to teach your children is by example. Children love to learn and they are always emulating adults. Here are some ways to pass on love and valuable success skills to your kids:

- **Involve them in the business.** To increase their self-esteem and sense of responsibility, give your kids a title in your business and print out business cards for them. When my friend Theresa opened her travel agency, she sent her kids throughout the neighborhood to hand out flyers and brochures about the new business. Who could resist a bunch of cute kids?

- **Teach them wealth-building skills.** Give your children checkbooks to balance and have them pick and follow stocks. Teach them to invest 10 percent of their allowance. Play games that teach them how to develop their business skills and handle their finances, such as Robert Kiyosaki's Cash Flow Board Game. Have your children choose a charity for donating their old toys before they get new ones.

- **Create a family wish jar.** A woman I know wanted to go to Disneyland with her family. She started a family wish jar. It worked on the same principle as the tip jar at the coffeehouse. Whenever my friend and her husband got small amounts of change back from their purchases, it would go into the jar. Their kids pitched in, and the parents matched their children's contributions. Then they all picked a stock together and invested the proceeds of their "family wish fund" on a regular basis. When they actually took their dream trip to Disneyland, it had much more meaning to everyone, especially the kids. Instead of just being along for the ride, the children felt that they had contributed to the vacation.

- **Lead by example.** Children learn by modeling. They love to emulate their parents and they want role models that they can look up to. Speak to your kids' school on career day. Help your children learn to conquer their fears and achieve their greatness by your example.

- **Don't overschedule.** One way to achieve balance is by not overscheduling your children. Kids need quiet time to be alone, think, and imagine. Today, kids have so many different activities they need their own dayplanners. When I was a child, I was given a coloring book and an empty cardboard box to play with. An after-school activity for me and my sister was jumping on my parent's king-sized bed and pretending it was a trampoline.

- **Tuck them in at night.** Even if your schedule is busy, take the time to tuck your children into bed so that your love is their final memory of the day. Read a story together. Ask them what they liked about their day. You can even "tuck in" a teenager by having tea and conversation at night. If you're not a parent, close your day by "tucking in" someone you love—a friend, your mother, an aunt, a neighbor—by telephone or letter.

Your Parents

We'll never stop being children to our parents. We are full-grown adults with the expanding waistlines to prove it, running our own businesses and caring for our own families, but when we walk through the front door of our parents' house we're suddenly thirteen years old again and having slumber parties.

> *Nothing affects our children as profoundly as the unlived lives of their parents.*
> —Carl Jung,
> psychologist

Parents are masters at inflicting guilt. I know from experience. I'm the survivor of a Jewish mother: "Don't be a stranger. Call your mother once in a while." And mothers do not possess the exclusive rights on guilt infliction. Fathers can do a pretty good job, too.

Our parents worry about us, and they still need us. They may not understand how your business can totally consume your life. They may not even understand why your business is so important to you. The reality is that as an ambitious, professional woman, you can find yourself getting frustrated by your parents. They grew up in a different time. They are getting slower. They have special needs and they may even need help walking and doing simple tasks you take for granted. When you take them to the movies, you have to let them off near the ticket booth and then go park the car.

I used to do other tasks while talking on the phone to my mother, such as typing on the computer. But then I spoke to Mary Marcdante, the author of *My Mother, My Friend,* which she wrote after she lost her mother. After realizing how lucky I was to have a mother who was still alive and wanted to be in touch with me, I decided that multitasking is good for business but not for sharing time with someone you love. Now I give my mother my full attention on the phone.

Your Friends and Extended Family

According to entrepreneur and radio commentator Terri Murphy, "Friends are the gems in the jewel box of life." Friends are your angels on earth. They are your safe harbor in life's storms. They know you inside and out and love you anyway.

Friendships between women are special. They remind us of who we really are and shape who we are yet to be. They soothe our tumultuous inner world and fill the emotional gaps in our marriage. Make time for your amazing women friends. Don't cast your girlfriends aside when you're in love. I knew a woman who always had time for her girlfriends—until she met her man of the month. She figured her friends would be there after the demise of her romantic dalliances, and usually they were, but maybe with a bit less intimacy and trust.

Your friends may not be interested in entrepreneurship. Their center may be home and family. *Vive la difference.* It's a wonderful exchange—you give them a glimpse into the business world, and they show you what real devotion to family is all about.

You probably have other family members—sisters, brothers, cousins, aunts, uncles, nieces, and nephews—that you enjoy spending time with and who light your life. It's all too easy to lose contact with these eminent people in your life. If you find yourself continually rescheduling outings with them, it may be time to reorganize your life and your priorities.

Your Pets

Society has changed. After marriage, it is no longer assumed that couples will become parents. Today, many couples elect not to have children; instead, they become what Brian Devine, the CEO of Petco, calls "pet parents." They don't just buy discount food from the grocery store, they read the ingredients on the label and buy veterinarian-approved nutritional supplements. They agonize over choosing the vet and the pet sitter. They pick up pet toys on their way home from the office. How else could you explain the meteoric rise of the specialty pet retailers, amazing animal stories on television, and pet bakeries that sell gourmet treats like "pup cakes"?

I confess: I'm a pet parent. I carry pictures of my two cats, Carmella and Sneakers, with me all the time. My husband and I refer to them as "the girls." Pets need your time and caring, and they give a tremendous amount in return. Having your own business allows you great opportunities to accommodate your pets. You can have a furry office mate. You can take breaks for a romp in the dog park or to brush the cat and relish in the soothing purring.

Your pets can even help you develop your business acumen. Mary Hessler Key has a theory that cats have the same qualities as entrepreneurs. In her book *The Entrepreneurial Cat: Thirteen Ways to Transform Your Work Life,* she says, "Cats take charge of their lives. Persons rarely do." Cats know how to do what comes naturally, find their instincts, focus completely, and prowl for opportunity.

An Active Mind

When your mind is active and healthy, you're eager to learn new things and move forward with your life. You're exhilarated about the challenges and changes ahead of you. You're also willing to take risks, make mistakes, and learn from your experiences

Practice Lifelong Learning

"School is never out for the pros," says Joe Polish, president of Piranha Marketing. Just because you're not in school anymore doesn't mean that you don't thirst for more knowledge. Read books, trade and business magazines, and the newspaper. Listen to tapes and talk radio. Attend seminars and surf the Internet.

Teleclasses and webcasts are a new way to learn and sharpen your skills. With a teleclass, all you need is a comfy chair and a willingness to learn. You simply call on a phone line at a specific time and listen to an instructor. The classes are totally interactive—you can ask questions and relate personal experiences. Webcasts are virtual classrooms with infinite possibilities, conducted on the Internet.

> *The truth is that, like every other part of nature, human beings have an internal imperative to grow.*
> —Gloria Steinem, feminist and human rights activist

Don't be afraid to approach people you are in awe of as part of your course in lifelong learning. Successful people are usually very open and helpful. Take people you admire out to lunch and pick their brains. Talk, fax, and email them on a regular basis to let them know how important they are to you and that they have improved your life.

Your Mind at Work

The wonder of starting your own business is that you can choose a line of work that truly suits your strengths. You are using your greatest talents and stretching your wings. When your mind is alert and engaged, your concentration is phenomenal, and your production shows it. Best yet, you're meeting your financial needs on the strength of your talent and perseverance.

A HEALTHY BODY

Your body is the vessel that carries you through this marvelous adventure of life. And yet, in today's hectic world, we frequently treat our automobiles more lovingly than our bodies. Is your body in balance? Do you sleep well and wake up refreshed? Are you happy with the way you look, comfortable in your skin? Listen to your body. If something hurts, figure out why. If you're getting sick more often than usual, maybe it's time to look for more balance in your life.

Eat Right

Enjoy your food, but remember that food is the fuel that keeps your body running. Certain foods have high nutritional value and create vigor and vitality. Others have empty calories and deplete the body's energy. Notice what foods work well with your metabolism, digestion, and weight management. Also pay attention to those foods—typically greasy and fatty foods—that deplete your energy and make you want to take a nap instead of working.

Exercise Regularly

Exercise is a tremendous stress reducer and mood enhancer. It stimulates brain function and helps prevents disease. Yes, exercise takes time, but the time investment in your exercise program will reap enormous returns. You will have more energy and mental clarity. Your lean healthy body will boost your self-esteem and confidence. An overwhelming feeling of accomplishment will fill your psyche and give you a sense of well-being.

Which doesn't necessarily mean exercise is fun when you're doing it. Personally, I hate it, but I love the benefits, so I exercise first thing in the morning. It gives me a sense of accomplishment that I carry through my whole day.

Utilize Your Senses

Your five senses connect you to the world. Did you listen to some beautiful music today, or notice the sound of a loved one's voice? Did you enjoy your food, rather than simply eating on the run?

Take pleasure in your senses and all they have to offer. Look around you. In the course of your day, your eyes spend much of their time on a single plane—a computer screen, a newspaper, even the road in front of you as you drive. Take some time to look at the distance, at the depth of things. Marvel at the layers of leaves in a tree. Look at the clouds in the sky. Take in the sights of the home or office you've lovingly decorated.

Each of your senses offers wonderful experiences. Feel the warmth of the sun on your face, the texture of grass or tile under your feet. Smell the flowers. Smell the coffee. Smell the wet pavement after a rain and the marvelous scent of the new car you bought to celebrate your last big sale.

Your Body at Work

As much as you love your new business, work can be hard on your body. Don't forget to take care of your body as you build your business. If your job keeps you on your feet, be sure to sit down occasionally. If your job keeps you at your desk, be sure to move around occasionally. Whatever your work, make a point from time to time to take a few deep breaths. Breathing brings oxygen to your brain and clears your mind. It relaxes your muscles and soothes your nerves.

> *I seldom think about my limitations, and they never make me sad. Perhaps there is just a touch of yearning at times; but it is vague, like the breeze among flowers.*
> —Helen Keller, blind and deaf author and activist

Computer work in particular can wreak havoc on your body. Develop some simple stretching exercises to do at regular intervals. Consider hiring an ergonomics specialist to come look at your workstation and make suggestions for minimizing the impact of repetitive motion and long periods at the desk.

Your body, if you listen, has a lot to tell you about whether you're on the right track with your work.

AN OPEN SPIRIT

The word *spirit* derives from the Latin word for "breath." Your spirit is the very core of your existence, the place where you feel the poignancy of life. When you're in balance spiritually, your intuition is in tune. You are able to let go of preconceptions and embrace uncertainty, with all its wondrous potential. Even your experiences of grief and loss enable you to grow.

Be Good to Yourself

Women will always be nurturers of others, but we need to remember to nurture ourselves as well. Georgette Mosbacher, author of *It Takes Money, Honey*, writes, "It's okay to want for our family, it's admirable to want for our children. It's understandable to want for our mothers and our husbands and even our best friends. But somehow we're not good people if we want something for ourselves. It's not in our job description as nurturers and caregivers—and we pride ourselves on a job well done."

To feed your spirit, indulge yourself without guilt. Block out time at least once a month to be good to yourself. Remind yourself, "I deserve this. This is good for me."

Spend money on yourself from time to time—not on something you really need, but on something you truly want. Don't wait for the man in your life to buy you that great new scent. Get the perfume for yourself. You'll feel wonderful about yourself and the way you smell. Indulge yourself not to fill a void, but because it feels good.

Sometimes indulgence purchases—things we don't overly obsess about but choose to acquire because of their beauty or some other intrinsic reason—become our most special possessions. Think of the things in your home that were purchased from favorite vacations or days out with friends and family. A good warm feeling flows over you when you look at these treasures.

A spa day is wonderful for reenergizing your body and spirit. You can fantasize freely about your upcoming goals and visions. Or take a mini vacation at an opulent setting. Denise Michaels, author of *Testosterone-Free Marketing for Women: Seven Secrets Why Old Boys Marketing Doesn't Work for Women*, goes to the most elegant hotel she can find and does her creative visualizing for her business. She sits in the beautiful lobby, has a cup of tea, and warms her soul in front of the toasty fire. She even picks the places with the best looking waiters.

Being good to yourself also means setting limits. Cell phones, email, and call forwarding were supposed to liberate us from the office and give us more free time. Instead, they increased our workload because people know we're always accessible. Draw a line in the sand and let people know what your business hours are. Don't feel guilty when you're on vacation or spending time away from your business. Be in the moment. Don't always think about the other activities you need to be doing. When you're reading a book to your child, concentrate totally on the heartwarming experience.

> *I don't know the key to success, but the key to failure is trying to please everybody.*
> —Bill Cosby, comedian

223

Pursue Tranquility

Our spirits need quiet time in order to flourish. Have the courage to cut out the "monkey chatter," the fifteen hundred words going through your head every minute. If your mind is constantly processing obligations and deadlines, your creativity and intuition won't be able to surface. Quiet time allows you to listen to your own inner voice and move forward with the wisdom it communicates. Here are some ways to pursue tranquility:

- **Meditate.** Meditation simply means to empty all thoughts from your mind. Some practitioners find it helpful to focus on something else, a word called a mantra, to help quiet all the monkey chatter in your mind. When you are meditating, don't expect some cosmic experience to occur. Simply enjoy the sense of peace you are left with at the end of your quiet time.

- **Change your scenery.** Years ago, I was having terrible sinus headaches. I went to an accupressurist. She told me that I needed a "reference for purity." There is so much pollution in the city—even thought pollution with billboards and constant advertising messages—that she encouraged me to go up to the mountains and look at purity. I needed to see nature in its purest form for miles around me. Engage in a relaxing exercise. Many women find a walk through tranquil scenery, along a beach or through a forest, a great way to provide the quiet space they need. Nature is a catalyst for free-flowing thoughts.

- **Renew your faith.** Get involved with your religion. Becoming a member of your local church, synagogue, or other house of worship will renew your spirituality and give you a sense of community.

- **Engross yourself in a hobby or household task.** Being involved in a hobby or an artistic pursuit puts you in an altered state. Many times, when I was drawing or painting, I was so engrossed in the work that when the instructor came up and put his hand on my shoulder, I almost jumped to the ceiling. Single-minded focus on a creative or even mundane task allows in a higher form of consciousness.

Solitude can be a creative stimulator. Many artists and writers take creative retreats by themselves to realize their true creative genius and bring out what is inside them. I know many people who are so afraid of quiet that the minute they walk into the house, they turn on the television or the radio. Quiet does not mean loneliness. It means self-discovery. It is the genesis of many great ideas, removing the cobwebs from your mind so that the hidden treasures can be brought out.

An open spirit, a healthy body, an active mind—balance these elements and reap the rewards of a peaceful life.

CHAPTER 18

Be the Hero of Your Own Life

At one time we've all had a dream of how our life would be, but our dreams often get buried in the everyday frustrations of life. Most people feel that the events of the world control them. They get caught up in making a living rather than designing a life.

A study quoted on NBC says that half the people in the United States feel the only way they can get ahead financially is to win the lottery. Can you believe it? The chance of getting hit by lightning is nine hundred times greater than winning the lottery.

We live in the greatest country in the world, surrounded by opportunities for success at every turn. Yet most Americans are too stuck in their ruts to try something new. To succeed in life, you have to forget about most people. If you want to rise to the top, you have to disregard the opinions, reactions, and warnings of others.

You need to believe deep down in your soul that you can run a successful business. Wealth and success come to those who live their passionate lives and do it bravely. Use the tips and techniques in this book to get you into the no-fear zone. Incorporate the seven secrets of success into your daily life. Give wings to your dreams.

> "Never lose sight of the fact that the most important yardstick of your success will be how you treat other people—your family, friends, and coworkers, and even strangers you meet along the way."
> —Barbara Bush,
> American First Lady

226

YOUR HERO'S JOURNEY

The great mythologist and philosopher Joseph Campbell has described what he calls the hero's journey. During our life's progress, as with every hero's quest, we have to suffer certain losses, leave the predictable comforts of our home, and set into unfamiliar terrain to realize our dreams and our goals. Out of these struggles the hero emerges with a grail or jewels or wisdom that she shares with others.

As you walk the more difficult stretches of your hero's path, look for the positive. Your subconscious, since it moves in the direction of the brain's dominant thoughts, is very open to suggestions that are similar to your previous

TURNING TRAGEDY INTO TRIUMPH

Georgia Durante's extraordinary life exemplifies the story of a true survivor. At seventeen, she had a successful modeling career. She was the Kodak Bikini Girl, whose full-sized cardboard image graced many camera stores. She then married one of the most notorious men in the Mafia.

We've all heard of the Mafia and read about mobsters, but Georgia Durante saw them up close. She lived with them. She drove their getaway cars. She survived their wars. Her struggles and victories are chronicled in her book, *The Company She Keeps*.

Georgia's husband was physically and mentally abusive, and she was threatened at gunpoint many times. She finally escaped with her young daughter, Toni, with only $7 in her pocket. She considered going back to modeling, but feared if her husband or his Mafia buddies saw her, they would track her down and kill her.

Georgia remembered the days when she drove getaway cars, and she noticed that stunt car drivers never showed their faces. She had a talent for fast performance driving, and it was totally anonymous work. She started doing stunt double work for Cindy Crawford and other celebrities. Knowing nothing about business, she launched her own company, Performance Two, providing stunt and performance drivers for Hollywood. According to Georgia, "Crashing cars for a living is a walk in the park compared to my days as a Mafia wife."

beliefs. In other words, your mind is always looking for validation. When you look for the bad, that's what you'll find. When you look for the positive, you'll find it in abundance.

You may have experienced tragedy in your life. That doesn't mean your life will be tragic. There are so many amazing women in the world who have turned tragedy into triumph, overcoming enormous obstacles to succeed. These women are true heroes. If they can conquer adversity and start their own businesses, so can you.

GIVE BACK TO OTHERS

Perhaps the most powerful way to be the hero of your own life is to be a hero to others. Your ultimate task as a hero is to bring knowledge, energy, and power back to the people you love and share it with them. In discovering your greatness and cultivating your inborn talents to share with the world, you can make your contribution and fulfill your mission. You can help those you love and help the society we live in. You will leave a magnificent legacy to future generations.

I encourage you to develop outrageous goals. Maybe your dreams are global, fighting against evils such as domestic violence and child abuse, or maybe you desire to make life better for the people you love. Your aspirations could lead you to buy a home for your parents, a favorite family member, or a friend. You could be the one in your inner circle who has the financial ability to say, "Don't worry, I'll take care of it."

> *If you breathe air, you bring a gift to life's party.*
> —Sheryl Nicholson, author and motivational speaker

Building a successful business is the ultimate opportunity for creating a glorious legacy. Women business owners are philanthropic leaders. High net worth women business owners and executives are more active and generous philanthropically than their male counterparts. More than half contribute in excess of $25,000 or more annually to charity. Seven of ten women business owners volunteer at least once a month. They are more likely than men to serve on nonprofit boards and in volunteer pursuits.

Catalog maven Lillian Vernon, after celebrating her company's fiftieth anniversary in business, partnered with Habitat for Humanity to provide housing for needy low-income families. Designer Diane von Furstenberg, whose mother Lily survived three different concentration camps, helped raise money for the National Holocaust Museum. She and her mother attended the inauguration of the museum in Washington, D.C., in April 1993. Lily had taught her daughter never to give in to sorrow but always to try to celebrate life.

You already know the importance of mentors in fast-tracking your success. Now may be the time for you to give back and become a mentor to others. Look around you for women who have great potential and could gain if you shared your experiences. You could mentor a young woman just coming into her own, or another woman just starting out in business.

Honor the people in your life in small ways whenever you can. Think about the people you love, the business people you admire, your loyal employees, and your favorite customers. Call them when you think of them. Give them gifts. Take them to lunch and acknowledge their special qualities. Tell them about the traits that you admire in them and how much they mean to you.

PROFITS WITH PRINCIPLES

Anita Roddick grew her business, The Body Shop, from a single "hippie" store in England to a multinational company with 1,366 stores in 46 countries. Anita's success has grown as well. In 1993 she was one of the five richest women in England. She has received many awards. She was named London's Business Woman of the Year in 1985 and honored with an Order of the British Empire award in 1988.

The success of The Body Shop demonstrates that one person can make a difference. Who would have guessed that her $6,500 investment would grow into more than $145 million? Perhaps the "profits with principles" theme is one that more companies should follow. Anita continues to promote social and environmental awareness. "I wake up every morning thinking . . . this is my last day. And I jam everything into it." According to Anita, "There's no time for mediocrity. This is no damned dress rehearsal."

GIVE WINGS TO YOUR DREAMS

In closing, I would like to leave you with an awesome quote by author Marianne Williamson. These powerful words were used by Nelson Mandela in his 1994 inaugural speech:

> Our deepest fear is not that we are inadequate.
> Our deepest fear is that we are powerful beyond measure.
> It is our light, not our darkness, that most frightens us.
> We ask ourselves, who am I to be brilliant, gorgeous, talented,
>   and fabulous?
> Actually, who are you not to be?
> You are a child of God.
>
> Your playing small doesn't serve the world.
> There's nothing enlightened about shrinking so that other people
>   won't feel insecure around you.
> We are all meant to shine, as children do.
> We are born to make manifest the glory of God that is within us.
> It's not just in some of us, it's in everyone.
> And as we let our own light shine, we unconsciously give other
>   people permission to do the same.
> As we are liberated from our own fear, our presence automatically
>   liberates others.

According to Marsha Sinetar in her book *Do What You Love, The Money Will Follow*, "Wings are those things that keep us moving and growing, going beyond where we've been and what we've done. Our dreams, our visions, our willingness to risk, our need for adventure and improvement all urge us to become airborne. Wings prompt us to discover the meaning and purpose of life."

Go out and write your life's story. As the young Anne Frank said, "How wonderful it is that nobody need wait a single moment before starting to improve the world." Improve your world. Be the hero of your own life.

Get out there and build your successful business. Live your passionate life and do it bravely. Make your contribution and give back to humanity. Discover your greatness. Get out and let your light shine for the whole world. I'll be waiting to hear your story . . .

Author's Note

I would love to hear from you . . .

I hope you were elevated and inspired by this book. I've dedicated it to the winning spirit of women just like you.

If you have any comments, questions, insights, breakthroughs, and stories that you would like to share, please email me at info@WealthyBagLady.com. You can also call 1-888-286-0602 or write to Wealthy Bag Lady, P.O. Box 83639, Los Angeles, CA 90083. Please note that any stories submitted may be used in a future publication. Individual stories may or may not be acknowledged. However, as in this book, names and other details will be camouflaged to protect your privacy.

The entrepreneurial passion has been enflamed. You've got outrageous goals and visions. You've researched your business, thought about it . . . dreamed about it. Now it's time to take action. Go for it, girl!

I wish you the best of luck with your business. Live well, have fun, discover your greatness, and share your gifts with the world!

REFERENCES

Abraham, Jay. *Getting Everything You Can Out of All You've Got: Twenty-One Ways You Can Out-Think, Out-Perform, and Out-Earn the Competition.* New York: St. Martin's Press, 2000.

Allen, Debbie. *Confessions of Shameless Self Promoters: Sixty-Eight Marketing Gurus Share Secrets, Tools, Tips, and Unique Ideas That Will Take You to the Next Level of Success.* Tempe, Arizona: Success Showcase Publications, 2001.

Allen, Robert G. *Multiple Streams of Income: How to Generate a Lifetime of Unlimited Wealth.* New York: John Wiley & Sons, 2000.

Amos, Wally. *The Cookie Never Crumbles: Inspirational Recipes for Everyday Living.* New York: St. Martin's Press, 2001.

Berkley, Susan. *Speak to Influence: How to Unlock the Hidden Power of Your Voice.* Englewood Cliffs, New Jersey: Campbell Hall, 1999.

Blum, Deborah. *Sex on the Brain: The Biological Differences between Men and Women.* Harmondsworth, England: Penguin, 1997.

Boylan, Michael A. *The Power to Get In: A Step-by-Step System to Get in Anyone's Door So You Have the Chance to . . . Make the Sale . . . Get the Job . . . Present Your Ideas.* New York: St. Martin's Press, 1997.

Campbell, Joseph. *The Power of Myth.* New York: Doubleday, 1988.

Card, Emily, and Adam Miller. *Business Capital for Women: An Essential Handbook for Entrepreneurs.* New York: Macmillan, 1996.

Carter-Scott, Chérie. *If Life Is a Game, These Are the Rules: Ten Rules for Being Human.* New York: Broadway Books, 1998.

———. *If Success is a Game, These Are the Rules: Ten Rules for a Fulfilling Life.* New York: Broadway Books, 2000.

Clason, George S. *The Richest Man in Babylon.* New York: Dutton, 1955.

Desberg, Peter. *No More Butterflies: Overcoming Stagefright, Shyness, Interview Anxiety and Fear of Public Speaking.* Oakland, California: New Harbinger, 1996.

Diamond, Claude. *The Mentor: A Story of Success.* Winter Park, Colorado: Claude Diamond Publications, 2001.

Donaldson, Mimi and Michael. *Negotiating for Dummies: Packed with Strategies for Achieving Win-Win Solutions!* Foster City, California: Hungry Minds, 1996.

Durante, Georgia. *The Company She Keeps.* Nashville, Tennessee: Celebrity, 1998.

Friedman, Jack P. *Barron's Dictionary of Business Terms.* New York: Barrons, 1994.

Fripp, Patricia. *Make It So You Don't Have to Fake It! Fifty-Five Fast-Acting Strategies for Long-Lasting Success.* Mechanicsburg, Pennsylvania: Executive Books, 2000.

Furstenberg, Diane von. *Diane: A Signature Life.* New York: Simon & Schuster, 1998.

Gerber, Michael E. *The E-Myth Revisited: Why Most Small Businesses Don't Work and What to Do about It.* New York: HarperBusiness, 1995.

Glaser, Connie Brown, and Barbara Steinberg Smalley. *More Power to You! How Women Can Communicate Their Way to Success.* New York: Warner, 1995.

———. *Swim with the Dolphins: How Women Can Succeed in Corporate America on Their Own Terms.* New York: Warner Books, 1995.

Hall, Stacey, and Jan Brogniez. *Attracting Perfect Customers: The Power of Strategic Synchronicity.* San Francisco: Berrett-Koehler, 2001.

Hill, Brian E., Dee Power, and Bob Bozeman. *Attracting Capital from Angels: How Their Money—and Their Experience—Can Help You Build a Successful Company.* New York: John Wiley & Sons, 2002.

Hill, Napoleon. *Think and Grow Rich.* New York: Fawcett, 1987.

Jaffe, Azriela, and John Gray. *Honey, I Want to Start My Own Business: A Planning Guide for Couples.* New York: Diane Publishing Company, 1996.

———. *Let's Go Into Business Together: Eight Secrets to Successful Business Partnering.* Franklin Lakes, New Jersey: Career Press, 2001.

Key, Mary Hessler, and Jazzie the Cat. *The Entrepreneurial Cat: Thirteen Ways to Transform Your Business Life.* Tampa, Florida: Jazzie Publishing, 1997.

Kiyosaki, Robert T., with Sharon L. Lechter. *Cash Flow Quadrant: Rich Dad's Guide to Financial Freedom.* Paradise Valley, Arizona: TechPress, 1999.

Kremer, John. *1,001 Ways to Market Your Books.* Fairfield, Iowa: Ad-Lib Publications, 1989.

Kushell, Jennifer. *The Young Entrepreneur's Edge: Using Your Ambition, Independence, and Youth to Launch a Successful Business.* New York: Random House, 1999.

Kushner, Malcolm. *Public Speaking for Dummies: Tried-and-True Tips for Dazzling Speeches and Presentations.* Foster City, California: IDG, 1999.

Lauder, Estée. *Estée: A Success Story.* New York: Random House, 1985.

Levinson, Jay Conrad. *Guerilla Marketing: How to Make Big Profits from Your Small Business.* New York: Houghton Mifflin, 1985.

Litman, Mike, and Jason Oman. *Conversations with Millionaires: What Millionaires Do to Get Rich That You Never Learned in School!* New York: CWM Publishing, 2002.

Marcdante, Mary. *My Mother, My Friend: The Ten Most Important Things to Talk About with Your Mother.* New York: Fireside, 2001.

McDonald, Kathy, and Beth Sirull. *Creating Your Life Collage: Strategies for Solving the Work/Life Dilemma.* New York: Three Rivers Press, 2000.

Michaels, Nancy, and Debbi J. Karpowicz. *Off-the-Wall Marketing Ideas: Jumpstart Your Sales without Busting Your Budget.* Holbrook, Massachusetts: Adams, 2000.

Moir, Anne, and David Jessel. *Brain Sex: The Real Difference between Men and Women.* New York: Delta, 1989.

Mosbacher, Georgette, with Diane Harris. *It Takes Money, Honey: A Get-Smart Guide to Total Financial Freedom.* New York: HarperCollins, 1999.

Murphy, Joseph. *The Power of Your Subconscious Mind.* Revised by Ian McMahan. New York: Bantam, 2000.

Nemeth, Maria. *The Energy of Money: A Spiritual Guide to Financial and Personal Fulfillment.* New York: Ballantine, 1999.

Nicholson, Sheryl. "Working Women Are Working Wonders." Marina del Rey, California, 1991.

Parker, Roger C. *Looking Good in Print: A Guide to Basic Design for Desktop Publishing.* Chapel Hill, North Carolina: Ventana Press, 1990.

Pflug, Jackie Nink, with Peter J. Kizilos. *Miles to Go before I Sleep: My Grateful Journey back from the Hijacking of EgyptAir Flight 648.* Center City, Minnesota: Hazelden, 1996.

Pinskey, Raleigh. *101 Ways to Promote Yourself: Tricks of the Trade for Taking Charge of Your Own Success by Viz-Ability Marketing.* New York: Avon Books, 1997.

Popcorn, Faith, and Lys Marigold. *Clicking: Seventeen Trends That Drive Your Business—and Your Life.* New York: HarperCollins, 1998.

———. *EVEolution: The Eight Truths of Marketing to Women.* New York: Hyperion, 2000.

Ries, Al, and Jack Trout. *The Twenty-Two Immutable Laws of Marketing: Violate Them at Your Own Risk.* New York: HarperBusiness, 1993.

RoAne, Susan. *How to Work a Room: The Ultimate Guide to Savvy Socializing in Person and Online.* New York: Quill, 2000.

Roffer, Robin Fisher. *Make a Name for Yourself: Eight Steps Every Woman Needs to Create a Personal Brand Strategy for Success.* New York: Broadway, 2000.

Sherman, Aliza. *Power Tools for Women in Business: Ten Ways to Succeed in Life and Work.* Irvine, California: Entrepreneur Press, 2001.

Silverman, George. *The Secrets of Word-of-Mouth Marketing: How to Trigger Exponential Sales through Runaway Word of Mouth.* New York: Amacom, 2001.

Sinetar, Marsha. *Do What You Live, The Money Will Follow: Discovering Your Right Livelihood.* New York: Dell Publishing, 1989.

Sivertsen, Linda. *Lives Charmed: Intimate Conversations with Extraordinary People.* Deerfield Beach, Florida: Health Communication, 1998.

Stanley, Thomas J., and William D. Danko. *The Millionaire Next Door: The Surprising Secrets of America's Wealthy.* New York: Pocket Books, 2000.

Stanny, Barbara. *Prince Charming Isn't Coming: How Women Get Smart about Money.* New York: Diane Publishing, 1997.

Stansell, Kimberly. *Bootstrapper's Success Secrets: 151 Tactics for Building Your Business on a Shoestring Budget.* Franklin Lakes, New Jersey: Career Press, 1997.

Sylver, Marshall. *Passion, Profit, and Power: Reprogram Your Subconscious Mind to Create the Relationships, Wealth, and Well-Being That You Deserve.* New York: Fireside, 1995.

Tracy, Brian. *The Twenty-One Success Secrets of Self-Made Millionaires: How to Achieve Financial Independence Faster and Easier Than You Ever Thought Possible.* San Francisco: Berrett-Koehler, 2001.

Varga, Kenneth J. *How to Get Customers to Call, Buy, and Beg for More!* Verdi, Nevada: World Wide, 1997.

Walters, Dottie and Lily. *Speak and Grow Rich.* New York: Prentice Hall, 1997.

Weiss, Alan. *Million-Dollar Consulting: The Professional's Guide to Growing a Practice.* New York: McGraw-Hill, 1998.

Winter, Barbara J. *Making a Living without a Job: Winning Ways for Creating Work That You Love.* New York: Bantam, 1993.

RESOURCES

Education for Women on Raising Capital

American Woman's Economic
Development Corporation (AWED)
216 E 45th Street, 10th Floor
New York, NY 10017
Tel. 917-368-6100
www.awed.org

Capital Connection
P.O. Box 18460
Fountain Hills, AZ 85269
Tel. 480-837-9590
Fax. 480-837-6680
www.capital-connection.com

Springboard Enterprises
2100 Foxhall Road NW
Washington, D.C. 20007
Tel. 202-242-6282
Fax. 202-242-6284
www.springboardenterprises.org

Women's Business Development Center
(WBDC)
8 S Michigan Avenue, Suite 400
Chicago, IL 60603-3306
Tel. 312-853-3477
Fax. 312-853-0145
www.wbdc.org

Women's Enterprise Development
Corporation (WEDC)
235 E Broadway, Suite 506
Long Beach, CA 90802-7804
Tel. 562-983-3747
Fax. 562-983-3750
www.wedc.org

U.S. Small Business Administration
(SBA)
Tel. 800-8-ASK-SBA
www.sba.gov

To find the nearest SBA Women's
Business Center, go to
www.sba.gov/WomenInBusiness/
wcbs.html

To find the nearest SBA Small Business
Development Center, go to
www.sba.gov/sbdc

Financing Your Business

Angels with Attitude
6541 36th Avenue SW
Seattle, WA 98126
Tel. 206-932-3850
www.activeangels.com

Count Me In for Women's Economic
Independence
22 W 26th Street, Suite 9H
New York, NY 10010
Tel. 212-691-6380
www.count-me-in.org

Business Publications

Barrons
Business 2.0
Business Week
Entrepreneur
Executive Female
Fast Company
Forbes
Fortune
Inc.

Business Training for Women

Wealthy Bag Lady
P.O. Box 83639
Los Angeles, CA 90083
Tel. 888-286-0602
Fax. 310-641-5823
www.WealthyBagLady.com

Women's Small Business Expo
4214 Glencoe Avenue
Marina Del Rey, CA 90292
Tel. 866-Women-Biz
www.WomensSmallBusinessExpo.com

Copyrights, Trademarks, and Patents

Patent and Trademark Office (USPTO)
Tel. 800-786-9199
www.uspto.gov

Getting Your News Releases on the Web

PR Web, the Free Wire Service
P.O. Box 333
Ferndale, WA 98248
Tel. 360-312-0892
www.prweb.com

Promotional Products and Corporate Gifts

The Bag Ladies
4214 Glencoe Avenue
Marina Del Rey, CA 90292
Tel. 800-359-BAGS
Fax. 310-574-9960
www.Bag-Ladies.com

Linking Partners for Your Web Site

www.linkleads.com

Learning by Phone

www.teleclass.com

Photography

Straight Shooter Photography
28576 W Lindbergh Drive
Barrington, IL 60010
Tel. 847-304-4446
Email. JaredSSS@aol.com

Autoresponders and Broadcast Email

www.infogenerator.com (mention #9402)

World Wide Web Hosting

www.internexions.com

Wealth Training for Women

Millionaire Women
15 E Putnam Avenue, Suite 289
Greenwich, CT 06030
Tel. 914-749-9331
Fax. 203-532-1961
and
120 Village Square, Suite 105
Orinda, CA 94563
Tel. 925-746-1912
www.MillionaireWomen.com

WealthyWomen.com
5580 La Jolla Boulevard, Suite 467
La Jolla, CA 92037
Tel. 858-638-0030
Fax 858-638-0033
www.WealthyWomen.com

Women Online

www.ivillage.com
www.oxygen.com
www.women.com

Women's Associations

eWomenNetwork
14900 Landmark Boulevard, Suite 540
Dallas, TX 75254
Tel. 972-620-9995
www.eWomenNetwork.com

National Association of Female
Executives (NAFE)
260 Madison Avenue, 3rd Floor
New York, NY 10016
Tel. 800-634-NAFE
www.nafe.com

National Association of Women Business
Owners (NAWBO)
1595 Spring Hill Road, Suite 330
Vienna, VA 22182
Tel. 703-506-3268
Fax. 703-506-3266
www.nawbo.org

A

Accounting, 111–12
Addresses, 78–79, 93
Advertising, 173–76
Advisers, 42, 75
Affirmations, 28, 151
Alert Staffing, 191
Ambler, Aldonna, 153
American Woman's Economic
    Development Corporation
    (AWED), 43–44
Amos, Wally "Famous," 49
Angel investors, 126–27
Apple, 65, 132
Artists, 91
Ashley, Evelyn, 66–67
Attitude, importance of, 23–33

B

The Bag Ladies, 3–5, 20, 65, 114, 117,
    173, 202
Baker, Carol, 69
Balance, maintaining, 214–25
Banks
    choosing, 70–72
    loans from, 128–30
    opening account at, 63–64
Barbie, 179
Bartering, 116–17
Benefits, 104
Bloomingdale's, 96
Body, maintaining a healthy, 220–22
The Body Shop, 52, 229
Bootstrapping, 122–26
Borgnine, Tova, 160
Brainstorming, 36, 66
Brandi, JoAnna, 203
Brands
    location and, 88–91
    personal, 87–88

Breakthroughs, 33
Brochures, 178–80
Brogniez, Jan, 13, 158
Buffet, Warren, 33
Burnett, Iris, 130
Bushey, Marilyn, 128
Business cards, 92–94, 155
Business directories, 175
Businesses
    buying existing, 52
    categories of, 50–51
    finding ideas for, 48–49
    researching, 53–54
Business licenses, 76
Business names, 64, 65–68
Business plans, 72–76, 122
Buyer's remorse, 200

C

Campbell, Joseph, 227
Cassatt, Mary, 30
Catalogs, 178–80
Cats, 219
Celestial Seasonings, 169
Cell phones, 78
Chambers of commerce, 154
Childcare, 17. *See also* Family
Circle of influence, 40–42
Classified ads, 175
Clients. *See* Customers/clients
Clothes, 88
Cluff, Sheila, 191–92
Coaching, 137–38, 141
Cold calling, 194–96
Collections, 200–201
Color, 179, 180
Competition, 74–75, 159, 161–62,
    190–91
Complaints, 207–9

Computers, 79–80, 83–84, 222. *See also* Email; Internet marketing; Websites
Conaway, Chuck, 118
Consultants, 141
Contact information, collecting, 151, 153
Copyrights, 86
Corporations, 69–70, 112, 215
Cost-plus pricing, 162–63
Count Me In for Women's Economic Independence, 130–31
Covey, Steven, 171–72
Credit cards
    accepting, 84, 192
    financing with, 124–26
Customers/clients. *See also* Prospects
    building a base of, 159–60
    buyer's remorse by, 200
    creating lifetime, 203–10
    dissatisfied, 207–9
    following up with, 205–6
    loyalty and referral programs for, 209–10
    making ordering easy for, 192–93
    payments by, 116, 200–201
    recessions and, 117–19
    relationships with, 84
    trophy, 201–2
Customer service, 204–5
Cybergrrl Inc., 79

D
Daigle, Ellen, 98
Dart, Iris Rainer, 35
DBA (doing business as), 64
Debt
    financing, 128–31
    paying off, 139
Deductions, 113, 140
Determination, 23–24

Diamond, Claude, 80–81
Direct mail, 176–80
Disney, Walt, 136
Divorce, 16–17
Dixon, Gigi, 129
Dogs, 219
Dreams
    dreaming big, 27–30
    giving wings to, 230
Dunkin Doughnuts, 207
Durante, Georgia, 227

E
Eating, 221
Echevarria, Pegine, 40
Eldercare, 17
Elevator speech, 149–50
Ellen's Silkscreening, 98
Ellerbee, Linda, 102
Email, 183–84, 188
Employees, 97–106
    alternatives to full-time, 99–100
    benefits for, 104
    expectations for, 102
    finding and hiring, 102
    job descriptions for, 98
    nonproductive, 105
    paying, 98–99
    praising and criticizing, 105
    respecting, 103
    terminating, 105–6
    work environment for, 100–101
    workers' compensation, 82–83
Employer Identification Number (EIN), 65
Empowerment, 14–15, 31
Entrepreneurship
    benefits of, 12–15
    quiz, 10–12

Entrepreneurship *(cont.)*
    self-improvement and, 47
    women and, 9
Equipment, 77–80
Equity financing, 126–28
E-trade, 118
Evaluations, 206
Events, 173
EWomenNetwork, 43
Executive Portrait Specialists, 136–37
Executive suites, 55–56
Exercise, 221
Expenses
    reducing, 113–17
    tracking, 113, 157–58
Eye contact, 152, 156

F

Face-to-face communication, 145–46
Factoring, 133
Failure
    fear of, 18–19
    learning from, 23–24
    Faith, renewing your, 224
Family
    business planning and, 61–62
    extended, 218–19
    financing from, 123–24
    negativity from, 20–21
    support from, 34–35
    valuing, 213, 215–19
Fax machines, 77–78
Fear, 18–19, 230
Financial documents, 76
Financial potential, 13–14
Financing, 120–33
    bootstrapping, 122–26
    business plans and, 72, 122
    debt, 128–31
    equity, 126–28
    government loans, 131–32
    other options, 133

Flexibility, 13
Florestano, Ernest J., 163
Flyers, 178–80
Follow-up, 196–98, 205–6
Food, 221
Franchises, 52
Freedom, 12
Friends
    financing from, 123–24
    negativity from, 20–21
    support from, 34–35
    valuing, 213, 218–19
Future, thinking toward, 52–53

G

Gage, Christina, 59
Garland, Kathy, 58
Gatekeepers, 147
General Electric, 101
Gianforte, Greg, 122
Gifts, 95–96, 205. *See also* Philanthropy
G II Design Group, 58
Goals, 28–30, 228
Goldie, Rhoda, 103
Gore, Shelly, 59
Government loans, 131–32
Grant, Paige, 38
Grants, 123
Graphic designers, 91
Greene, Fran, 115–16
Greystone, Nancy, 170
Growth businesses, 50, 121
Guarantees, 192–93
Guli, Maxine, 58

H

Hall, Stacey, 13, 161
Handler, Ruth, 13, 179
Hart, Roseanne, 128–29
Hero's journey, 227–28
Hobar, Debbie, 171
Hobby businesses, 50, 121

Home-based businesses, 54–55
Hope, Audrey, 145
Husbands, 58, 61–62, 215–16

I

IBM, 73, 180
Ideas
    for businesses, 48–49
    protecting, 85–86, 173
Image, 87–96
Income streams, multiple, 134–41
Independence, desire for, 12
Independent contractors, 99
Insurance, 82–83
International Directory of Young
    Entrepreneurs, 94
Internet marketing, 180–85
Internet Service Providers (ISPs), 181
Interns, 100
Introductions, quality, 41–42
Investments, 138–41
IRAs, 140
Isolation, avoiding, 36

J

Job descriptions, 98
Johnson, Judy and Doug, 162
Jones, Jacqueline, 155
Jones, Naimah, 132

K

Karpowicz, Debbie, 174
Kerr, Ken, 85
Key influencers, 41
Kinnare, Shahid, 162
Kmart, 118
Knowledge, lack of, 21
Krispy Kreme, 32
Kushell, Jennifer, 94

L

Lane, Sam, 60
Lapin, Yona, 208
Lauder, Estée, 67, 87, 95–96
Laura Ashley, Ltd., 61
Learning, lifelong, 219–20
Leasing, 55
Legal structure, 68–70
Lesonsky, Rieva, 55
Liability, 68–70
Licenses, business, 76
Licensing, 135–37
Lifestyle businesses, 50, 121
Limited liability companies (LLCs), 70,
    112
Line of credit, 129
Loans
    bank, 128–30
    from friends and family, 123–24
    government, 131–32
    home equity, 123
    micro-, 130–31, 132
Location
    branding, 88–91
    choosing, 54–56
    friendliness of, 89–90
    music and, 90–91
Logos, 92
Loss leaders, 161
Lowe, Victoria, 191
Loyalty programs, 209–10
Lucky Duck Productions, 102

M

Madonna, 87–88
Magazines, 175
Maher, Carin, 191
Mail, 78–79
Mail box rentals, 78, 93
Mailing lists, 176
Mail order, 180
Mandela, Nelson, 230

Manufacturing, 51, 135
Marcdante, Mary, 218
Marketing, 166–88. *See also* Image
   advertising, 173–76
   direct mail, 176–80
   importance of, 166–67
   Internet, 180–85
   measuring results of, 187–88
   octopus vs. elephant, 211
   pieces, 94, 177–80
   publicity, 170–73
   during recessions, 118
   target markets, 167–68
   trade shows, 185–87
   word of mouth, 168–70
Martz, Gayle, 125
Mathieu, Tracy, 59
Mattel, 13, 179
Media kits, 172, 174
Meditation, 224
Mellinger, Doug, 39–40
Mental bank, 26–27
Mentors, 39–40, 229
Merlino, Nell, 130
Microloans, 130–31, 132
MillionaireWomen.com, 59
Mind, maintaining an active, 219–20
Mirroring, 146
Mission statement, 27
Money. *See also* Accounting; Expenses;
   Financial documents; Financial
   potential; Financing; Taxes
  effects of, 109
  multiple income streams, 134–41
  relationship with, 110
  spending on yourself, 223
  women's needs for, 16–18
Morgan, Colette, 89
Murphy, Terri, 16, 218
Music, 90–91

N

Naimah Cosmetics, 132
National Association for Female
   Executives (NAFE), 43
National Association of Women Business
   Owners (NAWBO), 43
Naysayers, 20–21
Nemeth, Maria, 138
Networking, 41–42, 153–56
Newspapers, 171, 175
News releases, 172
Nicholson, Sheryl, 198
Nordstrom, 206

O

O'Donnell, Erin, 160
Ordering process, 192–93
Organization, importance of, 80–81
Organizations, useful, 42–45
Orkin Pest Control, 119
Outcault, Richard, 136
Oversensitivity, 21–22

P

Parents, 217–18
Partners (business), 56–61, 69, 112
Partners (domestic), 58, 61–62, 215–16
Part-time employees, 100
Patents, 85
Patrick, DeLyn, 155
Peak experiences, 31–33
People Puzzle, 198–99
Pepsi, 215
Perfect Customers Unlimited, 13
Perfectionism, 18, 22
Permits, 76
Pets, 219
Pflug, Jackie Nink, 24
Philanthropy, 228–29
Phones, 77–78, 90, 146–48
Polish, Joe, 219
Post office boxes, 78

Preselling, 116
Presentations, 150–51
Pricing, 157–65
   costs and, 157–58
   low, 159–61
   raising, 164–65
   self-worth and, 157, 158–59
   strategies, 161–64
Print advertising, 174–75
Printed material, 91–94, 177–80
Problem solving, 36
Procrastination, 18, 19, 63
Professional employer organizations
   (PEOs), 100
Professionals, hiring, 42
Profit, pricing for, 157–65
Profit centers, 134–35
Promotional items, 95–96
Prospects. *See also* Sales
   cold calling, 194–96
   decoding personality of, 198–99
   following up, 196–98
   identifying needs of, 193
   listening to, 194
   researching and qualifying, 190–91
Prosperity circles, 38
Publicity, 170–73
Public speaking, 149–52

Q

Quick, Edith and Roy, 157
Quiz, 10–12

R

Radio, 170–71, 175–76
Real estate investments, 139–40
Recessions, 117–19
Reel Women, 145
Referral programs, 209–10
Refunds, 209
Regan, Patti, 39
Reichert, Stacy, 215

Rejection, 18–19, 21–22
Relationships, importance of, 213,
   214–19
Reliability, 204–5
Responsibility, taking, 208–9
Responsiveness, 204
Retail businesses, 51
Retirement plans, 140
RightNow Technologies, 122
Risks, taking, 81–82, 121
Roadblocks, 18–22
Roberts, Joel, 171–72
Roddick, Anita, 52, 229
Roffer, Robin Fisher, 87, 90
Royalties, 135–37
Rudolph, Vernon, 32

S

Sales, 189–202
   closing, 198–200
   importance of, 189
   landing trophy clients, 201–2
   nurturing and, 143, 189
   opportunities, 191–92
   presentations, 193–96
   setting the stage for, 190–93
Sales letters, 177–78
Scenery, changes of, 224
Search engines, 182
Secretaries, 147
Securities, 139
Self-esteem, building, 26–27
Self-improvement, 47
Self-talk, 25–26
Self-worth, acknowledging, 157, 158–59
Seminars, 150–51, 154
Senses, utilizing your, 221
Sensory anchoring, 31–33, 150
SEP-IRAs, 140
Service businesses, 51, 160
Sher, Robert, 164–65
Sherman, Aliza, 79

Sherpa's Pet Trading Co., 125
Shyness, conquering, 144–45, 149
Siegel, Mo, 169
Silver, Jared, 136–37
Small Business Administration (SBA), 44–45, 127, 131–32
Small Business Investment Companies (SBICs), 132
Social security numbers, 84
Sole proprietorships, 68–69, 112
Southwest Airlines, 114
Spirit, maintaining an open, 222–25
Springboard Enterprises, 44
Subconscious
    affirmations and, 28
    power of, 24–27
    sensory anchoring and, 31–33
Success teams, 35–39
Suppliers. *See* Vendors
Support, sources of, 34–45

T

Tag lines, 88
Target markets, 167–68
Taxes, 69–70, 99, 112–13, 140
Telephones, 77–78, 90, 146–48
Television, 170–71, 175–76
Temp workers, 99
Testimonials, 152, 168–69
Thank-you notes, 205
Theme songs, 31
Time management, 80–81
To-do lists, 81
Trademarks, 67, 68, 86
Trade shows, 154, 185–87
Tranquility, pursuing, 224–25

U

Universal Studios, 202
U.S. Copyright Office, 86
U.S. Patent and Trademark Office (USPTO), 85, 86

V

Value, perceived, 160
Vendors, 115–16, 133
Venture capital, 127–28
Vernon, Lillian, 228
Victoria's Secret, 167–68
Visions, 28–30
Voice mail, 148
Von Furstenberg, Diane, 136, 229

W

Watson, Tom, 73
Wealthy Bag Lady, 5–6, 65–66, 88, 177
Websites, 64, 79, 181–83, 188
Weiss, Allan, 204
Welch, Jack, 101
Wholesaling, 51
Wild Rumpus, 89
Williamson, Marianne, 230
Winfrey, Oprah, 13, 29, 87–88
Women
    empowerment of, 14–15
    entrepreneurial advantages of, 9
    financial needs of, 16–18
    financing and, 120–21
    friendships between, 218
    longevity of, 17–18
    motivations of, 107
Women's Small Business Expo, 1, 6, 35
Women's Small Business Month, 1, 6
Word of mouth, 168–70
Workers' compensation, 82–83
WowGlobal, 59

Y

Yancey, Kym and Sandra, 43
Yellow pages, 175
Yona Skin Life Products, 208